# THE CREATIVE CITY

# The Creative City
## A Toolkit for Urban Innovators

*Charles Landry*

London • Sterling, VA

First published in the UK and USA in 2000 by Earthscan Publications Ltd

Reprinted 2000, 2001, 2002, 2004

A catalogue record for this book is available from the British Library

ISBN: 1-85383-613-3

Comedia
The Round, Bournes Green
Near Stroud, GL6 7NL, UK
Email: creativecity@hotmail.com
http://www.comedia.org.uk

Typesetting by MapSet Ltd, Gateshead, UK
Printed and bound by Creative Print and Design (Wales), Ebbw Vale
Cover design by Susanne Harris
Cover illustration by Christopher Corr

For a full list of publications please contact:

Earthscan
8–12 Camden High Street, London, NW1 0JH
Tel: +44 (0)20 7387 8558
Fax: +44 (0)20 7387 8998
Email: earthinfo@earthscan.co.uk
http://www.earthscan.co.uk

22883 Quicksilver Drive, Sterling, VA 20166–2012, USA

Earthscan publishes in association with WWF-UK and the International
Institute for Environment and Development

This book is printed on elemental chlorine-free paper

# Contents

## PART THREE: A CONCEPTUAL TOOLKIT OF URBAN CREATIVITY

# PART FOUR: THE CREATIVE CITY AND BEYOND

# List of Case Studies

# Acronyms and Abbreviations

| | |
|---|---|
| ASMARE | Street Scavengers' Association (Brazil) |
| CCI | Creative City Initiative |
| CIK | Cultural Services in Kirklees |
| CIS | Creativity Investment Services |
| CTI | Creative Town Initiative |
| EU | European Union |
| GDR | German Democratic Republic |
| IBA | Internationale Bauaustellung Emscher Park |
| ICLEI | International Centre for Local Environmental Initiatives |
| LETS | local exchange trading schemes |
| MAFIA | Merton Association for Independent Access |
| MHP | Marketing Huddersfield Partnership |
| NGO | non-governmental organizations |
| NLP | neuro-linguistic programming |
| PUBLIC | People United for Better Living in Cities |
| SAD | seasonal affective disorder |
| SME | small and medium-sized enterprises |
| TEC | Training and Enterprise Council |
| TQM | total quality management |
| UN | United Nations |
| UNCHS | United Nations Centre for Human Settlements (Habitat) |
| UPP | Urban Pilot Projects |

# Preface

*The Creative City* is an ambitious book. It should inspire people to think, plan and act creatively in the city and to get an ideas factory going that turns urban innovations into reality. Its aim is to make readers feel: 'I can do that too' and to spread confidence that creative and innovative solutions to urban problems are feasible however bad they may seem at first sight. A central message is that cities are changing dramatically in ways that amount to a paradigm shift. If we keep trying to solve urban problems with the old intellectual apparatus and mindset we will come up against the same obstacles. In spite of the urban crisis *The Creative City* is positive about cities, because they offer so much scope for communication, new ideas and wealth creation. Taking a bird's-eye view of cities around the world, it is astonishing how many ordinary people show leadership qualities to make the extraordinary possible when given the chance.

*The Creative City* treads a path between being practical and playing with ideas and is unashamedly conceptual in parts – concepts have immense power to shape how we view the world and to simplify the seemingly complex. When change is deep-seated, understanding its underlying dynamics is crucial. It involves thinking afresh about the concepts we use and logics we apply in solving problems and harnessing opportunities. Some things said may have been said many times before but not necessarily in the context of the city and this is what, hopefully, gives the book a distinctive feel.

# Setting the Scene

*The Creative City* describes a new method of strategic urban planning and examines how people can think, plan and act creatively in the city. It explores how we can make our cities more liveable and vital by harnessing people's imagination and talent. It does not provide definite answers, but seeks to open out an 'ideas bank' of possibilities from which innovations will emerge. Most of us sense that where we live could be a better place. Many of us know of places that show how cities can be made more human and more productive. Yet cities balance on a cusp – decision-makers can repeat past policies in a climate of slow decline, or they can seek to reinvent their city as a vibrant hub of creativity, potential and improving quality of life. Undoubtably, for the most part, old approaches do not work. We cannot solve 21st century problems with 19th century mindsets: the dynamics of cities and the world urban system have changed too dramatically.

Yet the urban utopia already exists in the dispersed experience of global best practice. Here are innovative ways of creating employment or applying technology and unleashing the skill of the young or the elderly. There is inspiring architecture that speaks to a city's soul and identity, and there are clever energy-saving devices or public transport that is a joy to use. There are retail environments that merge entertainment and learning, and public spaces that encourage urban buzz and celebrations that capture the unusual, the uplifting and the creative.

Since these good examples are widely dispersed they are hard to recognize and difficult to learn from. Instead we see the city as a place of fear, crime, pollution and degradation, forgetting that cities are the wealth creators – over 80 per cent for developed nations – generating the prosperity of nations, however unfairly distributed or shared. Cities provide opportunities and interactions which can solve their own problems and improve the quality of life of whole regions. Yet urban life is still seen in a derogatory light.

## The Century of Cities

*The Creative City* is a call to action because the 21st century will be the century of cities. For the first time, over half the world will live in cities – in Europe the figure is already over 75 per cent and in the developing world it will shortly reach 50 per cent, whereas two decades ago it was 29 per cent worldwide. Yet most live in cities through need not desire. In 1997 a survey showed that 84 per cent of people in the UK wanted to live in a small village compared to 4 per cent who do. We cannot create enough villages to meet these aspirations. Instead we must make cities desirable places to live and be in, partly by recreating the values that people perceive to exist in a village – a sense of place and belonging, continuity, safety and predictability – and partly by nurturing distinctly urban possibilities – buzz, interaction, trade, unexpected delight and much more.

## Creativity: the Lifeblood of Cities

Cities have one crucial resource – their people. Human cleverness, desires, motivations, imagination and creativity are replacing location, natural resources and market access as urban resources. The creativity of those who live in and run cities will determine future success. Of course this has always been critical to cities' ability to survive and adapt. As cities became large and complex enough to present problems of urban management, so they became laboratories that developed the solutions – technological, conceptual and social – to the problems of growth.

Yet there are special reasons for thinking about the problems of cities today in terms of creativity and innovation – or lack of it. Today many of the world's cities face periods of transition largely brought about by the vigour of renewed globalization. These transitions differ from region to region: in some areas, like Asia, cities are growing, while in others, such as Europe, old industries are disappearing and the value added in cities is created less through what is manufactured and more through intellectual capital applied to products, processes and services.

## PARADIGM SHIFTS AND BEYOND

*The Creative City* outlines the fundamental changes occurring in the city at every level; in their entirety they represent a paradigm shift from the typical city of 30 years ago and the city of today. In this situation, older solutions do not work. What might seem an impenetrable problem from within one mindset might be eminently solvable from within another and the new thinking and conceptual toolkit outlined aims to help readers think through the dilemmas.

Examples are cited only to illustrate a point: *The Creative City* is not intended as sourcebook of urban good practice but many references to those will be found. Many of the cases come from my own experience of working in Europe and the rest of the developed world. While the story of urban dynamics is told from a worldwide view *The Creative City* is written from a European perspective – not because European cities are more creative, but because I know more about them. I am aware of the great creative cities of yesterday and today in China, India, Africa and South America, yet am deeply etched by my own European culture and have an image of the 'good city' that reflects European urbanism. It includes ideas such as that the city centre matters as the neutral meeting place for all parts of the city; the sense that publicly shared space adds to the wealth of cities by enhancing interaction, connections, trade and urban buzz; the feeling that urban life itself has a self-sustaining quality beyond the individual; the notion that mixing, diversity and culture create potential.

Some of these views are shared worldwide, others perhaps not. Nevertheless the concepts, principles and ways of analysing urban problems can be used by anyone and should apply anywhere. The toolkit seeks to enable citizens, policy-makers and decision-makers to grasp opportunities which may only be possible in a city. Once you explore below the surface nearly every place has its creative potential, but in many cities it is blocked. Surprisingly little is known about the conditions necessary for creativity and innovation to emerge – the formal and informal structures that have helped Silicon Valley, Los Angeles, Barcelona, the Third Italy around Emilia Romagna, the advanced technology enclaves surrounding Tokyo or Bangalore develop world reputations for creativity and generation of new businesses and services. *The Creative City* will seek to explore the underlying dynamics of creativity and in so doing show the need to get beyond the idea that creativity is the exclusive domain of artists or that innovations are largely technological: there is social and political creativity and innovation too.

## CREATIVE SOLUTIONS TO URBAN PROBLEMS

At the heart of creativity are creative people and organizations who have particular attributes: when these come together in one area they establish a creative milieu. *The Creative City* asks how such a milieu comes about, enabling cities to become innovative hubs. It assesses how new forms of business and banking get off the ground and what the principles are of organizations such as a South Shore Bank in Chicago, which provides banking services to the deprived. I looked at how ecological approaches to urban development, like those undertaken in Emscher Park in the Ruhr in Germany, got off the ground. I studied the mechanisms of arts solutions to create civic pride and gain momentum like the Love Festival in Berlin. I asked what triggers the imaginative uses of technology for urban development as in Helsinki and new forms of governance as in Tilburg. I wanted to discover the ways in which creativity can be organized and how creative people can be managed; and whether the Huddersfield Creative Town Initiative is the right way forward. It is important to find out how government can work best with business and NGOs and how links between formal and informal networks can be fostered to produce the best results. I was interested too in the role of technology in developing a creative city and considered whether other forms of creativity are more important.

## A TOOLKIT FOR PRACTITIONERS

*The Creative City* argues above all that changes in mindset can generate will, commitment and energy which allow us to look afresh at urban possibilities. A range of approaches and methods to 'think creatively', to 'plan creatively' and to 'act creatively' are described. In their entirety they provide a new way of addressing urban planning. Once taken on board the techniques can be absorbed subconsciously and naturally embedded in day to day decision-making, as well as applied in more formal, methodical ways. A set of new terms and concepts for talking about cities runs through the text: civic creativity, a creativity harnessed towards the public good; the cycle of urban creativity and how it can be developed, implemented and made virtuous; the lifecycle of urban innovation concept; urban R&D and how pilot projects can be developed, mainstreamed and replicated; cultural resources and how they can be applied; how to think of the city as a learning organism and, finally, the creation of a new form of literacy – the capacity to 'read' and understand cities, whoever you are – called urban literacy.

## WHY THIS BOOK?

*The Creative City* was written with three primary aims:

1. To provide readers with a more integrated and holistic approach to thinking about and analysing cities. In the longer run this will change the way decision-makers consider the assets and potential of cities as well as how cities might be organized and managed.
2. To offer a 'mental toolkit' that provides readers with the cornerstones of a new mindset and so stimulate readers' own ideas and solutions for their city.
3. To engender a critical debate amongst decision-makers at different levels and to influence the policy, strategies and actions undertaken in cities.

# Acknowledgements

I wish to thank a number of people who have helped me. Franco Bianchini for his generosity with ideas and with whom I have frequently discussed and written about many of the themes covered. (Sir) Peter Hall with whom I co-wrote *Innovative and Sustainable European Cities* and who has given me sustained encouragement. François Matarasso whose constructively critical comments and help in editing the book have been invaluable in clarifying its arguments. (Lord) Trevor Smith and the Joseph Rowntree Reform Trust whose trust in me over the years, as well as co-funding for this project, I hope I can now repay. Phil Wood, the coordinator of the Creative Town Initiative in Huddersfield, who had the courage to implement a 'creative city' project and co-funded the writing of this book through the European Commission's Urban Pilot Project scheme.

Others I would like to thank include my Comedia colleagues Ken Worpole and Liz Greenhalgh who have a long-term interest in the future of civilized cities as well as Geoff Mulgan and his other collaborators in Demos such as Perri 6 and Charles Leadbeater. The book has been influenced by writers and thinkers such as Howard Gardner, Gareth Morgan, Jane Jacobs and Art Kleiner. Important too have been Comedia clients and especially Harry Schulman and Timo Cantell from Helsinki who have supported the Creative City work for over six years, as well as friends with whom I have debated themes such as Tom Burke, Bob McNulty, Jude Bloomfield, Marc Pachter, Jonathan Hyams, Deborah Jenkins, Ilid Landry and Lia Ghilardi. Thanks too to Pauline Matarasso for her editing help; Tom Fleming, Helen Gould and Annabel Biles who helped to provide case studies and Rob Lloyd-Owen who helped with the chapter on creative techniques and Jim Lister who helps run our annual Creative City course at the Amsterdam Summer School.

I especially thank Susie, Max and Nancy to whom I can now devote myself much more as well as my canine friends, Daisy and Bertie, for their constant companionship.

# Part One

# URBAN GROUNDSHIFTS

# 1

# Rediscovering Urban Creativity

## WHY ARE SOME CITIES SUCCESSFUL?

The origin of the Creative City concept lay in thinking about why some cities seem to have adjusted to, even surfed the wave of, change over the last two decades. Cities like Barcelona, Sydney, Seattle, Vancouver, Helsinki, Glasgow, Bangalore, Ahmedabad, Curitiba, Rotterdam, Dublin, the cluster along the Emscher river in the Ruhr in Germany or around Zürich, Karlsruhe, Strasbourg – these and other thriving cities seem to have made economic and social development work for them. Others seem to have been passive victims of change, simply allowing it to happen to them.

In reflecting on my work in various places, from the well-known and glamorous to the obscure and seemingly hopeless, some lessons emerged. Successful cities seemed to have some things in common – visionary individuals, creative organizations and a political culture sharing a clarity of purpose. They seemed to follow a determined, not a deterministic path. Leadership was widespread, permeating public, private and voluntary sectors. It expressed itself in courageous public initiatives and often risky business investments, and in a tissue of interconnected projects whether for profit or the public good.

An appreciation of cultural issues, expressing values and identity, was key to the ability to respond to change – especially organizational culture. The recognition of a culturally informed perspective was crucial to making urban planning work and that no one can shape urban change alone was vital to bridging divisions between disciplines, institutions and public, private and voluntary sector approaches. New forms of alliance had to be set up. Interdepartmental cooperation and corporate working in local authorities alone could not harness urban potential. The distinct worlds of planning, economic, social, educational and cultural policy had not learnt enough from each other to affect their fundamental assumptions, ways of operating and goals. Recognition of the limits of Comedia's own work persuaded us that successful urban policy and management demanded far more attention to cultural issues and approaches which are creative, holistic, anticipatory and people-based. Sustainable success depends on developing the thinking of policy-makers and urban agents.

The key actors in those places which have exhibited growth share certain qualities: open-mindedness and a willingness to take risks; a clear focus on long-term aims with an understanding of strategy; a capacity to work with local distinctiveness and to find a strength in apparent weakness; and a willingness to listen and learn. These are some of the characteristics that make people, projects, organizations and, ultimately, cities creative.

It is easier to conceive of creativity in individuals or even organizations than in a city which is, by definition, a complex amalgam of diverse people, interest groups, institutions, organizational forms, business sectors, social concerns and cultural resources. Given that the term 'creative' itself is not simple, and is still largely associated with the arts and science, it may help if I begin by tracing my personal route to the creative city. Two major issues shaped my understanding of creativity: first the power of thinking and ideas which shape our mindset, and secondly the importance of culture as a creative resource.

## Thinking Creatively

We all carry deep-seated cultural baggage – mine is a European mixture, which affects my mindset, thinking, scale of values and enthusiasms. The mix is German, British and Italian. Their characteristic ways of thinking have affected how I have thought about the creative city: readers may sense that these sometimes pull in opposite directions. The more dialectic German approach searches for theoretical frameworks, assesses dynamics, seeks synthesis and the reconciliation of opposites, while the Anglo-Saxon approach is more empirical, highlighting examples and real life best practice; a subtle imagination and a richer understanding of culture is legitimized in the Italian context.

The fundamental question for the creative city project is: 'Can you change the way people and organizations think – and, if so, how?' One response is to highlight the power of our thinking and ideas to create change. Changing a mindset – so that we grasp the need to address urban problems in an integrated way – can be worth a thousand persuasive reports so often seen gathering dust. A mindset is the usual, easy way of thinking that guides decision-making and represents the order within which people structure their worlds. One priority was to apply creativity to shift thinking – for example to overcome the habit of thinking in binary opposites which is such a common barrier to imaginative problem-solving.

*The Creative City* highlights the value of a creative urban climate in transcending narrow thinking. For example:

- Should urban solutions be conceived by combining a holistic thinking and a categorizing approach?
- What would a feminine rather than a masculine approach to the city imply?
- Can country models of living offer anything to the city?
- How can a balance be struck between fostering tradition or innovation, allowing drift and spontaneity or concentrating on order?
- Should instinct-based or rational decision-making processes be encouraged?
- How much distinctiveness is useful or is the tried and tested more comforting?
- Does the city need slowing down or speeding up?
- How can these choices be sorted out so that the city moves forward without destroying the social base from which it has emerged?

To take slowness and speed, there may be a 'slow' solution in one circumstance, a 'fast' solution in another, something in between in yet another: but a fourth problem might require us to go beyond the 'slowness–speed' continuum altogether and find another way of addressing the issue. Careful observation, based on a cultural approach to urban potential, as outlined below, usually suggests the most appropriate ways of dealing with a problem.

A list of binary opposites is not an imaginative way of present-ing ideas about a creative city – we have to recognize that these opposites are parts of a broader whole. *The Creative City* argues that a more integrated approach provides unexpectedly rich solutions. Urban creativity thrives when those in charge can be open-minded and centred, can link the capacity for focus with lateral thinking, can combine practical with conceptual thinking. If these qualities do not exist in one individual they can be present in a team. Urban problem-solving teams need new ways of combining people who like to master one area in detail before going on to another with holists who learn best by mastering the whole picture before filling in the details.

## CULTURE MOVING CENTRE STAGE

A further route to the creative city came from an interest in culture. Two significant connections were how cultural evolution shapes urban development and the intrinsic link between creativity and the development of culture.

Much of Comedia's early work in Britain involved fostering new, independent, mostly urban media. We produced research, feasibility studies and gave advice on the production, distribution and reception of private and community radio; publishing and book-selling; film, video and multimedia, music, design, crafts and theatre industries. We emphasized the value of cultural industries which, as an interconnected sector, are perhaps the fastest growing in modern urban economies. With the decline of existing resource and manufacturing industry, culture was seen as a saviour for many cities in Europe and increasingly elsewhere. In trying to understand the dynamics of the cultural industries and how the cultural resources of cities could be used to maximize a city's potential, I became increasingly aware of their wider importance and impact.

I also constantly encountered the power of cultural heritage and tradition. Why, in the rush for change, do we find solace and inspiration in the buildings, artefacts, skills, values and social rituals of the past? Is it because in a globalizing world we seek stability and local roots? Cultural heritage connects us to our histories, our collective memories, it anchors our sense of being and can provide a source of insight to help us to face the future.

Cultural heritage is the sum of our past creativities and the results of creativity is what keeps society going and moving forward. Each aspect of our culture – language, law, theories, values, knowledge – needs re-assessing as it is passed on to the next generation. 'Creativity is the cultural equivalent of the process of genetic change' and adaptation and 'most new traits do not improve survival chances ... but a few do and it is these that account for biological evolution' (Czikszentmihalyi, 1997, p7). The same with creativity – not all experiments or pilot projects work, yet historically for the cities which have survived their lifeblood has been their creativity which has allowed them to push at the boundaries of tradition. Culture and creativity are intertwined.

Culture is the panoply of resources that show that a place is unique and distinctive. The resources of the past can help to inspire and give confidence for the future. Even cultural heritage is reinvented daily whether this be a refurbished building or an adaptation of an old skill for modern times: today's classic was yesterday's innovation. Creativity is not only about a continuous invention of the new, but also how to deal appropriately with the old.

## Cultural Resources

Cultural resources are the raw materials of the city and its value base; its assets replacing coal, steel or gold. Creativity is the method of exploiting these resources and helping them grow. The key problem was not how to identify them, but how to limit the imagination, as the possibilities were endless. The task of urban planners is to recognize, manage and exploit these resources responsibly. Culture, therefore, should shape the technicalities of urban planning rather than be seen as a marginal add-on to be considered once the important planning questions like housing, transport and land-use have been dealt with. By contrast a culturally informed perspective should condition how planning as well as economic development or social affairs should be addressed.

Recognizing culture as a resource was a personal revelation and thereafter I began to think of cities and assets in completely different ways. Every crevice in the city had a hidden story or undiscovered potential that could be re-used for a positive urban purpose. This led to a new form of urban asset audit. By taking a broad sweep of a city's economy, social potential and political traditions, we assessed how cultural assets could be turned to economic advantage. How an old skill in carpentry or metal working could be linked with new technology to satisfy a new market for household goods or how a tradition of learning and debate could be used to market a city as a conference venue. We even considered the 'senses' of the city from colour, to sound, smell and visual appearance, also taking a broad sweep through mutual aid traditions, associative networks and social rituals as we saw that these could make a city competitive. This approach to the concept of cultural assets made me think of the city as a malleable artefact shaped both by built projects and by activity; I thought of the city as having a personality and emotions, with feelings uplifted at one moment and depressed in the next. The city conceived of in this way was a living organism, not a machine.

Along the way some conceptual tricks were learnt that at first sound simplistic. One was the idea of 'turning a weakness into a strength'. Focusing attention on how to make the most of a problem reinforced the idea that potential raw materials were everywhere. For example, Kemi, a town in the Finnish Arctic circle, suffered from high unemployment, its industry dominated by a declining paper mill. The main asset was coldness and snow and it built the world's biggest snow castle whose impact exceeded the wildest expectations. I heard that Glasgow's tourism officer, recognizing that the city was drier than Iceland, had promoted the city as a kind of Riviera to Icelanders: it was only seeing a group of merry Icelanders drinking in a Glasgow pub that brought the story home.

As the world of cultural resources opened out it became clear that every city could have a unique niche and 'making something out of nothing' became totemic to anyone trying to develop or promote ugly cities, cold or hot cities or marginal places. The realization dawned that every city could be a world centre for something if it was persistent and tried hard enough – Freiburg for eco-research, New Orleans for the blues or Hay-on-Wye for bookselling. In identifying urban resources much could be learnt from the Italians renowned for their 'feste' or 'sagre', which celebrate whatever resource their region is known for from mushrooms to pasta to literature.

It became clear that cultural resources were embodied in peoples' skills and talents. They were not only 'things' like buildings, but also symbols, activities and the repertoire of local products in crafts, manufacturing and services, like the intricate skills of sari makers in Indian cities, wood carvers of Bali or dyers of Djenne in Mali. Urban cultural resources are a historical, industrial and artistic heritage representing assets including architecture, urban landscapes or landmarks. Local and indigenous traditions of public life, festivals, rituals or stories as well as hobbies and enthusiasms. Amateur cultural activities can all be rethought to generate new products or services. Resources like food and cooking, leisure activities, clothing and sub-cultures that exist everywhere are often

---

**MONTPELLIER: A STORY IN SIGNS**

A visit to Montpellier showed how simply a city could tell the story of its aspirations. At the airport a sign welcomes the visitor in a dozen languages saying, in effect: 'Montpellier is an international city'. On the road to the centre are signs announcing tree planting schemes, the use of indigenous flowers in civic beds or the creation of cycle paths; the message is: 'Montpellier is an ecological city'. Further on, a district with streets named after Alfred Nobel and Albert Einstein, housing companies like Synergy, Diagnostics or Digital indicates a new tech area: 'Montpellier is a new tech city'. In the central square stands a health screening vehicle symbolically proclaiming: 'Montpellier is a healthy city'. Subsequent discussions with city officials revealed that Montpellier's key strategies were to be an international, innovative, ecological and healthy city. Consciously designing an urban narrative into signage revealed the power of using intangibles in urban development.

---

neglected. And, of course, cultural resources are the range and quality of skills in the performing and visual arts and the newer 'cultural industries'.

## The Impact of Culture

Culture provides insight and so has many impacts; it is the prism through which urban development should be seen. The cultural industries, hotbeds of creativity, are significant economic sectors in their own right and employ between 3–5 per cent of the workforce in world cities such as London and New York or Milan and Berlin. Tourism feeds off culture, yet most tourism focuses on a narrow conception of culture – museums, galleries, theatre and shopping. We could see the positive glow from cultural institutions and how the cultural sector had a direct impact on inward investment by attracting international companies who seek a vibrant cultural life for their employees. In assessing the social and educational impact of culture we saw how they help foster the development of social capital and the organizational capacity to respond to change. Culture can also strengthen social cohesion, increase personal confidence and improve life skills, improve people's mental and physical well-being, strengthen people's ability to act as democratic citizens and develop new training and employment routes.

## CREATING SOMETHING OUT OF NOTHING: HAY-ON-WYE BOOK TOWN, UK

Until 1961 Hay-on-Wye was a fairly unprepossessing Welsh border town, dependent on declining farming and agricultural markets for its economy. Richard Booth owned the half-ruinous castle and started to deal in second-hand books, which quickly filled up the castle, and when other buildings became redundant and went on the market – the cinema, the fire-station – there was always a ready buyer. The idea that a whole town full of bookshops could become an international attraction was before its time. The Cinema Bookshop quickly became the 'biggest second-hand bookshop in the world' and was later sold on to a London businessman. By the early 1970s Hay had established an international reputation and there are now 42 bookshops in the town. They cover specialisms as diverse as cinema, the arts, the occult, history, militaria, poetry, children, Americana, philosophy and economics. The publicity (and visitors) which the town and its eccentric trade attracted allowed more and more bookshops to be established, by Booth and others.

Richard Booth's personal investment in Hay – with his staff of 26 workers and around 220 employed elsewhere – has brought it economic sustainability in a way that no chemical agriculture, factory farming, or supermarket retailing would bring to a rural area. Hay's population is now just over 1,400. It supports 15 large guesthouses and four hotels, plus plenty of Bed and Breakfast accommodation in the town, with more such places in the adjacent surrounding countryside. A dramatic rise in the number of cafes and restaurants has been seen, with 12 opening in the last four years. Ten antique shops have sprung up in Hay over the same period. Over 110,000 visitors come through the town each year; with a slight concentration during the weeks of the Literature Festival in May. Hay has not suffered the retail blight experienced by many rural towns in the 1980s.

Richard Booth has helped set up an international book town movement as a means of revitalizing small towns, which include Montolieu in Southern France, Bredevoort in Holland, Redu in Belgium, Becherel in Brittany, St Pierre de Clages in Switzerland, Stillwater in the US, Fjaerland in Norway, Kampung Buku in Malaysia and Miyagawa in Japan.

*Source:* Landry, 1996

But our attention was drawn particularly to some impacts of culture because they seemed to be powerful sources for creativity – the value of distinctiveness. By looking at every aspect of culture as an imaginative resource we could see how the meanings embodied in traditional or current culture create the identity and values of a place. The local distinctiveness they express is vital in a world where cities increasingly look and feel the same. Beirut has focused on its massive city centre rebuilding project by Solidaire to overcome its image of strife and to re-establish itself as the Middle Eastern banking and meeting centre, building on its cosmopolitan past. Riga in the Baltics has drawn on its maritime and Hansa League tradition to re-establish an identity for itself separate from that of a vassal city in the former Soviet empire.

We noted how culture has gained an increasingly significant position. Countless times it was the threat of cultural losses that brought urban citizen groups into action. These campaigns were about more than saving buildings, they were about empowerment. The Calcutta-based PUBLIC (People United for Better Living in Cities) has become an India-wide campaigning group and used cultural heritage campaigns, such as for the railway station, the town hall and entrance to the city park, as a resource for democratization and celebration of local identity. In Singapore, by contrast, the Chinese quarter has practically disappeared; it is nearly too late to value and a visitor can wryly note how certain Chinese buildings have been recreated in the local urban theme park. Manila, which has exploded out of its original confines and become a mega city of 10 million is belatedly recognizing the cultural value of the Intramuros area. Both cities know that fostering cultural understanding has an important bonding effect. Civic pride can, in turn, give confidence, inspire and provide the energy to face tasks that may have nothing to do with culture.

## THE VARIETIES OF CREATIVITY

### Unravelling Complexity

The more I focused on creativity the more complex the concept became. I saw its essence as a kind of multifaceted resourcefulness involving the capacity to assess and find one's way to solutions for intractable, unexpected, unusual problems or circumstances. Creativity seemed like a process of discovering and then enabling potential to unfold. It was applied imagination using qualities like intelligence, inventiveness and learning along the way. But then I understood its dynamic aspect, and relationship to context: a project which might be creative in one period or situation was not necessarily so in another. Although being creative was mostly associated with artists or sometimes scientists, I met increasing numbers of people working in social, business or political arenas whose way of addressing problems was clearly creative. The ambit of creativity and innovative action continually broadened yet there seemed to be qualities that were cutting across the boundaries.

In the complexity I could identify creative people working as individuals, in groups, teams or organizations. In projects or organizations I could see creative processes and structures that seemed to release skill and motivation, implying that everyone can be creative under certain conditions. I could discern too that conventional administrations often did the opposite, making people play safe and avoid using their capacities to the full. I could see firms and public administrations slowly losing a grip on their priorities and in so doing missing opportunities. As I began preaching the creativity message I inevitably stumbled across deep-rooted and complex obstacles to it – linearity and box-like thinking were the words that came to mind, particularly in discussions with property developers, planners and accountants, many of whom did not seem to understand how to value what they could not calculate.

## The Power of Ideas

At the same time I came across creative concepts like 'Factor Four – Doubling Wealth and Halving Resource Use' or ideas like the Institute for Social Inventions' Global Ideasbank or services like the *Big Issue*. It became clear how many of the creative projects led by outsiders became mainstream once proven. I saw the power of concepts to change our priorities and began to ask what social conditions encouraged these new ideas. Discussions on how to nurture a conducive environment for urban revitalization in places as different as Brisbane, Johannesburg, Durban, Sofia and Barcelona led to the question: How do you establish a creative milieu?

As I spoke with people who had undertaken creative projects and worked with creative institutions it became evident that creativity depended on qualities which could be thought of as belonging to individuals, organizations or cities – qualities such as resourcefulness and problem-solving capability based on thinking

## THE *BIG ISSUE*: CREATIVE SOLUTIONS TO HOMELESSNESS BY ALLOWING PEOPLE TO BECOME ENTREPRENEURIAL

The *Big Issue* is a magazine sold by homeless people in the UK so they can earn a living and re-integrate into society. Launched in 1991 through the help of the Body Shop Foundation, a key strength is that the idea is easily replicated. It has grown from a monthly to a weekly publication with a circulation of 350,000 copies and has paved the way for street papers in 13 European countries, as well as the Americas, South Africa and Australia. The *Big Issue* has had a substantial impact on the perception of the homeless and is a unique experiment based on the philosophy of self-help – helping the homeless help themselves through earnings from selling the paper. The homeless are elevated out of a traditional hand-out mentality and are able to develop self-esteem. Since its inception the *Big Issue* has helped 7000 homeless people, has changed the relationship between the homeless and the public, keeps the issue of homelessness in the media and has led to partnerships with the police. The profits of the *Big Issue* are mandated back to the Big Issue Foundation, which in turn funds projects to aid the homeless.

*Source:* Hall and Landry, 1997

in an open-minded way; a disposition to take intellectual risks, to approach problems afresh and to be willing to experiment; and crucially, the capacity to be reflexive and generate a cycle of learning that leads to creation and re-creation.

This is a frame of mind which questions rather than criticizes, which asks 'why is this so?' and is not content to hear 'it has always been like this'. Creativity challenges not just what is a problem, but many things which are now thought of as adequate or even good. Creative people and institutions are willing to rewrite procedures or principles and so to imagine future scenarios, conditions, inventions, applications, adaptations and processes. They look for common threads amidst the seemingly disparate, bringing together unthought-of combinations that solve a problem. Most important, perhaps, is the capacity to look at situations in an integrated, holistic way, laterally and flexibly. Creative people and organizations think flexibly but with a focus and a readiness to take measured risks. As David Perkins notes, 'Creative people work at the edge of their competency not at the centre of it' (quoted in Fryer, 1996). Being creative is an attitude of mind and a way of approaching problems that opens out possibilities, it is 'a particular flexibility which can invigorate all mental functions' (Egan, 1992).

Crucially creativity is a journey not a destination, a process not a status. Every creative output has a lifecycle and as time and experience of the innovation in action unfolds, it will itself need to be adapted and reinvented again. I felt that creative people validate multiple viewpoints and approaches – not only the linguistic, logical and scientific, but also the visual, the musical, the interpersonal and the spatial. They acknowledge the creativities of different age groups, women and men and people of different cultural backgrounds. This allows them to tap into a rich resource by putting together different capabilities and knowledge in new ways.

Creativity is also value-free. It can be used positively or negatively, or with mixed results. The purpose to which creativity is put is what determines its value – which is why the concept of civic creativity is central to this book. I have realized too that creativity alone does not necessarily lead to success. Creative qualities need to be allied to others to ensure a creative idea or product passes a reality check. A combination of other characteristics – testing, trialling, management, and implementation skills – have a role. Yet in observing many good ideas and intentions fail, I saw the dangers of limiting creativity to the ideas stage of projects. It must run consistently from first insight to implementation, consolidation, dissemination and evaluation. The world does not divide into creators and the dull doers and boring support staff.

At times I came up with creative ideas for cities in my role as advisor, but they often lay dormant without the right people in the client city to make them happen. Our ideas only succeeded when I found creative implementers able, for example, to link cultural industries to job creation and spatial regeneration as in Glasgow, Mantua and Barcelona. There are degrees and types of creativity and everyone can find their own. Exercises can help us find out whether we are creative and unlock the dormant capacity.

I have looked at the difference between creative people and creative institutions, processes and structures and conclude that the qualities needed are similar although their focus and weighting may be different. They include personal communication, listening, team building or diplomacy, brokering and networking skills. You cannot have a creative meeting nor a creative institution without creative people. Equally you cannot have a creative milieu without creative organizations – it is the setting within which creative people, processes, ideas and products interact. Establishing such an innovative milieu is a key challenge of the Creative City.

But the more I defined creativity, the more it eluded me. Complications and qualifications emerged with every conclusion. Creativity and innovation seamlessly interweave, the first generating ideas which, if many may prove impractical, at least provide a basis with which to work. Creativity is the pre-condition from which innovations develop. An innovation is the realization of a new idea in practice, usually developed through creative thinking. An innovation exists when it passes a reality test; the creative idea on its own is not enough.

Creativity involves divergent or generative thinking but innovation demands a convergent, critical and analytical approach and these ways of thinking oscillate as a project develops. Innovations and creativity are both context-driven. What was creative in one place or time, such as using the cultural industries to regenerate Split in Croatia or Burgas in Bulgaria, was common knowledge in Sheffield or Melbourne. What was creative in the public sector – such as project-based working or acting across departmental and disciplinary boundaries – was the norm in some private companies, arts organizations or campaigning groups. The reverse was also true – I saw employment practices in relation to minorities in the public sector that the private sector found difficult to implement.

Although the literature on creativity – derived from psychology via management studies – is vast, there is little on urban creativity. Nor is there much on creativity in other areas relevant to urban success, such as economic development, community development, social affairs, education or urban governance in spite of the tremendous creativity applied to problems in these fields – like new forms of accountability, new approaches to skill-building in the arts sector or the micro-loan system tailored on the Grameen Bank's ideas.

While cities were grappling with the failure of rigid structures to achieve innovation-led economic and social development, I could see business increasingly focused on creativity. They saw it as a new form of capital reinforced by interest in the idea of the learning organization. I asked whether different forms of creativity were to be expected from different kinds of organization: for a commercial food producer, the introduction of eco- or social auditing may be an innovation; for a public authority, the establishment of a public/private partnership to deliver a service; for a voluntary organization, it may be the creation of a commercial wing to recycle

### COURAGEOUS AND IMAGINATIVE REORGANIZATION OF CITY ADMINISTRATION, TILBURG, THE NETHERLANDS

Tilburg, with 165,000 inhabitants, is the seventh largest city in The Netherlands. Fifteen years ago, it chose a completely new form of city administration which became known as the Tilburg Model with the city seen as a 'holding company' with separate divisions; including state-of-the-neighbourhood auditing to test performance, resulting in major cost savings. This is analogous to a private firm. The divisions operate like profit centres generating clearly defined urban services and 'products'. The political system (City Board and Council) decides upon the products, their quantities and according to which quality standards. The civil service (city administration) is responsible for the production at the lowest possible costs according to specifications, criteria and indicators defined within the political system. The Council does not, however, interfere with the way city products are made or delivered. The departments are contracted by the city authorities and inform the councillors through a transparent information system about progress and any deviation in the production process.

The basis for city management and implementation is set out in the City Management Plan. This annual project seeks to achieve a balance between what is technically possible and what residents feel is necessary through input from residents in the form of neighbourhood consultations, which are aligned to the City Plan and basic quality plans. The main integrating concept is a mutually agreed set of quality standards. Most city services now require only watchful normal maintenance. The City Plan is implemented through the annual City Programme setting out management tasks for different areas of the city as well as a 'rough draft' for distributing funds. After consultation and adoption, the City Programme is fixed each spring as an element of the city budget. The previous year's results are also audited through the political and neighbourhood consultation machinery.

The results are striking: from 1988 until the present day, Tilburg has had money left over every year. The surplus is invested in the city, for instance for co-financing a new soccer stadium and a concert hall. The city has been able to limit its own running costs: once the seventh most expensive city in The Netherlands, it is now thirtieth, one of the cheapest cities in the country.

*Source:* Hall and Landry, 1997

profits back into the community. If different types of creativity are needed to address the urban complexities, so are the criteria for success. For public bodies, the criteria might be reductions in resource use or pollution levels, and for the profit-making sector market share. Yet lack of debate of this kind shows that creativity in the public sphere is an underexplored terrain.

Some crucial issues are barely discussed. Social creativity is a forgotten dimension, undervalued and not seen as innovation. New social institutions are as vital to renewal as new products, services or technology. The same is true of political, environmental and cultural creativity. It is time to move investment away from technologically driven innovations to how we live, how we organize and how we relate to each other. If not, we will struggle to absorb the changes of a globalizing world without the R&D to guide us.

The problem with identifying new forms of creativity is that it is already an overused concept, often applied to things which are not creative at all, devaluing the concept, and neglecting real creativity. Two parallel themes of urban creativity seem to be clearly emerging: around environmental concerns and the cultural sphere, where my own involvement has been strong.

## Investigating Creative Places

Investigating innovative and sustainable European cities with Peter Hall, I found new environmentally conscious milieux based on a rethought idea of urban quality of life. There were geographical clusters of cities innovative in transport (Karlsruhe–Freiburg–Mulhouse–Basel–Zürich or Bologna–Perugia–Orvieto–Spoleto) or in energy (Saarbrücken–Zürich–Vienna). Other innovations – bicycle priority, solar heating, or separate collection of organic waste – seem to be more widely diffused. Perhaps the explanation lies in local pressures: southern Germany has among the highest rate of car ownership in Europe, but it is hard to generalize.

There have also been culturally driven creative milieux such as the axis around Sheffield, Huddersfield, Manchester and Birmingham in the UK or along the Rhine in Germany (Cologne, Düsseldorf, Dortmund) while a conscious attempt is being made to create a 'pop' cluster in Tilburg in The Netherlands. They have tried to respond to industrial restructuring by regeneration through a focus on music as a means of generating wealth, jobs, identity and image.

## A Special Urban Form of Creativity?

These clusters made me feel there was a special urban creativity, deriving from the problems and potential of cities and the unique response they require. Urbanity itself – critical mass, diversity and interaction – pushes forward a certain type of creativity character- ized by specialisms and niches as well as hybrid ideas. The urban projects I was involved in with Comedia illustrate the point.

Mantua, for example, is a somewhat inward-looking Italian city where local policy prioritized new technology projects without recognizing a link with its strong tradition of publishing and book- selling. Yet the cooperation between bookshops in Mantua was exceptionally good, often based on personal friendships between booksellers. Their desire to cooperate rather than compete combined with critical mass was a starting point. Five years on Mantua is becoming a book city, with Italy's largest literature festival, exten- sive job creation and good links with new media companies.

In Glasgow it was possible to use music and film as a branding device, both to bolster an internal sense of identity and to reflect new images of the city to the wider world. These resources have wide possibilities in industrial development as research in sound and new audio-visual techniques have applications well beyond its own field: software is used to help the deaf hear or to decode under- water images while leading-edge film and animation technologies help expand the industrial base in fields from plumbing to bio- medicine. Yet an area like Candleriggs can only become a focus for music industry activities because of the multiple interactions of performers, managers, technicians and venue operators.

Huddersfield could imagine the idea of a Creative Town Initiative – which attempts to make the town a creative environ- ment where the potential of its citizens is fulfilled – only because of the dense networks of individuals and organizations who had previ- ously worked together and formed a basis of trust.

Helsinki's creativity in rethinking the city's assets lay in public events like the Night of the Arts, the Total Balalaika Show or the Forces of Light which showed how the city could be re-used and how surprising economic and social opportunities emerged from these events.

It gradually became clear that our cultural strategies were being tasked with solving far more complex problems from the economic future of the city to its urban identity or the promotion of liveliness to recasting its employment profile. Success or failure related less to tangible assets and more to how cities approached their problems; once thriving places like Adelaide could go down and basket cases like Huddersfield could go up.

I realized too that understanding cultural resources required a new form of consultancy working with local teams, with diverse backgrounds, in a more participatory way. Being the detached observer was not enough: to get a feel for the city you had to be engaged, to see the factories, speak to the new entrepreneurs; to look at the night clubs and the alternative scene.

I began to see the limits of reports, so often stuffed into a drawer largely unread. I saw that changing someone's mind and their way of looking at a problem could be worth ten thousand words. But this is not an easy process. How do you change thinking about cities? I began to ask people about places they liked, about their dreams and personal utopias, and I incorporated this approach to personal visions into day to day work. It revealed the gap between aspiration and current reality and highlighted the obstacles to achieving the ideal. Three factors became critical. First, given deep-seated changes affecting cities, a new way of thinking was required. Secondly, we needed real models to show what is meant by the creative city, which is why the Creative Town Initiative in Huddersfield and the Emscher Park project are highlighted: neither is perfect – failure and success run side by side, but at least they are thinking about their urban future in a new way. Thirdly, there needed to be training opportunities to reflect on and develop ideas and practice with a peer group: this has now taken place annually since 1997 at the Amsterdam Summer School.

# 2

# Urban Problems,
# Creative Solutions

## THE CONTEMPORARY CITY

### A Globalizing Dynamic

Cities are caught in a whirlwind of change affecting urban life in
the challenges thrown up and solutions found. As a result it is
necessary to look at cities afresh and rethink priorities, requiring
an understanding of the nature of urban trends, their paradoxes
and contradictions if solutions for tomorrow's world rather than
yesterday's are to be found. The problems of cities in the North
and South differ in kind and degree, yet even these differences
provide opportunities for mutual learning. The solutions have often
shared underlying principles, such as:

- the need to involve those affected by a problem in implementing solutions;
- providing an environment for problem-solving that permits
  open-minded learning opportunities both for decision-makers
  and those affected by them;
- generating solutions that are culturally, economically, socially
  and environmentally sustainable.

Yet the differences are important: The speed of urbanization in the
South has created a gap between needs and expectations, resources
and response; infrastructures like sewage, water, housing or roads
have not kept pace with the demands of growing urban popula-

tions; insufficient wealth is generated to provide living standards that are deemed tolerable in the North.

Surpluses produced in Northern cities facilitate the creation of 'higher' standards of living. Having thus metaphorically climbed the Maslowian scale of need, the inhabitants of these cities are able to consider quality of life issues such as clean air, the public realm or cultural facilities. Such issues can seem like luxuries in poorer places, and breed misunderstanding between nations: for example, the North, having passed through its stage of intensive industrial development, can appear hypocritical in seeking to impose higher standards of environmental protection on the South.

Yet key trends affect both. Communication technology costs 100 times less than it did 50 years ago while computing power has grown a million-fold and transportation costs are a tenth of what they were in the 1940s. The consequence is greater globalization resulting in a new interlocking, interdependent economic system of cities, each playing different roles within an overall hierarchy of economic, political or symbolic power. Some, like New York, Tokyo or London, are world leaders, others like Buenos Aires or Singapore are regional barons. Cities have become the 'junction points for global flows of people, cargo, information and finance' (Nigel Harris in *Urban Age*, Washington, Spring 1999) providing control, command and logistical functions and facilities to tie together, direct and smooth the passage of goods and services. To create and operate this system effectively requires ingenuity, imagination and creativity.

A pair of trousers may be made from components sourced from cities in five countries; the design of a Walt Disney cartoon may start in Hollywood and end in Manila. Cities in developing countries are competing with each other to catalogue for libraries or process land and law records in developed countries. A dozen or more cities in Asia do Silicon Valley's software programming. The battle lines are drawn between competition on labour costs, new technology and expertise and creativity. This symbiotic dynamic is largely unseen, yet its implications are felt everywhere – a financial blip in Bangkok has reverberations in Atlanta, Stockholm or Cape Town; the opening of a new factory in Kuala Lumpur can close another in Newcastle.

In spite of urban competition there are so many specialist roles and niches that cities can fill, whether in the North or the South, and the challenge is for cities to assess how adroitly to identify and exploit their unique selling points, whether as centres of technology; finance, fashion and heritage or more importantly adapting the creative skills of their people to whatever demands and opportunities that may emerge. Seen in this light cities compete and complement each other as in the world of finance where Tokyo hands the baton to London and then New York as one time zone seamlessly opens out into the next.

## Layers of Connection

There are layers upon layers of urban interconnections – personal, political or economic – often based on historic migratory patterns such as the bamboo network of expatriate Chinese, who from Vancouver to Sydney are part of a China-based trading system. Yet the connections are not always obvious. Some, like the control of financial trading, can be detected, yet most are invisible to us unless we are avid readers of supermarket labels.

And new connections are made all the time as a result of economic booms, skills shortages or of war. The Albanians and Turks dominating the 'Fressmarkt' in Vienna; the 200 Afghani drivers who control the taxi route from Washington Dulles airport; the Korean, Japanese or Russian enclaves in Los Angeles; the one million Cubans who make Miami one of the largest Spanish cities in the region; the 300,000 Greeks who make Melbourne the largest Greek urban community after Athens – each group reinforces internationalized trade, first to supply its own needs, then by seeking broader commercial opportunities. New outsider populations take time to become integrated into the host city: they can be a source of creative potential and of conflict. In an increasingly multi-cultural world, finding innovative ways of bridging cultural divides will become an increasing priority for cities that want to be successful.

The organization of this intense flow of interaction, trade and finance requires innovations in logistics, management and regulatory structures at city and national level. The mobility of capital creates shifting fortunes. Cities need to be alert to stay competitive. Each new source of advantage requires a mass of creative inventions and interventions: good governance; the ability to build trusted partnerships; the availability of support facilities such as health care, housing or culture. Creativity is required to address the fabric of global governance; international trade agreements; environmental balance; equity issues; cultural identity and basic infrastructures in the developing world from health facilities to housing.

Here issues of scale impose themselves dramatically. Linear trends like population growth create a new dynamic demanding innovative solutions of a different order. In 1900 there were a dozen cities of over one million inhabitants: today there are over 300 and urbanization continues apace unabated. Infrastructures are not keeping up with population pressure, especially in the developing world. The availability and price of land largely determines urban development patterns and processes and, in their wake, structures of disadvantage and discontent embed themselves into the urban fabric.

## Intensely Global; Intensely Local

Yet the most significant urban figure is the individual human being, buffeted by global trends but mostly unaware of them or seeing them as personal experiences concerned with the exigencies of daily life and survival – going to the shop, dealing with a puncture, posting a letter, walking the dog, seeing neighbours, going to work or getting the children to school. The typical urban manager seeks to ensure that the multiple transactions of such daily experience unfolds trouble-free. Each small element has the potential to be done better.

But at the local level the bigger issues impact too. Daily transactions in the city now involve negotiating across cultural differences from eating foreign foods to sharing space with tourists, so more distant interactions occur alongside the more local, traditional interactions of a city, district or street. For the most part, the

---

### TEXTURED PAVING STONES TO GUIDE THE BLIND, JAPAN

An example of responsible, socially inclusive planning is textured street paving. In many Japanese cities, specially textured paving stones are embedded in pavements to guide blind pedestrians along safe routes. Changes in texture indicate changes in direction, stairs or obstructions. They are also used to mark the edge of platforms, helping sighted people too. This practice is being replicated and is increasingly common in European and North American cities.

*Source:* Global Ideas Bank

## Reducing complex bureaucracy through a Welfare Smart Card, Campeche, Mexico

In Campeche, south-east Mexico the complex bureaucracy of processing 18 different subsidy schemes to socially and economically marginal groups has been greatly simplified through the introduction of a smart card which can be charged with each individual's entitlements.

This scheme reduces alienation through its simplicity and it helps improve general health care since cards are recharged in specific places such as health centres. Individuals are obliged to receive regular, preventive medical check-ups if their cards are to be recharged.

*Source:* Global Ideas Bank

## Linking garbage collection to education, Bangalore, India

In Bangalore, a recycling initiative is interwoven with public education, health, economic and anti-social exclusion programmes to establish a multiply-sustainable initiative. Citizens are encouraged by the city corporation to separate their waste into 'wet' and 'dry'. Previously marginal 'rag-pickers' (many of whom are children; all of whom are exposed to a high risk of disease) are trained as 'waste retrievers'; travelling by tricycle they 'retrieve' the waste for a wage. Their literacy skills are also developed.

Wet waste is composted in lined pits in city parks and later sold; dry waste is sold at affordable prices to local industry and soiled/toxic waste is safely disposed by the city corporation. Citizens' forums monitor the process to ensure and perpetuate local agency. A city-level committee – *Swabhimana* – of city corporation officers, and health and education workers maintain the initiative as part of a comprehensive and coordinated city-wide strategy.

*Source:* Habitat

daily life of the city is a mix of interactions, different in form and extent, embracing both the local and the global.

Our capacity to be connected and mobile is counterpointed by our physical rootedness. It is the immediate environment that throws up hourly, daily, weekly pressing needs, although at the touch of a button on a keyboard there is an infinite amount of unconnected information and ideas available. It is here, like mending the drain, cleaning away the street garbage or alleviating the tedium and anger of living next to impossibly loud neighbours, as much as in the larger realms, that creative solutions are required.

The urban problem is made up of personally experienced dilemmas which are part of a larger shared experience where individuality is submerged in a civic, public life.

Encompassing and enveloping this civic life are the financial, economic and political structures of nations and multinationals,

---

### REGENERATING AN URBAN TRAVELLER COMMUNITY THROUGH CREATIVE ACTIVITIES, DUBLIN, IRELAND

Every city has itinerant groups, including travellers, squatters and the homeless. A personal development course for ten women became the starting point for the regeneration of a traveller community on the outskirts of Dublin, Ireland. The women's group urgently needed better living conditions: their existing site was unsanitary and vandalism was rife; there were no toilets or public lighting, and there was one fresh water tap serving 40 families. The site was scheduled for redevelopment but the local authority had not consulted the community about it. Through a series of empowering activities – model-making, drama, embroidery, pottery, quilting, photography, video, literacy and numeracy – the women planned a new site, produced a model and embroidered a quilt with the design; used photography and video to record the project, and persuaded council officials to develop their design. The site has become a model for traveller site design and is well-maintained because of the strong sense of ownership among the local community. The remit of the original group, now known as Clondalkin Travellers' Development Group, has been extended and it now runs advice services in social welfare, housing and health, literacy development, youth and children's projects.

*Sources:* Planning a Travellers' Site, 1998, Community Arts for Everyone, Dublin. Simeon Smith, Community Arts for Everyone, 23/25 Moss Street, Dublin 2. Tel: 353 1 677 0330 E-mail: cafe@connect.ie

with dynamics over which the individual has no control. Their effects cut across the lives of individuals leaving them disempowered and unwilling participants in representational or corporate structures governed by nameless – public or private – organizations. Re-establishing these links is perhaps the primary task for creative action.

## The Urban Manager's Dilemma

The urban manager has a thankless task. Pushed and pulled in many directions, the problems he or she faces are interconnected and the role involves a series of intractable strategic dilemmas in matching individual desires with political, social and budgeting priorities. The urban manager's problems include the following:

- Everyone wants a car, but without reinventing what a car is, the problem of pollution can only increase – not to mention ambient pollution like light, noise, traffic jams and parking problems.
- Developers' demands can result in skyscrapers blocking out light or distorting historic townscapes.
- Lack of resources and carelessness can lead to degraded natural landscapes with earth submerged under miles of asphalt.
- Effluents souring the air or poisoning the water supply – the environmental list could go on.

As the city bursts out of its original confines, a response becomes almost impossible: in Manila just getting in to and out of the suburbs can be an eight hour round trip. Such extra stresses and burdens are largely borne by the worst off who cannot afford to live near centres of activity. Such frustrations with poverty and unemployment can breed hopelessness, unfulfilled expectations, and boredom can change whole areas into ghettos with self-reinforcing cycles of deprivation. Meanwhile the rich create their own ghettos, like Forbes in Manila, to protect themselves from the perceived or real threat of the poor. If this becomes more extreme in some areas than others, an increasing separation develops between the middle classes and employed working classes and those whom we now call the 'socially excluded', as is evident in large British cities like London, Manchester or Newcastle.

In areas like Queens or Brooklyn in New York, the favellas of Brazil and the townships of South Africa it is often the strongest or

## LEARNING CITIZENSHIP THROUGH UNDERSTANDING ACROSS THE AGES, NEW YORK, USA

The increasing loss of traditional community makes intergenerational understanding crucial for settled urban life. Elderly people have often lost employment, income, respect and authority and become isolated in cities. For over a decade the Elders Share the Arts (ESTA) project in Brooklyn, New York has been doing intergenerational work linking cultures and generations, its largest growth area, with astonishing results. One project is called 'Why Vote?'. It brings together students from Brooklyn Congregational High School and seniors from the Bushwick Community Roundtable Senior Centre in a collaborative effort to create a play about voter education. The play, a series of songs and monologues, contrasts the history of voter education in the struggle for the right to vote in the rural South to urban apathy today. All the material is based on life experiences with elders and the young sharing true stories researched from authentic sources.

The Pearls of Wisdom are a group of older story tellers in ESTA selected by their communities to gather stories and tell them to others. The Pearls tour widely in New York City asking questions like 'what is community?, how do you define it?, how do you make it viable?'. In their recent 'Learning to see' project a group of seniors and young people each drew a map of their neighbourhood contrasting the places that provided special meaning to them: the doctor's surgery for one group, the video store and school for the other. Discussing their area they drew a composite map as part of a visioning exercise about the changes they wanted to see in the neighbourhood and which they then lobbied for.

*Contact:* Elders Share the Arts, 57 Willoughby St, Brooklyn, New York 11201. Tel: 718 488 8565 Fax: 718 488 8296

*Source:* Creative Communities

most violent who take hold. This collapse of established order can suffocate the generation of a civil society and independent action from which many creative solutions may grow. Yet there are examples across the world to show how even from such hotbeds of possible disintegration come positive answers. In almost all of these places are hard working community leaders, youth workers, priests, men and women of vision who, given the opportunity and support, could begin to address their problems. But such possibilities are

## EVEN THE POSTMAN CAN COLLECT RUBBISH, MIKKELI, FINLAND

Small settlements like Mikkeli in Finland have been left outside recyclable waste collection schemes, because of the high costs, yet the region has set stringent objectives for waste recycling: 70 per cent of the waste is supposed to be utilized. The central idea is brilliantly simple: waste paper from households in sparsely populated areas should be collected by the postman. The purpose of the pilot project was to discover its logistical possibilities and how much paper waste could be recovered. Each household was given a cloth bag, which was taken from next to the mailbox once a week.

The pilot project was successful at the time of reporting: it seems that it is possible to recover almost 80 per cent of waste paper, and the system could be suitable for collecting other kinds of recyclable and reusable waste. The main problem is cost. Mikkeli does not yet pay for the services of the Post as the profit from the collected paper is not yet sufficient.

*Source:* Hall and Landry, 1997

stifled by entrenched interests, inflexible bureaucracies, corruption or maladministration. When control lies in the hands of narrow interests and the public good falls prey to private greed the very solution causes further problems.

Over the last 30 years many cities have seen the arrival of large populations from other parts of the world, sometimes at a pace which has bred insecurity, fear and racism in the original community. In other cases the sheer number of incomers has left them adrift in a new environment without a sense of place or identity, particularly where migrants have been catapulted from rural life into an advanced industrial society. Citizens of the North have experienced similarly rapid change as a result of recent technological advances. In this world, traditions – even those newly invented – are a backbone of healthy survival, but attention to cultural identity and expression is the last thing on the urbanization agenda. How individuals adapt, negotiate and make choices are cultural questions. In the past our cultural and social values had time to develop and mature; today, the pace of change can overwhelm people and lead to reactive, impulsive responses.

> ## Innovative design creates commitment to education: Deepalaya school for slum children, Okhala, New Delhi, India
>
> Rather than suppress the imagination of 'slum children' in Okhala by formalizing their education in dour compartmentalized classrooms, this school is built with novel materials to innovative designs attractive to the imagination of children. Bold colours are splashed across new (and low cost) materials such as shells and pre-fabricated blocks to generate a variety of stimulating forms in a somewhat magical setting. Socially marginal children are consequently more responsive to education – they are more likely to go to school; and their education improves – once at school they are more likely to learn. A measure of social sustainability is thus achieved, quite simply, by using an innovative, cost-effective approach to the design and use of materials to transform attitudes and behaviour.
>
> *Source:* Habitat

Finally, it must be possible to entrust governance to those directly affected. Outsourcing problem-solving leads to unsustainable solutions because the essential learning process has not been understood. The primacy of education, of self-help and of working from within the community is self-apparent.

In this maelstrom stands the urban manager, generically identified as a land use planner although these challenges involve overlapping issues. Some cities have mechanisms for integrated responses through joint decision-making structures or mixed teams, but most address problems individually. Employment, education, housing, crime, social welfare, health and culture are inextricably entwined, particularly since what people believe – for instance about crime – may be affecting their behaviour more than the reality.

Housing and land use present some of the most intractable problems. How well is the housing stock standing up? Is there enough? And are there sufficient resources to maintain quality? There are endless negotiations from individual house extensions to major housing and retailing developments or changes in patterns of use. At one time, industry was considered dirty, and indeed created high levels of air and water pollution, with the result that there

# The Hundertwasser Haus, Vienna: holistic
## architecture as a living artwork

The late Viennese artist Friedensreich Hundertwasser (1928–2000) focused his practice on a sustained critique of cheap grey concrete high-rise blocks proclaiming the rights of all people to choose their own type of dwelling and arrange it as they would their own clothes. In December 1977 the Mayor of Vienna offered Hundertwasser a derelict site in the middle of the city on which to build an apartment block which was finished in 1985.

His crazily unique house with 52 apartments makes architecture art. It is designed on organic lines throughout. Decorative ceramic tiles line the windows so each tenant can recognize their own flat from outside. The house uses traditional Viennese design by incorporating part of a facade of an old house previously on the site. Openings are irregular, there are many pillars and towers, and some rooms project out of the facade. The walls bulge and wave. The floor is slightly uneven providing 'melodies for the feet'. Staircases are inlaid with mosaic and ceramics. Each apartment is different and there are no edges or corners in the rooms. Windows are triple glazed for energy conservation and to reduce noise. Great attention has been paid to details such as door handles, taps and other fittings. No two lights are the same. There is a doctor's surgery, a cafe with terrace, a winter garden, which serves as the central core of the house, a children's playroom and a courtyard – the 'green lung' for the whole tenement. There are three communal roof terraces, a laundry room, store-rooms and a garage. Built mainly of concrete and brick, the house is insulated with green roof terraces. Trees in steel troughs between the house wall and the recessed windows enliven the facade. Hundertwasser called them 'the ambassadors of the forest in the town'. They provide oxygen, noise abatement and climatic regulation.

Reactions to living in the house are extremely positive. 85 per cent of people love the house and identify strongly with it. Construction costs were probably 15 per cent more and rents are 10 per cent higher than a comparative structure designed conventionally and built commercially, but the City feels that the Haus has more than repaid the investment because of the favourable response from all quarters, substantial tourism impact and the beautification of the city as a whole, which will last for decades. The success of the project has resulted in a plethora of similar commissions for a range of public buildings throughout the city and elsewhere in Austria.

*Source:* Landry, 1996

were environmental health reasons for keeping work, living and leisure segregated, but this is no longer always the case. The transition from manufacturing to services brings new urban requirements, yet balancing the needs of older industry with the desire for renewal is difficult.

How does the urban manager encourage new investment and development whilst safeguarding the interests of people by-passed or made unemployed by the change. Multiple deprivations create 'sink estates', where nearly everybody and everything is pulled down. Solving these interconnected problems to avoid creating 'dual cities' is not the responsibility of any single department or the public sector alone.

How does the urban manager balance these questions with the need to attract high flyers? Cities are brands and they need glamour, style and fizz. That means attractive commercial areas with brand name stores and vibrant cultural, sports and commercial events. But these can cause their own tensions: what is the right balance between high and popular culture; between the city centre and the edge; between visitors and residents? The city has multiple stakeholders and the local authority's role is increasingly to set up, manage and drive partnerships to come up with solutions.

This means dealing with the lobbies, vested interests and campaigning groups pulling in opposite directions – a housing project with associated road expansion can pit a property developer against a conservation group with local people divided on the issue. We know that people hate congestion but like cars, however managers have few resources to increase the attraction of other forms of transport. The urban manager knows that many desirable outcomes involve behavioural change – like living above the shop and higher density living – which he or she has little power to influence.

The urban managers' biggest headache is balancing these demands and making the most of the available budget, knowing that some issues are beyond the control of a single city. In the end, whatever the scale or complexity of any problem, creative responses have something to offer.

## FAULT-LINES IN URBANISM

The world is changing in ways that happen rarely. The new conditions include the ascendance of the marketplace as an arbiter of value and taste, the rise of the knowledge-based economy and the special position of the entertainment industry; a lesser role for the state and the emergence of political formations beyond the left–right continuum; a new demand from many quarters for partic-ipation in defining the values and purposes of society; challenges to the unified canon of knowledge in many fields and a blurring of intellectual boundaries; the growth of multicultural national communities; the reordering of relationships between the sexes; changing conceptions of place, space, and time, particularly driven by technological advances; a general sense of fracturing in the unity of a body politic; and a reconsideration of what identity means locally, regionally and nationally.

Traditional structures for work, organization and learning are proving inadequate to the new demands. Core concepts governing our lives, such as notions of time, place and space, are being recon-figured to accommodate virtuality and cyberspace. The revolution in how we live and work throws up all sorts of new possibilities and problems while existing systems of thinking cannot analyse, explain and solve current situations. Watchwords at the beginning of the 21st century are: change, overload and atomization. The latter undermines our capacity to deal with the overload caused by change as well as our ability to build new, shared institutions which are necessary to manage change so that the benefits outweigh the costs.

But the new envelopes the old. The emerging post-industrial system lives side by side with the old, the pre-industrial and indus-trial. We make transactions in the 24-hour world of cyberspace, yet the opening hours of most institutions continue to be based on a nine to five routine, and seasonal weather patterns determine our lives more than we would care to admit. On one level much will stay the same – people will still take buses and cars to work and houses will still look like houses – but the inner logic of the knowledge-based economic system will increasingly frame industrial society. Learned patterns of behaviour will overlap and at times collide with the new needs which emphasize fluidity, portability of skills and adaptability. Yet the absence of predictable patterns and structures proves to be too unstable in the long run and because change will not go away issues of culture, meaning and value will be increasingly important, with the danger of new fundamentalisms emerging.

There is a transitional quality to the current period, its form is unclear and its contours still unfolding. Change and risk will remain key aspects within a framework of principles which offer predictability and some direction for decision-making. More open structures, which enable greater participation in development processes, lie at the core of this new balance and locality will become more important in the context of a shared global humanity.

In transitional periods mistakes are inevitable. Solutions depend on experiments which can be managed by organizations open to new ideas. This is the cost of living through a paradigm shift on the scale of the industrial revolution: solving problems in the old way does not work and although not everything is thrown overboard, priorities have to be shifted. We still need principles and they may come from many sources; indeed the task in creative cities is to mine the ideas bank of the past to face the future. Culture and how society sorts out, prioritizes, gives value to and transmits its purposes and aspirations will be critical. It is time to look at some of these changes more closely.

## Economic and Technological Change

In the weightless knowledge economy, wealth is created by turning data into information, knowledge, even judgement. Competitiveness no longer lies in immobile, physical resources like coal, timber or gold but in highly mobile brain power and creativity. There is less value in labour, even in capital and more in applied creativity as software embeds information in every product transforming every manufacturing and service process.

Although knowledge businesses built on information capital are not new, it is only recently that information itself has shifted the whole economy. The power of the chip and reduced communications costs have created new rules for the networked economy. There are 400 million computers, but 6 billion encoded, communicating chips are already embedded in objects from door sensors to cash registers. Their multiple connections create innovations on which this economy thrives, and the most promising technologies are connectors. As Kevin Kelly reminds us this requires us to re-imagine the objects around us. 'With more chip power in them than most computers, we should be seeing cars as chips with wheels, planes as chips with wings and houses as chips with inhabitants'. (Kelly, 1999)

Kelly notes further that the industrial economy found value in scarcity so when things became plentiful they were devalued. The network economy reverses this logic: value lies in abundance and relationship. The fax, or e-mail, has worth when others have them too. In buying a fax machine you are purchasing access to a network. The value of standards and networks increases in direct proportion to reductions in the costs of hardware and software according to the so-called 'law of plenitude'. The 'law of generosity' illustrates how value is created by giving away access – as Netscape did with its Internet browser software. The goal is indispensability which allows other sales to be generated – eg ancillary products, upgrades, advertising.

Sealed systems have no future – communication, collaboration and partnership are key. Value explodes with membership, in turn drawing in more members. The concept of economies of scale is over-ridden by the 'law of increasing returns'. Competition in the industrial era meant producing more for less; today, in the networked economy 'increasing returns are created and shared by the entire network. Many agents, users and competitors together create the network's value ... and the value of the gains resides in the greater web of relationships' (Kelly, 1999).

Silicon Valley's greatest innovation may be its model of social organization rather than its products. Here the 'networked architecture of the region itself – the tangled web of former jobs, intimate colleagues, information leakage from one firm to the next, rapid company lifecycles and agile e-mail culture creates the social web ... that makes up a true Network Economy' (Kelly, 1999).

The knowledge economy is universal but its effects vary. In developed countries techno-parks proliferate on greenfield sites or in recycled industrial city cores, but in Bangkok, Djakarta and Mumbai sweatshops exist side by side with software outfits providing back office functions for the global economy. Call centres – which already account for 1 in 30 UK jobs – are the industrial factories of the 21st century where telephone operators sort out problems or sell products following standard scripts. Individuality is not valued, yet the work demands intelligence. Even in consultancy, another growing industry, mechanistic processes are often in place.

## Implications for Cities

The city has a special role in the new economy because, despite the proliferation of virtual communication, face to face interaction, networking and trading remains vital. The idea that the information economy can revitalize cities runs against received wisdom that modern telecommunications disperse work. Yet geographical clustering is a result of the economic phenomenon of 'returns to scale' creating a virtuous circle that focuses production largely in cities. The essential requirement is for a diverse population with knowledge and social skills to support whatever turns out to be the next growth sector. The city provides the possibility for interactivity which force-feeds the exchange of information, ideas and projects (see Graham and Marvin, 1998).

The portability of skills and mobility of people forces cities to compete through the quality of their amenities, services, public realm and entertainment. The needs of knowledge companies and workers calls for huge urban transformation. In the industrial age there was a need to separate dirty industry from work, home and leisure. But knowledge industries require urban settings that project space, openness and social interchange. Ironically this is often provided by redundant industrial buildings around the urban core. In the centre are high value services like finance, business, retail, and civic political or cultural institutions. The inner urban ring provides supply services to the hub – printers, couriers, catering. It is also usually the home of the less well-established creative and knowledge industries – such as design and Internet companies, young multimedia entrepreneurs or even artists – that provide the buzzing atmosphere on which cities thrive, experimenting with new products and services.

The inner urban ring tends to provide the clientele for the new restaurants and venues, to which the more conservative people from the hub will ultimately want to go to. The buildings in inner urban rings are usually a mix of old warehousing, small industrial buildings and older housing with a large element of mixed uses. Lower prices enable younger, innovative people to develop projects in interesting spaces that in the centre only companies with capital can afford. As these companies grow and become more profitable they move into the hub or gentrify their own areas. This inner ring provides a vital experimentation and incubation zone. As these inner areas themselves become gentrified the pioneers move out to new low rent, run-down areas, and the cycle turns.

Urban renewal battles often take place in the transition zone between the hub and the inner urban ring, as the inner ring community resists the encroachments of office buildings; an example is Spitalfields in London where the City of London is seeking to expand.

## Social Change

New wealth creation processes mean new work and jobs. Flexible production systems based on simultaneity and interaction demand adaptable, multi-skilled workers. Security now derives from individual employability rather than the security of a large company or protection of a trade union. Employability highlights core competencies and in particular the ability to communicate: the new jobs are for data manipulators, communicators and interpreters of the symbolic realm.

Innovative organizations are inventing forms that larger institutions need to imitate – they are light-footed, project-based, strong on networks and alliances, and unpredictable. Typically companies dealing in knowledge and creativity need pleasant, stimulating environments. Increasingly they cluster in urban areas, usually close to cultural industrial areas like Silicon Alley in Manhattan or Soho in London where face to face contact is convenient, useful and efficient. If bureaucracies want to keep pace they need to develop flatter structures which nurture motivation, loyalty and trust and so unleash talent, responsibility and risk taking.

### Implications for Cities

Communication technology thus determines organizational form; it shapes the pattern of cities too. The classic industrial organization made for manufacturing material goods was large, hierarchical, fixed in one place and was able to disperse once telephones and telegraphs ensured information could spread rapidly through the system. The supreme metaphor of the industrial age, the clock, describes the ethos – standardizing, regular, mechanistic. The visual icon of the industrial landscape is the belching red-brick factory. The icons of the city of the information age stand at two extremes: the clean, sanitized glassy greenfield palace or the fashionable studio in a refurbished warehouse at the inner city edge (see 'Liberation Technology', Demos Quarterly, 1994).

At the same time information technology has shown place to be an impermanent and opaque entity rather than a fixed one and increased mobility and virtuality can sever our sense of anchoring. A diminished sense of locality, of shared space and identity has meant that community is increasingly defined by interests as much as by geography. Even at the level of neighbourhood there may be little sense of community, because the factors which nurture it – social homogeneity, immobility and the need to cooperate – are gone.

Quality of life is strongly tied to place in environmental terms and more personal, subjective connections to a location. Place attachment is seen as a centre of felt value; much more than an environment, it provides meaning in life and is a fundamental human need, and is enhanced when people are involved in the shaping of places.

The physicality of place has been shaken by a virtuality which enables people to take part vicariously in distant worlds. Time and place now function on levels where they have never done so before, which is something everyone will have to come to terms with. The physical world has fundamental sensual qualities, which makes actually being there the greatest experiential effect.

These changes also produce a new geography of exclusion. Vibrant, wealthier enclaves stand beside ghettos of poverty where cycles of deprivation lock people in. The consumer citizen requires cash to participate in the urban spectacle, yet people's consumption and leisure patterns overlap less and less. The role of neutral space in city centres is undermined by corporate blandness, and patterns of use which exclude many people.

For those with the education and portable skills – the portfolio workers – the city offers excitement, freedom and energy; for those without such personal assets it has only hopelessness, impotence, discomfort and squalor. There is an urgent need for urban creative action to address social exclusion, which can best be measured 'by looking at how people are cut off from work, learning and other forms of participation and how they lack the most valuable form of capital today – human capital – not just formal qualifications and skills, but subtler ones: knowing how to behave at work, knowing how to please a customer, knowing how to work in a team … being able to spot an unexploited opportunity' and knowing how to network with other people – not just with people like yourself who are also socially excluded (Perri 6, 1997).

## Political Change

The systems by which cities are managed and accountable – governance – is receiving new attention. Though democracy is spreading, its promises of participation are not always fulfilled. Power is shifting, particularly towards subsidiarity from the state to regions and districts and within them to partnerships between the public, private and voluntary sectors, and upwards towards supranational bodies such as the EU (European Union). There is increasing discus-

---

### RENT A GRANNY: RECONNECTING GENERATIONS BY USING THE FREE TIME OF THE ELDERLY, BERLIN, GERMANY

Over-stretched working mothers in Berlin have found a novel solution to the expensive child care problem. For less than £2.00 per hour, and often at no charge at all, busy parents can call on a growing army of substitute 'grandparents' eager to dote on their children. The Grandparents Service founded in 1998 rapidly opened its second office to cope with demand. The agency matches families with elderly women or couples who often form lasting relationships with both children and parents. For the carers greater meaning is given to their lives. Grannies are available for a maximum of 20 hours per week. The director Roswita Winterstein believes the secret of their success is taking into account intellectual and social factors in making introductions. One worry is that real grandparents get jealous if the hired granny gets too close to the children.

*Source:* Denis Staunton, *Guardian*

---

sion of the rise of the city states matching that of Renaissance Italy. We now see cities as complex amalgams of stakeholders with overlapping leaderships. In the UK at least, the idea of an elected mayor has been revived, but not in the search for a city boss, but for a visionary negotiator who can harness talent and resources and provide strategic vision and focus.

Declining voter turnout has also raised interest in other forms of citizen involvement from referenda to voter juries, as well as the representation of non-geographic communities from educationalists to women, the elderly or ethnic groups. Once more, the homogenous is challenged by diversity and multiplicity.

But good governance is a competitive tool in urban affairs. It could be questioned whether unpaid councillors, drawn from a narrow section of the population and affiliated to a handful of political parties, should have ultimate control over urban affairs. Beyond such elected bodies there are always groups of committed individuals willing to contribute to making urban life better, which is allowing the concept of stakeholder democracy to gain currency, in turn leading to new forms of municipal departmental structures being set up.

## Cultural Change

Economic and technological transformation, mass movements of population and the effects of globalization have had searing cultural effects. Cultural institutions and the host of independent activities and expressions, are consequently changing. Homogenization and standardization of products, especially in the entertainment industry, is threatening local identities, increasingly making cities look and feel alike. Simultaneously the hybridization of cultures is a cause of both conflict and creativity. For some, culture represents a protective 'shield' to guard them against unwelcome change, for others it represents a 'backbone' with which to face the future.

Cultural heritage and contemporary expressions of it have provided a worldwide focus for urban renewal. In the midst of economic development we find inspiration in the buildings, artefacts, traditions, values and skills of the past. Culture helps us to adapt to change by anchoring our sense of being; it shows that we come from somewhere and have a story to tell; it can provide us with confidence and security to face the future. Cultural heritage is more than buildings – it is the panoply of cultural resources that demonstrate that a place is unique and distinctive. Culture lies at the core of creative invention. Culture is thus, ironically, about a living way of life that is reinvented daily.

Frequently in the past, expressive culture and its mediators, the cultural institutions, were aligned to the purpose and goals of society. Today the situation is different. Democratic society tends to be uncertain when making judgements about what is right or wrong, good or bad in cultural matters because many see choice-making in this context as inherently undemocratic and bound up in a traditional system of hierarchy and privilege. Until recently there was a more natural connection of culture with the dominant spirit of its era and a consensus as to its role. The greatest modes of expression in the Middle Ages in Europe, for example, went to the service of religion. In the Renaissance, they focused largely on the re-creation of the city in the service of princely or bourgeois power. By the Enlightenment, the emphasis switched to the development of knowledge in the service of establishing an improved citizenry and society. Out of that grew the 19th century cultural institution: the museum and gallery, the public library and the symphony hall. At the heart of the 19th-century cultural institution lay the notion of the democratization of knowledge, whose purpose was to uplift and improve the broader public to suit the emerging conditions of the industrial era and the nation state.

A key challenge for culture is to come to terms with living in a market economy and to assess whether what is valued can be given a price. Yet the market economy has already indicated its difficulty in generating meaningful purposes beyond consuming and has recognized other aspirations among its publics. Retail outlets from Sephora to the Discovery Store have begun to take on core attributes which are normally associated with cultural institutions such as museums, that is in seeking to meet educational goals through what they offer for sale. (Marc Pachter helped these formulations.)

## Conclusions

New understandings from fields as diverse as economics, psychology and biology and the socio-economic implications of new technologies from the digital to the biological, compounded by the effects of democratization and mass mobility have highlighted the limitations of past understanding. The recognition that everything is connected exposes the limitations of compartmentalized thinking, revealing possibilities neither fully understood nor exploited. Changing our perspective – eg seeing waste as an asset rather than a cost; bringing work to people rather than people to work; reassessing what should be deemed to be free or paid for; or focusing on outcomes rather than inputs in municipal budgets – can have massive effects. The internal logic of the unfolding world can seem counter-intuitive, because its operating rules are different, but the first step is to understand that the new challenges cannot be solved simply by drawing on lessons of the past and on traditional ways of thinking about the present.

---

### FORMALIZING SCAVENGING, PHILIPPINES

The Linis Ganda (Clean and Beautiful) Programme in Metro Manila formalizes scavenging. By focusing on environmentally sustainable measures such as waste management, it reduces social exclusion, increases employment and improves the urban environment. 500 waste dealers employ 1000 'Eco Aides' who work along fixed routes with fixed prices for different materials. Over 200,000 households separate their garbage into 'wet' and 'dry'; Eco Aides collect their recyclables for $5–20/day. Over 4,000 tonnes of recyclables are collected per month, with an economic impact of over $200,000 in 1998. A dangerous, unpredictable, marginal activity is coordinated to a stable, 'decent' occupation; local industry benefits from low-cost recycled materials; waste collection/transportation costs are reduced; landfill sites have a longer life span.

*Source:* Habitat

# 3

# The New Thinking

## Uncreative Urbanism

City managers want good solutions to their problems, but barriers to action always emerge. These underlying obstacles must be removed before we can build a creative environment. Most are generated by bureaucratic mentalities – from which the private and voluntary sector is not immune – and the rigidity of professional disciplines; the individual has control over only some of these.

In cities, formulaic responses thoughtlessly repeat what has gone before. Issues are approached from narrow perspectives and fail to capture reality. Solutions are driven by manageable financial calculation with no room for insight and potential. Uncreative urban acts are all around us in spite of the best practice exceptions and, as a result, mainstream town planning interventions tend to disappoint. People seem fearful of discussing what quality and 21st-century urbanism is or could be.

---

### BARRIERS TO CREATIVITY, HUDDERSFIELD, UK

I once asked a group of officials in Huddersfield whether they were creative. In unison they answered: 'yes'. When I asked why this personal creativity was not visible in the town for which they had collective responsibility, they said: 'At home, in my own surroundings, I feel more in control of my destiny. I can shape my life and aspirations and as I become stimulated ideas and connections emerge. When I focus on my work, my world view narrows; as I enter the office world of procedures, administrative systems and hierarchies my creativity somehow disappears.'

## Abuse by Sectional Interests

Lack of creativity by people whose job it is to plan cities is only part of the problem; in many countries far greater is the random abuse of the urban environment through lack of regulation or the power to enforce it. In the new democracies of Eastern Europe, in particular, building, signage, noise or pollution control systems are neither strong nor incorruptible enough to create coherent urban landscapes. Companies like Coca-Cola or Marlboro provide incentives for shops to carry their logo so plain streets in places like Sofia or Cracow now have an uncontrolled garish look that draws nothing from their own cultures. A high-rise building is punched into a traditional street pattern; a bright late-night disco beams its pulsating lasers across the Nevsky Prospekt in St Petersburg. Residents and visitors immediately know a questionable deal or a challenge to the law has taken place.

## Lack of Effort and Thoughtlessness

Out of town shopping centres are usually formulaic, lack local distinctiveness, have no real public space. They rarely retain natural features; the mix of shops is predictable; opportunities are rarely taken to integrate public buildings such as an arts centre or a library. Distinctiveness is key, for although cities draw from each others' experiences the danger is that pioneering cities around the world quickly become textbook case studies for city officials. Cities then tend to adopt generic models of success without taking into account the local characteristics and conditions that contributed to those successes. The result is a homogenous pastiche of buildings – aquariums, convention centers, museums, shops and restaurants – that prove to be remarkably similar the world over (see *Urban Age*, Winter 1999).

Public space is too often the left-over of planning. It is rare to see a network of spaces creating alternative walking routes as in Barcelona, Rome or Munich. In Munich the generation of a more pleasant environment has created higher property values which have contributed to the costs of underground car parking: most cities make do with cheap, surface car parks that depress values and people. Roads and intersections are part of public space and in the core of Los Angeles it represents a staggering 60 per cent of the space used, while elsewhere in the city it represents over 30 per cent, yet the Los Angeles road engineers don't seem to realise this. Conversely, Stuttgart's inner ring road illustrates the impact of good planting, while in the summer of 2000 the 'Peripherarock' festival closed Paris' main ring road to allow the segregated communities on both sides to re-engage again through rock concerts and community events.

Lighting is more than mere brightness: it shapes atmosphere, acts as a guide and a pathway and creates the conditions for safety. Whilst the strategic lighting of monuments has improved substantially in Lyon, Melbourne, Glasgow or Vienna, lighting is still not used creatively. The character of each urban area is varied; lighting should reflect the distinctiveness thematically. The 'Luci d'artista' programme in Turin in the winter of 1998 used astronomy as an overarching theme to tell stories. Solutions are available: if an urban area is unsafe, what about lighting routes through darker walkways; if an urban park is worrisome at night what about foliage and undergrowth lighting?

## Formula Thinking

City marketing is concerned with identity and distinctiveness, yet common formulae emerge from urban publicity. Cities always find a way of saying they are central. Birmingham implies it is as central as Frankfurt – one of Europe's largest transport hubs and the seat of the European Central Bank. Does it make sense to say you are central when you are not? A string of cities along the former fault-line between East and West Europe project themselves as gateways: Helsinki, Berlin, Warsaw, Cracow, Prague, Vienna, Budapest. Equally every city is the festival city. Finally, the surrounding area has beautiful nature. The imagery reflects these themes: greenery, steel and glass offices, a high-tech industrial estate outside the centre, a golf course, a photo of a cafe area with many people milling around. If you replaced one city name by another you would not know the difference. Little reference is made to genius loci. Exceptions do exist: Palermo subtly highlights its Arab heritage while Naples has appointed an *assessorato all' identita*, a councillor for urban identity.

## The Importance of Genius Loci

Promoting local distinctiveness can be difficult. In Liverpool, people appreciated the character of the place, its creativity and rebelliousness while outsiders liked that eccentricity, in a framework of security: city marketers emphasized either one or the other. If Liverpool is 'in your face' there is a feeling that Leicester is a dull place where ideas could come to die. The city marketing task is to show that, under the surface, the city is diverse and vibrant, but that is not immediately readable or dramatic. This calls for 'iconic communication' grasping and conveying complexity. The same applies to festivals which need deep meanings and local creativity, but tourism promotion can damage what makes a city attractive by pushing out local identity. York has softened its tourism impact through simple low cost means to handle crowds: a town crier draws people away from busy areas, while coach parties are given different maps to explore the town, sponsored by retailers. There is a need to broaden the talent base for marketing and to bring in historians, anthropologists, cultural geographers, etc who can think more deeply and originally. The place-marketing world is dominated by product specialists, who have good tips or formulas, yet rarely understand the complexity of the city.

## Under-exploiting Assets

Urban entry points like airports, bus and train stations are not used to celebrate the adventure of arrival or homecoming as they once did. Urban rivers – from the Thames in London to the Tiber in Rome and in the extreme case of the channelled Dimbovita river in Bucharest rarely contribute to urban life. Why are buildings such as underused churches not rethought to include inputs from a secular point of view? Why is nature not used as a beautifier of roads and simultaneously a barrier as in the Ruhr? Why is there still insufficient social participation when the evidence of its effectiveness is fully documented?

## Erasing Memory

We continue to erase memory – a particularly pointless form of urban vandalism. Memory is undervalued though it helps the anchoring process, it can be tapped as a creative resource, it triggers ideas, it helps make connections. Kuala Lumpur and Singapore, among many examples, realized at the last moment, probably too late, that they had erased practically every historic quarter from sight even as they created fake versions of their past in urban fun parks. In Berlin there are few surviving remnants of the Wall, and though locals may have wanted to forget, other solutions could have been found rather than the 'cancelling strategy' whose over-riding theme was the erasure of any memory of the GDR.

## *The Inner Logic of Uncreative Ideas*

### *Power and Political Will*

There are many incentives and regulatory structures which affect city life over which city authorities have no remit. In most cases they cannot determine taxation rates and fiscal structures; they cannot, for example, institute a tax break for innovation or an ecological tax reform. They usually have no power to determine the nature of the overall school curriculum which may have an effect on fostering the creative imagination; they do not normally have the authority to set their own legally binding standards for environmental control, building or materials; they may not have the power to determine the programme for larger roads in a city, which tends to fall to a regional authority; they cannot determine levels of expenditure in public transport provision that goes beyond city boundaries, such as rail. Cities are not islands with the power to shape their own futures. The degree of their control, however, depends on the country's structure: the more federal a country – as say the US, Germany or Italy – the more likely larger cities are able to determine their fate. German Länder can veto national legislation they do not like; Italy's new regions can levy income and transport taxes. Under the Scandinavian 'free commune' system, communities big and small can 'opt out' of central government oversight and run their own affairs.

### *Accountability as Liability*

Incorporating creativity into city management is problematic as cities are run by public officials who are accountable to electorates. Being accountable slows down the pace of response to problems, which tends to be faster in private enterprise. A radical democratic approach to accountability could turn this potential liability into an asset by creating new channels for a flow of creative ideas from the grassroots to city government. This happens rarely and in a limited way, because politicians and officers are afraid of raising public expectations which then cannot be met with adequate resources. They may also be afraid that this process will lead to their legitimacy being questioned and to the emergence of alternative power structures.

### *Bureaucratic Proceduralism*

The functions controlled by cities require complex regulations, including planning permissions, licences, by-laws and traffic restrictions which govern city life to ensure the civilized co-existence of competing interests for the common good. It is a slow and difficult process to adapt these systems of control to changing circumstances, especially when strategic working is still not the norm. Bureaucratic proceduralism often pervades city organizations, preventing the identification and exploitation of endogenous creative potential. Curtailed by rules, municipal managers are often unable to make full use of creative talent so there is a search for new forms of organizational working, including forms of intrapreneurship, segmenting organizations into task forces or setting up public–private partnerships to bypass restrictions and encourage inventiveness. As city governments are forced to slim down and shed inessential functions they are sometimes enabled to think and act strategically.

## Reactive not Proactive

The cliché 'If it ain't broke don't fix it' may have some truth, but it does more harm than good in modern cities. Where issues are addressed only reactively they are already problems if not crises, and responses are defined by the problems themselves, so we are forced to deal with yesterday's problem not tomorrow's opportunity. The pace of urban change demands that policy-makers be forward-looking, proactive and address issues which are not yet problematic. Trends need monitoring accurately to detect little changes that may become significant in the future.

## Short-termism and the Need for Glamour

The short-term logic of politicians, time-limited agencies or partnerships is aimed chiefly at quick and visible results rather than longer term solutions. There is a tendency to go for flagship projects like the Grand Projets in Paris or festival events to suggest that something is happening. While these can motivate, celebrate achievement or create momentum, a city's competitive position may benefit more from a simple training programme or new partnerships with the private and non-governmental organization (NGO) sectors. The urban strategist has to find ways of making such low-profile projects visible.

## Power and Patronage

Networks of patronage and long-established élites can reduce access to power and information, and limit creativity by excluding people who may have much to contribute. Every country has élite facilities whose members slide easily into positions of responsibility, but innovative talent may come from anywhere, including less well-regarded areas of higher education. New universities may be more creative because they want to make a name for themselves or have less to lose. Peter Hall's analysis of innovative cities shows how outsider cities cut off from the mainstream are often the most innovative – Los Angeles, Memphis or Detroit, Glasgow or Manchester at different periods in their lives. He also notes the significance of the outsider – the immigrant or radical – in pushing cities forward.

### Inadequate Training

Urban professionals often have access only to training which is too narrow to make creative connections. This is as true for town planners, steeped in the disciplines of land use and development control, as it is for engineers, librarians, leisure managers and environmental health officers. Neither professions nor city management have yet fully understood the open and flexible dynamics of tomorrow's cities nor the importance of 'urban software' such as identity, social development or network dynamics.

### Professional Self-justification

The internal languages of different professions makes communication with outsiders difficult and constrains their thinking. The self-protective systems by which professions justify their actions cannot always stand up to more holistic perspectives. Traffic engineers, for instance, have stressed the need for blank visual environments so as not to distract motorists using major roads in urban areas without considering the effect of such degraded environments on generating graffiti, crime or even accidents caused by boredom. The balanced solution taking all risks and costs into account requires multiple perspectives. If creativity is to flourish across disciplines, between professionals and with the community at large a common language is necessary.

### Lack of Integration

Planning still centres on land use issues rather than the social dynamics of cities. It is easier to plan within a controlling, rather than a developmental or permissive paradigm, but it is the latter which is essential now. Despite the emphasis on 'joined up thinking' planning remains insufficiently integrated with economics, social or cultural affairs, environmental matters or aesthetics, to the detriment of all our cities.

## Entrenched in Stereotypes

Contemporary complexities prevent simple control, forcing us instead into partnership and joint action. But even a combined effort is unlikely to be successful if its thinking is hampered by stereotypes about the inefficiency of the public sector, the rapaciousness of business or the unprofessionalism of NGOs. Each sector has its own domain of operation, purposes and values but, these are also changing: a voluntary group may be entrepreneurial, a private company may be public spirited. In all sectors, the same key principles operate: effectiveness – the achievement of stated aims; efficiency – the maximization of results; economy – the best use of resources, time and energy; equity – the fair conduct of work; excellence – the achievement of quality in work (Matarasso, 1993, p 41). But their meaning will vary in different sectors. Efficiency is not simply speed or rate of profit, but effectiveness of purpose. Profit is often seen as the purpose of business but many companies would prioritize longevity, influence, market share or fair trading more highly. Profit is simply another term for value: for Oxfam, saving lives is the benchmark.

## Cooperation in Word not Deed

There is a self-evident need for local authorities and universities to collaborate to soften the blow of economic change, yet how many universities are closely involved in identifying local needs, arresting decline, getting involved with local manufacturers and bringing them into the new world? How many local authorities plan with universities to create targeted courses that relate to local needs? Yet the kind of links established between Stanford, local entrepreneurs and venture capital is what made Silicon Valley. The need for partnerships is a mantra of the age, but how much do they really deliver?

## A Restricted View of Motivation

Because urban leaders so often have little faith in people or their motivation, they have little confidence in what might be achieved. We need to get beyond the incentives paradigm and develop approaches which recognize some of the other reasons we have for action. Successful societies with the 'greatest economic dynamism and viable social cohesion are the ones where a culture of high trust enables individuals ... to take personal responsibility but also to sustain long-term co-operative relations in trading with and employing people who are strangers to them' (Perri 6 Missionary Government, *Demos Quarterly*, 1995). So crime will not be reduced by tinkering with sentencing policy, but through public re-engagement; environmental or health improvements through lifestyle changes.

## The Dynamics of Capital

Capital restrictions inexorably push out low value uses from the city. Changes in land use from lower to higher values – typically from light industrial or artisanal use to offices – decreases diversity and creates monotonous urbanism. The ability to build upwards, when allowed, becomes a license to print money, and only rarely are air rights or other land use changes costed and the value returned to the community. There are quirky exceptions, by-laws and traditions which can curtail this impregnable logic, but these are continually challenged. The observant can identify these easily as they determine the look of the city: in Washington there are no skyscrapers because nothing is allowed to be higher than the Capitol, so the city spreads laterally. Melbourne has sought to control the height of its Victorian street patterns pushing skyscrapers into the courtyards within the grid blocks; so pedestrians walk along Victorian streets, yet the skyline is of a cosmopolitan 21st-century city.

The workings of capital produce tension between reducing cost and increasing value and quality. This assessment shapes the built environment where there is a constant temptation to focus on short-term profits by reducing quality rather than generating longer term value. Governments can create incentives to enhance quality, for instance by greening a building and blending it into the natural landscape or by creating a car park that looks like a piece of art. These would pay for themselves if buildings were not valued in isolation. This requires doing 'context evaluations' of real cost and benefits going beyond the project itself. The real cost of dealing with graffiti or crime generated through lack of consultation and low quality, badly designed environments should be calculated.

# INNOVATIVE THINKING FOR CHANGING CITIES

This section falls into two parts: the first looks at overarching issues impacting on fresh thinking while the second outlines the characteristics and qualities of the new thinking. There are opportunities arising from the social, technological, economic and political transitions noted and from new conceptual approaches. New thinking is a precondition to recognizing and exploiting creative possibilities. The new thinking is a strategic tool and self-reinforcing mechanism through which people can find their own tactical solutions. It adapts the best of what we have, and adds to it. To maximize the potential of re-thinking it is essential to understand different types of thinking and action, such as the usefulness of different levels of abstraction, forms of communication, like the narrative and the iconic, and the deeper difference between ends and means or strategy and tactics.

## The Foundations of New Thinking

### Developing Coping Capacity

The idea that the future will resemble the past is long gone. Our capacity to cope is stretched when so many key ideas and ways of doing things are changing at once. We need new skills well beyond new technological literacy, including new approaches to thinking. People cope with the opportunities of change much better than the responsibilities. They cope well with some localized and personalized aspects, adapting to things like e-mail easily. People cope less well with structural aspects of change and at times do not even address them. These are intrinsically more difficult, but it is only structural responses that will create stable solutions.

For example, the funding of pensions is based on the concept of many younger people paying their current pension contributions now. What happens when the demographic pyramid is about to reverse? This fact has been known for at least a decade, yet the response remains limited. Another example is the emerging world water crisis caused by urban growth which contains the seeds for future warfare. Sana'a, the capital of Yemen, has grown from 160,000 people to 1.5 million in 30 years and ground water supplies are about to disappear. The crisis was predictable.

New thinking can help find responses, but it is inhibited by the mass of information cascading over us. The city itself is an incredible information source that can lead to sensory overload. This is why attention – the capacity to concentrate, listen and absorb – is increasingly seen as a factor of production like labour, capital and creativity. We need to know what information is for and remember that technology is an enhancer, a means rather than the end. We need filters, interpreters, decoders – not only in a technological sense, but also people who help sort, catalogue and discard – super-librarians with judgement. Physical environments can help filter too when there is the right balance of places for reflection.

## Understanding Mindset, Mindflows and Mindshifts

Managing the potential of cities will require a re-assessment of how we think and learn, of what we learn, of intelligences harnessed, of the types of information used and disregarded. It will demand new criteria to discriminate, judge and filter information and a broader perspective which embodies a more inclusive sense of possible resources and more free-flowing, lateral and creative thought processes in problem-solving. How can this come about? A changed mindset, rethought principles and new ways of thinking and generating ideas are the cornerstones. What is a mindflow, mindset and mindshift?

Mindflow is the mind in operation. The mind is locked into certain patterns for good reasons. It uses familiar thought processes, concepts, connections and interpretations as a means of filtering and coping with the world. The environment or context determines what is seen, what is interpreted and what meaning is implied. For example, when someone asks in English: 'What does S-I-L-K spell? The answer given is: 'Silk'. When one asks as question two: 'What do cows drink?' most people say, 'Milk!' Another example is the optical illusion of the combined picture of a young girl and an old woman. Beforehand one half of a group is shown the young girl, the other half the old woman. When combined into one picture it is rare for any one individual to see the image they did not see at first, as it is etched into his or her memory. The brain hears what it expects to hear; sees what it expects to see and discards what does not fit in. This is called 'contextual pre-conditioning', and it is especially powerful because it operates below the level of conscious awareness.

The same is true of more complicated thought processes. Someone with specialist training will look at a problem in a particular way due to that training and has vested interests in perpetuating current practices. A land use planner or traffic engineer will not want to be told that his or her discipline might become a less relevant way of solving urban problems and will fight to maintain the importance of that discipline. People will not relax and become creatively open if the result of such an exercise changes the authority of their profession. The creativity focus can be seen as dangerous and threatening. Power configurations are likely to change, say in local authorities, as those who can apply the new methods of thinking or organizing may improve their own status. Narrowly focused sector specialists will be reduced to a pair of technical hands unless they adapt and see their own specialisms in more flexible ways.

A mindset is the order within which people structure their worlds and how they make choices, both practical and idealistic, based on values, philosophy, traditions and aspirations. Mindset is an accustomed, convenient way of thinking and a guide to decision-making. It not only determines how individuals act in their own small, local world, but also how they think and act on an ever encompassing stage. Mindset is the settled summary of prejudices and priorities and the rationalizations we give to them.

A changed mindset is a re-rationalization of a person's behaviour as people like their behaviour to be coherent – at least to themselves. The crucial issue is how to get urban decision-makers at every level and those outside public structures who want to make an impact on their city to change their approach systematically – not piece by piece.

A mindshift is the process whereby the way one thinks of one's position, function and core ideas is dramatically re-assessed and changed. At its best it is based on the capacity to be open-minded enough to allow this change to occur. At times this happens through reflective observation of the wider world. At others, possibly more often, it occurs through external circumstance and is forced upon individuals and groups as when a crisis – say a dictator going too far – simply makes the need for democratic procedures more apparent. Alternatively an environmental disaster may immediately and with a sense of urgency create an awareness of sustainability – rather like a 'eureka effect'.

## Changing Mindsets

Changing a mindset is difficult, unsettling and potentially frightening. Transformative effects happen to differing degrees: by direct experience, by seeing things work and fail and through conceptual knowledge. The most powerful means is the direct experience of having to change behaviour, for instance by running an urban community development project according to sustainability principles. It provides the tangible experience to understand, to learn and to relate. By understanding directly a person internalizes learning and is able to repeat this learning in different contexts – it thus becomes replicable. Visiting an example of urban creative best practice provides indirect experience and is not quite as powerful. It can still have an impact though, especially if the project is based on different principles – eg using Internet technology as a means of empowerment and job creation. Conceptual knowledge derived by reading books or teaching at school conveys yet another understanding of city life and represents a powerful force when, by realigning thinking, it reshapes actions. Is education working to these ends? Are young people given enough opportunity to share in the experiences of others, to experience workplaces, to see diverse living conditions, to raise awareness of other environments? Only then will they understand their urban world.

## Changing Behaviour
There are six ways to change behaviour and mindset:

1   to coerce through force or regulation;
2   to induce through payment or incentives;
3   to convince through argument;
4   to con, fool or trick people;
5   to seduce – an odd combination of the voluntary and involuntary; and, finally,
6   to create and publicize aspirational models.

The urban decision-maker convinced of the need for creative change needs to plan a strategy of influence to change mindsets. Should it be bottom up or top down, given that directly experienced changed behaviour provides the greatest opportunities? It is not as straightforward as it sounds and is likely to be a combination of all persuasive devices, that takes into account immediate, short- and long-term impact. The most difficult and slowest way of changing a mindset is by argument, yet it is the most enduring and effective.

## Applications of New Thinking
The new thinking should impact on policy at three levels: the conceptual, the discipline-based and implementation levels. The first is aimed at reconceptualizing how we view cities as a whole and involves paradigm shifts in thinking. It is concerned with re-assessing the concepts and ideas that inform action, and is much the important as it determines how problems are conceived and handled at other levels. The idea of conceiving the city as an organism rather than a machine is an example. It shifts policy from a concentration on physical infrastructure towards urban dynamics and the overall well-being and health of the people, implying a systemic approach to urban problems. It is embedded in the notion of the 'sustainable city' – a notion which was itself a paradigm shift

when it first emerged in the mid-1970s as a response to the Club of Rome report on *The Limits to Growth* (Meadows et al, 1972). Another example would be re-conceiving transport as accessibility instead of mobility; this originally laid the foundation for the pedestrianization schemes of the 1970s. This level of thinking is concerned with changing mindsets and creating mindshifts.

Thinking about policy at the discipline level involves reviewing existing policies in known fields, such as transport, the environment, economic development or social services and considering the efficacy of existing models and ways of addressing problems. For example, in transport there may have been an emphasis on car transport, which might need to shift to a hybrid model combining the benefits of public and private transport. Or it might mean rethinking local authority departments away from titles like social services to community development, signalling a shift from the idea of the 'citizen as victim' to the 'citizen as potential', which has a far more positive focus.

Thinking afresh about policy implementation involves reviewing the detailed mechanisms to expedite policy, such as the financial arrangements or planning codes to encourage and direct development into certain directions. This might include considering how grant regimes are set up and to whom they are targeted; or what incentive structures such as tax rebates or fiscal encouragements are created or the nature of local plans and the priorities they highlight.

## The Characteristics of the New Thinking

### Integrated Approaches and Boundary Blurring

Box-like, bi-polar and compartmentalized thinking cannot generate the solutions to future urban issues. The greater the number of perspectives applied to a problem the more imaginatively it will be approached. To look at issues from many angles at different levels, depths of analysis and uncovering the assumptions of different disciplines will facilitate an understanding of how ingrained mistakes are made. This is not to deny the value of our existing specialist knowledge. The technical skills of an engineer or physical planner will remain essential, but to solve most urban problems they will need to be integrated with other skills, especially in the human and social sciences. Knowledge of history, anthropology, cultures, psychology has been lost in urban affairs. A traffic or zoning issue is never only about cars or land use. If transport planners had had a better understanding of psychology or culture or of the ideas of mental geography, they would have been more careful about building urban motorways with routes that scorch their ways through communities. The crime and social problems that ensue are then picked up by others who try to re-create some coherence for inhabitants.

We travel with a weight of history attuned to bi-polar thinking and are often sceptical of integrated, interdisciplinary and multi-disciplinary thinking. The bi-polar world looks for a trade-off, not win–win solutions. The 19th and 20th centuries saw a trend towards increasing specialization and hierarchies of knowledge with the result that we know more about less. We have neglected the connections between disciplines, the patterns and dynamics between parts and their self-sustaining system ecologies. This thinking is based on circularity and sustainability, where an input creates an output, which in turn becomes an input for a new cycle: in this pattern everything comes back in some form. This contrasts strongly with our overarching logic of linearity and the simplistic notion of inevitable progression which makes it difficult to grasp pervading patterns or contradictions that govern urban dynamics. For example, more motorways often lead to more cars and more congestion while restricting mobility can sometimes increase accessibility. We find it impossible to say what are the synergies between culture, economic development and environmental sustainability or how traffic and movement affect urban psychology. A further danger of the separation of knowledge is that a common language for urban discourse disappears so urban problem-solvers cannot talk to each other. When the capacity to communicate goes, a crisis point has been reached.

Looking at the effects of the globalization of cultures we can identify challenges to the unified canon of knowledge in many fields and a blurring of intellectual boundaries; and – often – imaginative recombinations. Valuing the worth of other disciplines is key. In multi-disciplinary planning several fields are brought together maintaining the integrity of each domain whilst taking into account lessons from other fields. Yet that is only the first step. Interdisciplinary planning, in contrast, truly interweaves forms of knowledge and creates innovative concepts and ideas through crossovers. In the process each discipline is changed and enriched by a broader perspective. For example if a mixed team generates a recycling project using unemployed people within a voluntary group structure, it has multiple impacts: the focus is environmental, it uses unemployed labour and is thus economically sustainable; because it works within a voluntary organization structure it may be more

## FROM NATO AMMUNITION DUMP TO HORSE PARADISE: IMAGINATIVE CONVERSION FEEDING OFF AN AREA'S TRADITION, TWISTEDEN, GERMANY

The NATO ammunition site Twisteden near Kevelaer in Nord-Rhein Westfalen, Germany, was closed in 1994, resulting in the loss of 196 local jobs and the soldiers' purchasing power in the local community. In 1995 the conversion into a Horse Park and Mushroom Cultivation Centre started. The site consisted of 370 acres, of which 160 were wooded, with 350 bunkers built out of reinforced concrete, and living quarters and administrative buildings. Returned to the community, the local authority encouraged innovative solutions.

Because the cost of bunker demolition would have exceeded the benefits of any alternative use, the idea of tearing down the 165 square metre bunkers was rejected. A solution had to be found that would convert the bunkers to some use without destroying them and their utility to the community.

One idea was storage use, another was mushroom cultivation. Yet neither was commercially viable on their own. An entrepreneur, Heinz Verreith, aware of the regions' horse racing traditions, detected a market gap as there was a lack of optimal training grounds. The dump was close to race tracks and serene enough for even the most highly strung horses.

Reuse of the site began in 1995 and the existing infrastructure of roads and paths eased reconstruction. Inside the wooded area a 1,300 metre race track was built. The former 6 km watch way became the jogging track for stamina training. The soldiers' former barracks were transformed into residential areas for trainers and staff, 110 bunkers have been converted to stables for 450 horses, 60 bunkers are used for mushroom cultivation and another 50 for storage. A veterinary hospital and restaurant have been built.

One hundred and thirty jobs, mostly local, have been created and another 190 are in the pipeline. The arrival of the horses has regenerated local agriculture. Neighbouring farmers provide horse feed and straw, retaining jobs in the primary sector. The hospitality industry has benefited from the influx of tourists who visit the park.

*Source:* Adapted from Elena Florin/Economic Development Abroad, Washington

empowering; and, by developing management skills, it has social and ultimately economic impacts. The integration embedded in the Emscher Park project which turned a weakness into a strength is another example. An area left degraded by former industrialization became a research and development zone precisely to invent the solutions to that degradation. Here the integration involves primary research in universities, product development in commercial laboratories, pilot projects in recycled buildings to maintain a sense of history and new forms of housing built on ecological principles.

It may not be easy for urban professionals to accept the loss of status implied in integrated thinking and planning. Technical, scientific and finance disciplines tend to have higher status compared to those like social affairs which involve people. In future the demand for urban leadership which combines an understanding of communication, social dynamics and networking with a grasp of finance and planning will reverse some of these conventions.

The recognition that the logic of scientific method cannot alone solve urban problems is a watershed: we shall need to link it with imagination, intuition, holistic thinking and experimentation. The strength of the creative imagination is 'the capacity to think of things as being possibly so, it is an intentional act of mind, it is the source of invention, novelty, and generativity ... it is not distinct from rationality but is rather a capacity that greatly enriches rational thinking' (Kearney, 1988). Looking for alternative views is a sophisticated form of rationality, something to be valued rather than feared. The different forms of knowledge need not be incompatible: they can spark off each other. The modern era associated with the rise of scientific rationality, 'was marked by a powerful obsession to impose a thoroughly rationalized order onto the world, an order that would efface all traces of the ambivalence that characterized earlier modes of life' (Clarke, 1997). This ambivalence encapsulates many solutions to urban problems by valuing connection and cooperation.

### Changing Metaphors: From Machine to Organism

Images and metaphors can have immense power, conditioning our mindset, structuring our thinking and the propositions we come up with. A machine mindset comes up with mechanical solutions, whereas one based on biology is more likely to come up with self-sustaining ideas for a city. The primary metaphor that characterizes the new thinking is that of the city as a living organism. It represents a paradigm shift in how cities are viewed, focusing us on balance, interdependence and interactivity within a sustainable whole. It contrasts with the modernist metaphor of the city as machine, and has implications as it shifts the focus onto health, well-being and people as well as the lived experience of cities rather than infrastructure, buildings and place. This biological image has far greater resonance, interpretative power and problem-solving capacity.

The city as machine is an authoritarian image reflecting a closed system with controlled and measurable causes and effects with little room for humans. Machine images have had a profound influence on how we think about organization, city planning, design, architecture and urban society. It betrays the assumption that someone must always be in charge, directing the machine, but the conditions for machine-like organizations no longer hold. Systems cannot be kept closed. A machine is inflexible, built for one function (Greenhalgh et al, 1998).

The organic metaphor, the city as body, is a better organizing principle and offers a new language for urban discussion: the bones might correspond to the topography; the arteries and sinews to roads, rail and paths; the intestines to water services; the nervous system to communication and electricity and so on. It is useful since it highlights the concept of a variable state of health. So a heart attack might be traffic gridlock where everything stops running and the blood stops flowing. Uncontrolled population growth might be seen as a tumour. The organic metaphor suggests a way of looking at cities in terms of diagnosis, prescription and cure.

Diagnosis suggests a health check, measuring the urban pulse and defining what problems exist. Its conclusion may be 'the city has a metabolic crisis and has reached the limits of its capacity for growth'. As a consequence the city cannot fulfil its purpose, role and potential – it is becoming dysfunctional. As we cannot see the interconnectedness – given our mindset – there is the danger of systems breakdown. Historically the city grew organically, meeting needs and supplying needs for others, but with a degree of self-regulation. With uncontrolled population growth, a massive strain is put on the system leading to economic, environmental and social breakdown. There are too many people in many cities and not enough resources, but like a malignant tumour the dynamics cannot be contained. As Herbie Girardet points out, the voracious demands of the city machine are 'beginning to outstrip the capacity of the planet'. Girardet argues for a shift to circular thinking with cities reconnecting inputs and outputs so that every waste output is re-used as an input. If recycling is integral and waste a potential

## HAWKS AS PIGEON PREDATORS: LETTING NATURE CONTROL POLLUTION, WOKING, UK

In Woking in the UK, like many towns over the world, pigeons cause considerable environmental degradation, their acidic droppings showering buildings, accelerating decay. Pigeons are also perceived as a nuisance by many townsfolk, causing inconvenience and anxiety. They have been cited as an attributable factor to the increased success of indoor malls and the deterioration of main shopping streets. Many towns conduct regular pigeon culls, yet for many people this is unacceptably cruel. A novel alternative has been developed in Woking. George, a Harris hawk, and his mate, Harriet, are used by Woking Borough Council to frighten away pigeons. The hawks rarely catch any pigeons, but their presence has greatly reduced pigeon presence and the associated problems. Main shopping streets are much cleaner, money has been saved from cleaning pigeon faeces, and the hawks themselves have attracted people into the town as a minor tourist attraction. A similar scheme has been introduced to London Transport's Northfield Depot. Managers realized they were spending more money cleaning pigeon faeces than repairing trains. Since the regular introduction of a 'fleet' of Harris hawks two years ago, it is estimated that hundreds of thousands of pounds have been saved.

*Source:* Global Ideas Bank

asset, cities can provide their own resources and reduce their environmental impact (Girardet, 1992a).

Following diagnosis we can looking at prescription. Is amputation the right remedy, perhaps by cutting up cities into urban villages? Or do we need medication? We may advocate the establishment of sensitive management of resources, more efficient use of roads, better design, pollution controls and tax incentives, but such responses cannot provide the answer on their own. These basic conditions of urban function are vital but they are only a starting point. The human aspects which might effect a cure may be helping people fulfil their potential or encouraging imaginative and sustainable ideas. Looking at the city from a sustainability point of view provides a basic redefinition of the problem and possible solutions. (see Kevin Lynch's work and especially *Good City Form*, 1981.)

## Enriching Concepts

Expanding our concepts of key terms like capital, assets, time and sustainability can help us to rethink urban development, perhaps by translating a concept that works in one area to another. Capital, for example, is conventionally applied only to financial resources, relating to money flows and assets such as cash, jewellery or land. Its value lies in its convertibility, so that it can achieve goals by purchase. If we see capital as one of a complex of assets that sustain or contribute to peoples' livelihoods, the focus shifts to the broader resource base governing people's survival. Financial capital becomes only one asset among many, including human, social, physical, natural and cultural capital. Human capital includes people skills, talent and health, while social capital includes people's networks and connections, their membership of groups, their relationships of trust that facilitate cooperation, reduce transaction costs and provide informal safety nets. Social capital enhances economic efficiency by facilitating the development and sharing of knowledge and helping innovation. Natural capital are resources from water to air to minerals, while physical capital is the built infrastructure. Cultural capital is the system of beliefs that holds a society together and their transmission mechanisms – the cultural institutions. Economics shape the dominant value system and by expressing social or cultural issues in these terms it gives them new legitimacy and metaphoric power. Yet quantifying the qualities expressed in these various forms of capital is a task for the new thinking (Sustainable Livelihoods Guidance Sheets, Department for International Development, London, 1999, was helpful for definitions).

Time seems like an anchor to everything we do; a set of fixed, regular points shadowing our activities and giving them order. Yet our concept of time is culturally specific and linked to economic formations. Time in the 21st century is different from pre-industrial or industrial time and our thinking about time as a resource needs to adapt. In the pre-industrial period, time followed nature and was essentially cyclical; in the industrial period, it was monitored against the clock or railway timetable. It required uniformity and the creation of time zones to facilitate trade. Industrial time was linear, regular and it standardized everything. If the seasonal clock could not meet the demands of the industrial era, we should not assume that concepts forged to meet industrial needs will serve the fluid pattern of post-industrial urban life. We always need reliable rhythms to balance the need for flexibility, but how we

---

### THE CREATIVE USE OF TIME: OVERCOMING SLACK PERIODS IN RESTAURANTS, HONG KONG

Eating quickly or slowly may not be good for your health. The prices in the Kowloon Hotel, Hong Kong, change depending on the time of the day. To maximize the use of slack times prices change each hour from $12.50 at 11pm to $33.00 at 7 pm. Clever eaters even take two meals in one, eating a late lunch and an early supper together. Hostesses punch time cards for guests, some of whom will spend hours eating, as they arrive. The idea has increased turnover by 30 per cent since the promotion began.

In Tokyo Tohtenko, by contrast, diners pay 35 cents per minute with a record of four minutes for one meal. The Tohtenko has spawned imitators. Many eat as fast as possible and a typical meal may take 12 minutes, costing $4.00 rather than $15.00 in a regular restaurant.

*Source:* Peter Hadfield, *USA Today*, November 1998

---

conceive and organize time in a global world is far from clear (see 'The Time Squeeze', *Demos Quarterly*, 1995).

One time change allows instantaneous communication across time zones, creating 24-hour markets, shopping, work and leisure. Urban life's multiple stimulations makes time feel as if it is crowding in on us. The new mental geography is unsettling. Too much information is packed into too little mental space compacting time. Mobility condenses time further, making us feel it physically as our bodies adapt with difficulty. Faraway places feel nearer because it takes less time to get there: for Londoners, Paris is nearer than Cornwall.

Time is an economic commodity, a form of capital which we cannot afford to waste in getting to work through the urban sprawl. It is also personal and felt, and reflects the other divisions in society, as many of the poorest people have the most time to kill, while the better-off feel they have no time in which to enjoy their wealth. As the emphasis shifts from wealth to well-being the capacity to use time well rather than merely fill it becomes paramount. The new rhythms of post-industrial time may come to include the right to time and an associated responsibility to use it.

Sustainability is the central concept of our age, it represents a new lens through which to interpret the world. It forces us to think about the effects of our legacy, and opens up the concept of inter-generational equity. It implies meeting the needs of the present without compromising the ability of future generations to meet their own needs, and fundamentally affects our concept of urban development. It is a richer concept that needs to be stretched beyond environmentalism to reconfigure conceptions of psychology, economics or culture. It should infuse the new thinking and allow the identification of sustainable forms of creativity.

The notion of creativity and sustainability may seem to be at odds. Sustainability shapes creative endeavour by stressing the need to test consequences and resilience in the face of external shocks. It extends into other areas as well: economic sustainability addresses the need to maintain an income stream over time, or the need for economic development initiatives to tackle issues such as crime, lack of confidence or inadequate educational facilities. Social sustainability demands that social exclusion is minimized and social equity enhanced, highlighting the need to ensure real participation by local communities. Institutional sustainability demands that structures can perform over a long time period.

Political sustainability is less often considered but projects depend on political commitment or tolerance for their long-term viability. Conceptual sustainability focuses on the need for activities to be internally and externally consistent to succeed over time, partly to help win political support, but more importantly to achieve the outcomes anticipated. Cultural sustainability highlights the fact that activities must take account of the cultural context, how people live and the values which inform the patterns of their lives. Finally, we should not forget emotional sustainability. We do all sorts of things for emotional reasons which we may scarcely be aware of: for example the sustainability of teaching depends at least as much on encouraging the positive feelings of those entering or in the profession, as on the remuneration offered (Francois Matarasso helped to clarify this point). What makes happiness is not higher income and at whatever level of development we prefer a sense of well-being to being well-off with its allied need for developed consumerism (see Argyle, 1987).

## Enriching Intelligence

Western societies have tended to value some forms of intelligence – particularly scientific–linguistic – over others, so that the belief that there is only one intelligent form of cognition has seeped into the fabric of our institutions. This linear thinking breaks everything down into component parts, arguing that logical reasoning is the only sound basis for decision-making. New knowledge is constructed on that restricted foundation and becomes caught in its own inner logic, so that organizations self-select people who exemplify the same thinking they already have access to. The value of this form of thinking often blinds us to other forms, and to the people who use them, which operate through unexpected connection, simultaneity and flexibility.

Education systems have been slow to recognize the validity of multiple intelligences in the curriculum (Gardner, 1993). Compared to cognitive–linguistic skills, other forms of intelligence – spatial, visual, musical, bodily-kinaesthetic, personal, psychological and interpersonal – remain marginalized. The written word is vital but there are vast unused resources which we can tap into. For every goal there is an appropriate set of intelligences to be applied, and others whose use would limit possibilities. We can only solve the city's problems creatively if we apply different understandings, perspectives and interpretative keys.

Different cultures and periods favour some blends of intelligences over others. During the early industrialization era, learning reflected the machine image of the age and valued rote learning. More industrialized and post-industrial societies value logical-mathematical, linguistic and intra-personal forms. In an age of creativity all forms of intelligence need bringing into the picture as sources of inspiration and vehicles for expression of thought, information and theory. A drawing can express a thought, a piece of music may echo a political sentiment or a film might expound a vision. The new communications media are forcing us to recognize the role these intelligences already play: we should be making more active use of them.

We also need to rethink when and where we learn. The pace of change has weakened the notion of fixed life-stages and linear life development. The model of life as composing just three periods – education, work and retirement – with supporting social and economic structures is passing. Now we recognize the need for lifelong learning, where learning occurs in a repeating cycle to help us adapt to new circumstances. This challenges the monopoly of traditional education service providers: opportunities for learning are increasingly varied – obvious, surprising but increasingly informal whether at home, at work, in libraries, universities or even hybrid situations.

## URBAN POOR ELDERLY HEALTH WORKERS, MANILA, PHILIPPINES

Elderly people rarely figure in the urban agendas of metropolitan cities. In Manila there are more than 200 groups responding to the needs of street children, while elderly people are virtually ignored. In this context, the 'Coalition of Services of the Elderly' (COSE) have set up an innovative project. Each 'squatter community' of Manila delegates two elderly people to become 'Community Gerontologists' (CGs). For three days they are trained by a doctor, dentist and nurse with an emphasis on ailment prevention for elderly people. 'Armed' with a medical kit containing a thermometer, blood pressure and sugar monitoring instruments, basic dental examination tools and common medicines, CGs work as a valuable and low cost interface between professional medical staff and sceptical communities. Regular monitoring ensures they maintain and develop their skills, communities are healthier and ownership/agency remains to a large extent with local elderly people.

*Source:* Habitat

This has also brought new talents into play, as people from much more diverse cultural and demographic backgrounds begin to play a part. The self-resourced University of the Third Age for the over-50s has presented a serious challenge to entrenched discrimination on the grounds of age. Whilst retirement may become a more porous concept, has it gone far enough in giving value to the diversity of experience? If these human resources are underestimated, cities are failing to tap into all their talent and are also creating costs in an increasingly ageing society. There is much imaginative work to be done that shows how one can both revalue older people as well as broaden our assessment of the potential of the young.

### Enriching Communication

Understanding the distinction between forms of communication – especially the narrative and iconic – is important. Narrative communication is concerned with creating arguments; it takes time and promotes reflection. Its 'band width' is wide as its scope is exploratory and linked to critical thinking; it is 'low density' in the sense of building understanding piece by piece. It is about creating meaning. Iconic communication by contrast has a narrow 'band width' and highly focused purpose; it is 'high density' because it seeks to 'squash meaning' into a tight time frame, creating high impact by encouraging symbolic actions that make what is being projected feel significant. A typical form of iconic communication is the promotional material of the charity Action Aid which does not aim to explain the causes of a situation but simply to trigger a response, expressed financially – now.

The challenge of creative urban initiatives is to embed narrative qualities and deeper, principled understandings within projects which have iconic power. Emblematic initiatives can leapfrog learning and avoid lengthy explicatory narratives through the force of their idea and symbolism. In this context visionary leaders, emblematic best practice projects and the work of campaigners, radicals and risk takers are all paramount. For example, the Calcutta-based PUBLIC (People United for Better Living in Cities) enhances living conditions through its direct action campaigns on litter, public transport and saving cultural heritage.

The decision to create the first directly elected mayor for London had huge iconic quality. It symbolized not just the creation of a leader committed to the city but a break with tradition and a new start. Another idea with iconic quality was that of Common Ground, who suggested creating new river-based songs for London, involving all communities along the river. The river divides and joins Londoners. Such a participatory event would change how they felt about London, enable people to meet and link with cultural and political regeneration, preparing the ground for addressing other tangible problems of London having enhanced commitment, civic pride and motivation. The Helsinki Forces of Light project, outlined in detail later, has similar qualities given the significance of light in Finland.

The idea of zero tolerance initiated in New York to combat crime is equally iconic. Everybody knows immediately the power of the word 'zero'. It is a packed phrase and people know what it means and what is expected without complex explanations: linked to the word 'tolerance' it provided psychological comfort.

Identifying the iconic trigger – whether light, a song or even a word like zero – is the most difficult aspect as communication needs to relate to the place, its traditions and identity. The cultural resources model described later is one approach to identifying these triggers. In an age where attention span is at a premium identifying projects that within them embody principled, fresh ideas yet can be communicated iconically is the challenge of the creative city. Iconic

## REVERSING ROLES: STREET CHILDREN TRAINING THE POLICE, ADDIS ABABA, ETHIOPIA

Police trainees in the Ethiopian capital Addis Ababa are learning to manage situations involving street children through workshops with young people from Adugna Community Dance Theatre. Adugna is part of the Gemini Street Symphony Youth Programme which works to improve the lives of street children in Addis Ababa through training in film and dance skills for community development and personal empowerment. The relationship between police and street children has traditionally been hostile, fuelled by perceptions of police brutality. The dance workshops use dance as a metaphor to explore and challenge issues of violence and the attitudes of those in authority. They create a safe environment in which street children can question police views and learn to understand the work of the police, and correspondingly offers police cadets an opportunity to hear the views of street children and learn to avoid strategies which may tolerate the brutalization of street children.

*Source:* Adugna Community Dance Theatre/Gem TV, project reports 1999. Andrew Coggins, Street Symphony Support Operation, 20 Wandsworth Bridge Road, London SW6 2TJ. Tel: 0171 736 0909 E-mail: apc555@aol.com

communication, if not leavened by an understanding and acceptance of deeper principles, can be dangerous and can turn into manipulation and propaganda. (I am grateful to Tom Burke for highlighting these distinctions.)

### Creating Cooperative Space

Integrated thinking depends on increasing respect, empathy and the understanding of collective goals. There are many routes to success so respect for difference and alternative viewpoints and a willingness to change one's own mind are essential. There are many ways to be a creative city. There are different ways of running a museum, a restaurant or internet service and difference can be a competitive advantage. An atmosphere which respects different contributions encourages ideas and maximizes potential. It creates an arena for dialogue and a space for common action. But that depends on being able to value difference without demanding that anyone should abandon their own core values – unfortunately not a characteristic of most political debate. Since it is easier for people trained in dialogue to operate in this cooperative space, teaching participation techniques should be part of new thinking strategies.

Respect fosters curiosity and the courage to take risks, and develops an attitude disposed to seeing solutions rather than problems. For example, emotional, psychological and aesthetic intelligence is underrated as a skill in management and policy-making – indeed most managers would not even know what they are – yet a person with these skills often makes a team work better. What counts is what works appropriately. Being creatively critical can help test arguments and risks while avoiding the caution that comes with fear of personal criticism. But creative criticism should come with proposed alternatives. Licensing experiment and valuing alternative views gives people permission to think afresh and explore, conceptually and practically, leading to pilot projects that can be mainstreamed. It encourages people away from black and white alternatives, when the solution may be to use parts of different alternatives.

## Widening Rights
The new thinking needs a system for making choices, discriminating and judging, but what is its underlying basis? Surely it is the recognition of our interdependence in a shared humanity – one earth that predominantly lives in cities. But what universalities and lasting values can we derive from this understanding of mutual dependence to provide anchorage, where certain things are incontrovertible, at least for a time?

At heart the principles relate to human rights: freedom of conscience, expression and religion – an acceptance of cultural diversity. Yet the United Nations (UN) charter model inevitably focuses on the individual: how might it help us to negotiate urban life? Most developed societies have accepted that the weaker of their members – children, the disabled, elderly and so on – are entitled to public support, and are not to be discriminated against. These and other rights are being extended into other areas, for example the concept of a right to clean air and water is developing. Are there other issues which, if conceived as rights, would affect our hierarchy of priorities and our decision-making? Our understanding of our rights changes from time to time, and is always subject to political negotiation between interested groups, but the concept can be powerful. We should not feel that rights are always universal: what is a right in one place may not be somewhere else. Cities can grant their citizens *de facto* rights – for example, as many have done through codes of service standards or Citizens' Charters – which they do not enjoy elsewhere, thus gaining a competitive advantage.

## The New Simplicity: A Focus on Ethos

It is a self-fulfilling truism to say that the world has become more complex, but we can choose whether to feed that complexity or to work towards simplicity in the way in which we plan, design or even discuss the future of the city. A knowledge economy, once we understand its rules, need not appear more complex than an industrial one: its confusing detail then fits into clearer patterns. The mass of information available through the media and Internet perplexes too, but once filtered and ordered, it disentangles and streamlines.

The replacement of firm belief systems by frameworks like postmodernism with its focus on relative value might lead us to feel that anything goes, except making judgements. Yet we do make value judgements which guide our choices and actions, and so make complexity intelligible. We prefer certain forms of expression, social goals, styles of living, concepts of integrity and purpose. The reassertion of fundamentalist belief systems or the range of beliefs generally referred to as 'New Age' are other ways of making life easier to grasp.

It is possible to simplify without being simplistic or making shallow judgements. The new thinking with its focus on holistic approaches is a route to appreciating complexity, because it involves the capacity to hold apparent opposites in mind. This might mean combining openness with rigour or being simultaneously focused and flexible. By honing in on underlying logics, principles, rules and systems, complexity can be reduced to comprehensible essentials. If we are firm on values, disorder achieves a focus through an ethical framework. The notion of ethos helps re-create coherence, which Geoff Mulgan summarizing Norman Strauss' ideas encapsulates well:

> *An ethos is a unifying vision that brings together a set of clearly comprehensible principles and a narrative account of what ... is to be achieved. Ethos is a tool for the regeneration of coherence. This is the first task of any organization. ... It requires self-understanding and that of its operating environment.*

> *It demands skills for the higher order integration of
> what may seem to be conflicting information and
> incompatible interest groups. ... Its response to a new
> situation is relatively easy to see when it has such an
> ethos. Its response is relatively predictable and its
> principles are transparent to everyone. ... Having
> defined an ethos a government has a very powerful
> tool: a guide to priorities and resources, a common
> identity and purpose that binds people together. ..
> Ethos is a decision making tool .. when new prob-
> lems arise they do not have to be considered from
> scratch. Ethos is a variety or complexity reducing
> tool ... that links the visionary and the practical. ...
> There are three layers that need to be coherent ... the
> meta or grand strategy of ethos, vision, ethics and
> transformation; the core strategy of management,
> control, rules, budgets, initiatives and monitoring,
> the base strategy of routine, repetitive operations*
> (Mulgan, 1995).

A strong ethos for the new urban leadership should focus on civic
creativity. The word civic is not normally associated with creativity
and we do not think of applying creativity to public purposes such
as economic development or combating racism. This ethos should
embed itself in the genius loci, chime with its culture and an assessment of the potential of its cultural resources. In this way the ethos
is both grounded and aspirational.

### Leadership as a Renewable Resource
Leadership needs to be treated as a renewable, developable
resource. The process starts with the recognition that boundaries
are blurred, admitting we do not know everything even in our
specialist fields. A culture that sees this as a strength has far more
resilience, honesty and need not operate on bluff. Partnership is
thus essential. 'Creating a culture for leadership involves saluting
those who have done extraordinary things and bidding them
farewell, so that stepping down forms part of the norm. This is a
pre-condition to preserve long-term commitment, to a vision, a
goal, and a strategic plan. ... A community that creates that kind of
leadership builds civic capacity – an infrastructure as essential as
roads and sewers. Civic capacity buttresses community in time of
stress and allows it to take bold new actions' (McNulty, 1996).

De-personalizing leadership is important, because it ensures that good ideas – which are essentially strategic opportunities – are part of a common agenda rather than the expression of a single person. It allows a good idea to have many parents, and allows for adoption without difficulty. Institutionalizing leadership helps it endure, but involves planning for burn-out, retirement, even death. It implies a process for training new leaders and there must be leadership opportunities for young people to develop new skills, to usher out older leaders and honour them for their contribution while the community moves ahead with a new leadership.

Leaders in business, civic organizations, culture, volunteer bodies or the professions typically play collective roles in their community as well as in their jobs. They become its unofficial trustees when they see they cannot focus solely on a single issue, but must deal with the related concerns of their community. Unfortunately, in many cases leaders are selected from old, traditional power structures, which might represent the past rather than the true diversity of tomorrow's city (see McNulty, 1994).

## Re-assessing Evaluation and Success

The new thinking demands that monitoring, evaluation and judgement on success and failure be re-assessed wholesale. Continuous and built-in evaluation is necessary to ensure creativity runs throughout project processes. Evaluation encourages reflexive learning and continuously revitalizes thinking. It is the capacity to absorb and gain knowledge, to build on the experiences of past lessons and to have a full and active awareness of what is going. In order to be effective and efficient, learning requires evaluation based on both divergent, generative or convergent as well as analytical and critical thinking.

Success or failure tend to come together; only very rarely is a project successful in all respects. The seeds of success lie in failure and vice-versa and we can learn from both through continuous feedback. People believe they can avoid failure by following best practices, yet this is often unreflective imitation without considering the context. Who decides how to assess success or failure is crucial. The limitations of simple financial calculus have already become apparent. To speak of people in the creative city as the most valued asset is one thing, but: 'accounting systems have not caught up with the shift that is needed. They have not moved from measuring only the use of financial capital to measuring the building of human capital. Within corporations financial measures can swamp other measures of performance and value and claim disproportionate time and attention' (Rose Moss-Kanter from a speech at the Commerce Labor Department summit on the Future of the Workplace, Washington, 1993). Generic headline indicators like urban versions of GNP are poor indicators of urban health, focused as they are on short-term profits or narrow definitions of urban dynamics rather than the long-term capabilities of a city.

Yet crucially, as David Yankelovich, the renowned American pollster, put it: 'The first step is to measure whatever can be easily measured. This is okay as far as it goes. The second step is to disregard that which can't be measured or give it an arbitrary value. This is artificial and misleading. The third step is to presume what can't be measured isn't really important. This is blindness. The fourth step is to say that what can't be easily measured really doesn't exist. This is suicide!'

## What are the Benefits of the New Thinking?

Applying this style of thinking opens a richer range of possibilities and a wider resource base of ideas with which to work. It allows policy-makers to research and map with a greater chance of discovering the uniqueness and specialness of a place rather than merely seeing a partial picture of problems and opportunities. It is a much more effective way of working within and beyond the organization and provides the opportunity to make mistakes without being damned. It provides a constructive working environment with people more involved and responsible connecting with a wider network of organizations and residents. It thus makes the city more competitive.

## IMAGINE A CITY

During the Amsterdam Summer School we imagine a place that sounds like an urban utopia, fulfilling most of our dreams about how we want our cities to be. We know it exists in the mass of urban best practices around the world, but we can't see this utopia because the imaginative solutions are not in one place. The urban dystopia by contrast – congestion, pollution, unease and soullessness – feels only too present.

### Common Concerns
Because of your age, interests and background your own utopia

may differ in details, but some aspects are likely to remain constant – a decent livelihood, somewhere comfortable to live, access to facilities. There is a growing understanding that we need to live more sustainably. Most of us agree that cities should have clear identities and a sense of community, that they should be distinctive and true to themselves. We would concede that participation and involvement in decision-making increases motivation, commitment and civic pride, but how many would take that so far as to accept that fairer distribution of resources and power leads to a decrease in crime and social stress? And who would take issue with the need for cities to be vital and vibrant – economically, socially and culturally?

## Movement

What might this mean? Let us consider movement around the city. We are wedded to our cars, convenience overriding hassle, cost and pollution. Alternatives seem forced, prescriptive, expensive. Can we imagine an approach to transport and land use which encourages us to reduce car travel willingly? One that makes us want to return to walking or cycling for enjoyment, where public transport is a pleasure and the use of 'para-transit', like shared cars, is normal?

Perhaps we could, with the right combination of policies and action, such as:

- extending user-friendly public transport;
- a 20-hour service at very frequent daytime intervals and guaranteed evening intervals;
- stops within easy walking radius;
- traffic calming in residential areas, but extending over time to all areas of the city or developing 'No Car' residential zones;
- integrating public transport so you can move seamlessly from one form to the next;
- upgrading the quality of the train, bus, tram and bicycle experience and giving priority to them, creating communication systems that deliver new routes and connections through the city;
- a parking regime that gradually reduces public car parking spaces in central and inner areas with priority to residents and short-stay parkers;
- park-and-ride at the periphery with a choice of public transport or bicycles;

- pedestrianizing central areas, with defined exceptions for quiet non-polluting public transport (trams, electric buses); even extending pedestrianization with people movers in hilly cities;
- creating noise protection zones, especially at night, with concessions for 'quiet trucks';
- shifting car transport to main roads;
- offering discounts or incentives, such as negotiating with employees – perhaps first in the public sector – to give up parking spaces in return for free public transport and bicycle facilities (shelters, showers, etc);
- creating computerized control systems and selective vehicle detection at traffic signals;
- and for those bold enough, raising extra tax revenue to pay for public transport investments.

## *Beyond a Fantasy?*
It sounds like a fantasy – easily proposed but impossible to implement. Yet everything proposed is already accepted common-sense in different European cities: just not all in the same place. In Basle, Zurich, Freiburg and Strasbourg most of this has been achieved and individual car use and energy consumption has declined sharply – even as the economy has expanded. In The Netherlands – The Hague, Groningen, Delft, Amsterdam – and in Copenhagen, Vienna and Bologna, similar initiatives have taken root because of a combination of public sector vision, initiative and consistent purpose, campaigning by pressure groups and finally private sector support. Resistant public opinion is being turned round by success: in Zurich, by 1987 61 per cent were in favour of drastic car reduction measures.

Taming the car has not made these places dull, slow-paced and uninspiring. It has not blunted their wealth creation capacity or the edge of their urban creativity. The car – 'the great connector' – has ultimately, in cities at least, restricted communication and human contact. Cities that encourage walking, the chance encounter and face to face contact foster creativity, wealth and well-being.

The car is the most visible symbol of the city, but our ideal contemporary city has similar creative solutions for energy saving or waste emissions: regular energy audits; district heating islands with co-generation of power; tariffs to discourage profligate users; the raising of standards to cut energy and subsidizing the purchase of energy saving devices; help for ecological housing cooperatives. Cities like Saarbrücken, Frankfurt and Helsinki are at the forefront here.

## Corporatively Creative

What about creating the conditions for an urban utopia beyond the environmental domain? There are companies who have accepted a responsibility to the society in which they operate, companies who are:

- promoting racial integration;
- identifying educational and work opportunities for street children;
- creating employment for disabled people to foster independent living and change attitudes;
- improving training for the hard-to-employ, adopting local schools, providing local scholarships, mentoring schemes or using company premises as a training ground;
- helping the unemployed set up shadow companies within a safe company umbrella;
- finding innovative means of avoiding redundancies such as job rotation and job sharing;
- fostering initiatives to help the regeneration of deprived areas;
- linking business to fair trade practices to give producers a fair deal;
- undertaking ethical auditing – an annual ethical accounting statement.

All these and more practices are already in place among businesses like Body Shop, Levi Strauss, 3M, Sparekassen Nordjylland in Denmark, Ahlers in Antwerp, ABN, AMRO, Neckelmann, Quelle, Hewlett Packard, MacDonalds, Piaggio, Starbucks, Thomson CSF, Zanussi, the Grameen Bank and South Shore Bank. They are also some of the most successful in their field as technological and product innovators. As Giovanni Agnelli, Fiat and Piaggio's former chairman notes: 'I cannot accept that the ultimate scope of an enterprise is profit. Of course, it is an essential part but I am also convinced that the role of industry is to improve society' (see European Business Network for Social Cohesion, 1996).

## Seeing Through the Eyes of ...

There are inventive initiatives to get new faces involved in planning and decision-making, with benefits for social sustainability. Women, the elderly, disabled people and children have been involved in urban planning through projects such as the 'Children as Planners' initiative in Kitee and Helsinki in Finland, Rouen and Locarno, Frauen Werk Stadt in Vienna, the Burgerziekenhuis Hospital, Amsterdam, Open Sesame in Liverpool or the senior citizens product label in Utrecht. Seeing the city through the eyes of different groups is crucial as a means of empowerment, and as a way of gaining an insight into different perspectives.

Urban planning remains largely in the hands of middle-aged men, whose ideas of need and priority are conditioned by who they are. The simple creative step of involving children not only gains a commitment for their own environment but develops civic pride and ownership. Taking a women's perspective has highlighted issues traditional planning tends to neglect: play areas, accessibility, spaces for social interaction, attention to lighting and safety, apartment interiors, etc.

## Cultural Pride Through Inspiration

A culturally rich place would have a critical mass of cultural activity from one-off festivals to organizations that regularly create work. Architecture would mix the old and new in an urban environment visually at ease with its contrasts. Such an approach, with creativity at its core, enriches identity, distinctiveness and confidence. In doing so it reinforces and adapts for modern purposes the characteristics of a place, its traditions, myths and history. It fosters cultural sustainability by recognizing the values and norms of different social or cultural groups.

Common Ground's local distinctiveness programme in the UK is a good example: it includes developing local parish maps to rediscover places and the reintroduction of 'Apple Day' in 60 British towns. Helsinki's Festival of Light draws on winter traditions to overcome darkness; Berlin's Multikulti programme sought to integrate immigrant groups by stressing there are '35 ways of being a Berliner' and strengthen social cohesion, intercultural and intergenerational understanding. Bologna's holistic youth programme has transformed old youth clubs into creative industrial centres using the arts to build life skills and employability. Building-based projects which exemplify this culturally sensitive yet imaginative approach include the revived Pei Pyramid in Paris, the rebuilding of the Bibliotheca Alexandrina in Alexandria or the re-use of a Baptist Chapel such as the District 6 Museum in Cape Town to celebrate the community violently forced out into townships under apartheid.

## Ideas out of Nowhere?

Taken together the examples sound utopian. Wherever you go leaders seem to appear out of nowhere, if conditions are right: here an entrepreneur, there a city official and there a mother driven into action by personal experience. Creativity thrives in every area, in every discipline; almost any urban problem has been responded to by an imaginative solution somewhere.

If best practice were gathered in one place, our 'dream city' would exist – perhaps. So a basic question is posed: Why, if a city is able to develop a working best practice in one sphere, and if it is well-aware of best practice elsewhere, can it not develop similar imaginative solutions across the range of urban concerns? What is the block to creativity, where is the resistance to taking up innovative solutions? Is it a result of a power play within bureaucracies? Is it intrinsic short-sightedness and narrow-mindedness of so much economic logic based on capital? Is it to do with individuals? Is it to do with organizations? Is it to do with how organizations interact? Is it that cities only have a certain quotient of creativity? But why are some places more creative than others? What makes a creative milieu where it is possible to have and to implement ideas?

Seeing urban creativity from a vertiginous vantage point packed and swarming with potential one must be struck by the power of the obstacles put in front of innovations – the power of entrenched interests, economic, social, political; the laming qualities of fossilized, closed mindsets; a lack of a culture of risk-taking. As a consequence there is a lack of mutual learning between citizens, projects and cities and the quality of urban life continues to atrophy.

So the central question is how do cities become more creative and innovative? How can they implement new ideas and anchor them in reality? What are the pre-conditions? How do cities sustain imaginative processes? How do they establish an operating environment that fosters joint learning, growth and fulfilment within and between organizations? How, in short, can we bring into being a 'creative city' across all the dimensions of urban life?

Part Two

# The Dynamics of Urban Creativity

# 4

# Creative Urban Transformations

Two long-term Comedia projects are worth looking at in detail: the Creative Town Initiative in Huddersfield and the Helsinki Maximizing Creative Potential Programme. In addition, we will consider Emscher Park and the European Union's Urban Pilot Projects programme, although this is one with which we have not been directly involved. They exemplify a series of issues:

- The extent to which the municipal urban policy framework can encourage creativity and innovation.
- The importance of developing a creative milieu which is reliant on a city's organizational culture and its capacity to be creative and innovative.
- The relationship between technological, economic, social and environmental factors on the one hand, and cultural creativity and innovation on the other.
- The long-term time scales needed for creative change to work itself through to the different levels of economic enterprise in the city.
- The effect of such policies in attracting to a city new skills that are self-sustaining, and the balance between external and internal creativity.

## EMBEDDING A CULTURE OF CREATIVITY IN A SMALLER CITY: THE CREATIVE TOWN INITIATIVE

Huddersfield is an industrial town of 130,000 inhabitants, located in the north of England, close to Leeds and Manchester and about

300 km from London. It grew rapidly in the 19th and early 20th centuries on an industrial and manufacturing base of woollen textiles, engineering and chemicals. In the 1980s it suffered, like much of the British economy, a severe recession leading to mass unemployment and industrial restructuring. From the early 1970s onwards, textiles and engineering declined by more than 75 per cent, a decline initially off-set by growth in chemicals, food and drink; there was however no growth in the high-tech sector. Huddersfield thus has more manufacturing than the national average, a less qualified workforce, lower pay and more unemployment. Commuting to neighbouring cities has been draining skills and talent, and there is a concentration of poverty amongst its mainly Asian ethnic minority.

Yet in 1997 Huddersfield was chosen as one of the winners of a competition, held by the European Union, to find Europe's most innovative urban initiatives. From an entry of over 500, a total of 26 were finally selected as Urban Pilot Projects with a brief to experiment in new forms of urban policy and development, to establish new models of best practice, and to disseminate the results to the rest of Europe. Huddersfield's project – the Creative Town Initiative (CTI) – emerged from discussions held with the author over several years about ways of extending creative ideas beyond the artistic sector. It was awarded 3 million ECU (about \$3.0 million), a sum matched from other sources, to run a programme of 16 separate experimental projects over a three-year period up to the end of the year 2000.

The Creative Town Initiative was the first urban strategy project of its kind. The proposal argued that creativity, a latent form of intellectual capital, exists in all walks of life – in business, in education, in public administration, in social care services. Using a series of pilot projects, it sought to establish an innovative spatial area as part of a process of extending creative thinking throughout the town – embracing ways in which the unemployed can regain the confidence to re-educate themselves, the development of routes to entrepreneurship, setting up, in fact, a network of creative thinking across all disciplines and sectors.

A number of projects were devised to achieve the aims of the 'cycle of urban creativity', as will be explained in Chapter 8. Some were aimed at enhancing the town's capacity for generating ideas, such as the Creativity Forum and the Millennium Challenge, which will have implemented 2000 innovative social and economic urban projects by the end of the year 2000. Others, such as the Creative

Business Development Training Company or Creativity Investment Services (CIS), were to aid business development in SMEs (small and medium-sized enterprises). The Create! project is at the centre of the network, designed to promote and bring together creative thinkers in the town. The Hothouse Units were set up to get innovative businesses to work together in a conducive environment, and various vehicles of dissemination were set in motion, which included discussion salons, a website, a database of creative projects, the magazine of northern creativity, *Brass*, and, lastly, this book. CTI is run by a team of two core people with project directors for each initiative. Many projects succeeded and some failed, such as the CIS and *Brass*.

CTI aimed to change the perception that Huddersfield had of itself. Its website tender states boldly: 'CTI represents a body of confident and ambitious people in Huddersfield who are prepared to challenge orthodoxy and bring about change. Everything about CTI, particularly its corporate branding, must exude this ethos. A creative town must vaunt its creativity every time it communicates – face to face, through its printed material and now, through its website.'

The impacts of CTI were unexpected. It led to a thorough reappraisal of the town itself by the Marketing Huddersfield Partnership (MHP) – an alliance of the leading private, public and community agencies. A strategy to rebrand the town was launched under the banner 'Huddersfield – Strong Heart, Creative Mind', with the full support of the formerly critical media. It sets out to establish – at regional, national and international levels – more favourable perceptions of Huddersfield, by identifying it as a town with a creative and innovative culture, a reputation for quality output, progressive businesses and institutions, active individual citizens and corporate bodies, a richness of multi-cultural diversity and an enterprising community spirit. CTI even influenced its own host body, Huddersfield Pride, a regeneration agency with an ambitious programme for social, economic and environmental renewal running from 1995 to 2002; this programme aims, in the spirit of CTI, to transform Huddersfield into a thriving and prosperous town, valued for its quality of life by residents, wealth creators and visitors.

## From Margins to Mainstream

In 1997 at the start of CTI, creativity was seen by the leadership in Huddersfield as something vague, woolly and of relevance only to the arts. Two years later, enabling people and organizations to be creative was recognized as a means of unleashing talent and harnessing intellectual capital. In a short time Huddersfield has become a regional centre of excellence for creativity, and the use of creativity as an urban revitalization strategy has moved from the margins to the mainstream. The national government minister for regional and local development, Richard Caborn, chose Huddersfield to launch a keynote speech in February 1999 for Britain's new Regional Development Agencies, in which, by stating that creativity was the greatest asset the new regions had, he gave national endorsement to the CTI. Kirklees Council, the authority within which Huddersfield falls, has incorporated the key CTI ideas into its programme for urban regeneration, called Platform for Change, in an attempt to infuse creative city ideas throughout the fabric of the town and getting down into the heart of communities. The Chamber of Commerce, the Training and Enterprise Council (TEC), the University School of Business have all sought to be associated with the CTI initiative. The concept has been internalized by major policy-makers.

Significantly, creativity is increasingly seen as an attribute that needs to be embedded in every process or project, and not merely in the new and obviously creative media industries. However, the existence of the Kirklees Media Centre was a crucial element, which gave visible and symbolic expression to the idea and acted as a centre for debate, meeting, eating and drinking. A business centre with 25 spaces for new media, it has been fully booked since its opening and subsequently doubled its space, contributing to the physical regeneration of part of the town. The idea of such a centre in Huddersfield, a town more associated with cloth caps and brass bands, was strange even as recently as the mid 1990s. The image of Huddersfield is changing in the media, and the experiment has been covered in the national press by both broadsheets and tabloids. Although the end-products have only been visible at the end of the 1990s, several thousand people have already been involved in events and training programmes, over 50 new businesses, mainly in the modern technology and media fields, have been set up, and new talent is being attracted to the town. Within the specialist urban regeneration field, Huddersfield is attracting foreign visitors on an unusual scale, particularly from large European cities, such as Bologna, Berlin, Vienna, Tilburg and Helsinki, anxious to be at the forefront of urban revitalization.

Huddersfield did not arrive at this situation out of the blue, but as the result of key changes and a deep reflection on its future. It realized that medium-sized and small towns like itself, whose original locational advantages, resource- and skills-base have long since disappeared, exist all over Europe and, indeed, the rest of the world. Many have gone into decline, after failing to adjust to the demands of the new globalized economy. Often suffering deep-rooted deprivation, with all the social consequences that entails, they live in a spiral of worsening difficulties. Huddersfield was in danger of becoming such a place, but over the last decade of the 20th century it has succeeded in breaking out of this cycle by recognizing and nurturing what the people of Huddersfield, in the face of adversity, could offer to their town's renewal. The town saw that it had only one resource – its people: their intelligence, ingenuity, aspirations, motivations, imagination and creativity. If these could be tapped, renewal and regeneration would follow.

Regeneration was increasingly seen to be a more subtle and all-encompassing process than had been previously understood. It was not merely a matter of improving the material environment, it involved the whole person. Material changes assist by helping to build confidence and by providing visible markers of progress. Yet if urban regeneration is to be self-sustaining people need to feel engaged, to have the opportunity to give of their best and be empowered. This means giving scope to people's creativity and harnessing their capacity to solve problems. This was the true source of urban competitiveness.

Huddersfield saw that what determines the rise and fall of cities is in part within their own control and in part dependent on the bigger economic, social and political forces against which a city cannot on its own do battle. Huddersfield's instability was in large part the consequence of major changes in the worldwide location of production, services and wealth-generating capacity. As textile production increasingly moved towards the Far East, Huddersfield saw the best of its local talent begin to move outward to places like London and Leeds, or even further afield. The impact of this was a breaking up the fabric of social life, with consequent loss of impetus and self-confidence.

This process, driven by the speed of capital movements, the globalization of production and the effects of information technology, meant that Huddersfield was going through a second industrial revolution whose overall impact on the town would be as dramatic as the first. In time it will transform every aspect of economic activity, spawn new products and new services. The current phase is primarily fuelled by the application of microchip technology to almost every sphere of economic activity, revolutionizing manufacturing, distribution and services.

Huddersfield saw that, for cities and companies hoping to keep up with the increasing rate of technological change, the quality of management and decision-making as well as that of the workforce acquire overriding importance, and a premium is attached to scarce and portable skills and to the capacity to be creative and innovative. Given the pace of change, people must become more mobile, more skilled, and more adaptable to the changing requirements which affect the role and operation of towns like Huddersfield and intensify urban competition. Some cities will founder and others will rise to the top in this maelstrom of change, which brings threats and opportunities to every industry and commercial sector in Huddersfield, as it does in its commercial rivals.

Huddersfield realized that many new opportunities were being created by these global shifts and, importantly, that the revolution was only just beginning. It sensed that there would be a new divide between, on the one hand, the intellectual and creative centres of the emerging knowledge-economy based on intellectual capital, where a high quality of life is considered an essential adjunct, and, on the other, the cities which would let themselves be bypassed by this dynamic. In trying to understand the implications of this paradigm shift, Huddersfield felt it could achieve its 'reinvention' by focusing on the core strategic competencies, necessary in the longer term to re-position a town, by moving its activities higher up the value chain, and so transform itself from a simple manufacturing centre into an intellectual and creative hub. In so doing it thought it could be a model for others to follow.

## Internal Change as a Trigger

The foundations which enabled Huddersfield to stake its claim as a creative city had been laid 10 years before. The Huddersfield and Kirklees municipality had been reviewed by Inlogov, a respected specialist public sector consultancy and its conclusions were stark. The authority was the worst they had come across; it was a 'basket case'. There was no corporate working; each department behaved like a self-contained barony; the political leadership was old guard Labour and controlled officials in such a way that they had no autonomy and so developed no motivation to do well; there was political infighting, a culture of fear and blame, practically no partnerships with the voluntary or private sector, no openness to new ideas and little knowledge about how to adapt to change.

Finally, after an internal political struggle within the Labour Party in 1986, a compromise leadership choice was made in the person of John Harman whom the old guard thought they could control. A new chief executive, Rob Hughes, was also appointed, and between them they instituted a palace revolution. They recognized the changing institutional map in Britain, which included competition within local authority services, the transfer of certain functions out of the Council altogether, and the growth of non-elected agencies – quangos controlling more resources than the local authority itself, such as National Health Service Trusts or TECs.

To operate in this new landscape the Council needed to build relationships with an ever-growing range of other agencies. It needed to influence, to collaborate, to orchestrate and to scrutinize – roles which are not easily balanced; it needed a public information service to show who did what, since the Council was increasingly commissioning services from others rather than supplying them itself.

Harman and Hughes acknowledged that the Council's urban management had to change dramatically. This required tenacity and a certain ruthlessness. They effectively got rid of the departmental barons and instituted corporate working. They separated strategy formation and overview thinking from operational management. A culture of internal training with strong mentoring, now well established, was instituted. New forms of partnership were created to accelerate regeneration. The overall purpose was to find means of responding to the then Conservative government guidelines and directives and to new possibilities, as well as creating the conditions for enterprise of all sorts to flourish – whether private, voluntary or public. Kirklees pragmatically turned government constraints into advantages and learnt that by collaboration it could win public resources. It ultimately generated the effective 'Kirklees bidding machine' which used bids for government money as a means of pulling the authority together towards a common vision. Over a seven-year period they competitively won £80 million of public resources for the town. Many of these approaches have been copied elsewhere and are being mainstreamed.

These positive responses overcame the despondency and cynicism of the 1980s. The town now takes more risks and shares responsibility for success and failure. The cultural sector has played a significant role in making Huddersfield a creative milieu in embryo. The voluntary sector and environmental divisions have also responded well to the changes, and until recently the major problem has been the lack of collaboration from the university, where personality difficulties were largely responsible for a certain academic isolationism.

A major supporter from the outset of the changes occurring in Kirklees was the Cultural Services Department and especially its deputy head, Phil Wood, now the coordinator of the Creative Town Initiative. From early on this department adopted a broad definition of culture, embracing issues well beyond the development of art forms – using, for example, the arts for community development and as a potential economic driver. In 1991 it helped to set up Cultural Industries in Kirklees(CIK), a locally based agency which used the arts to assist in economic and social regeneration and produced a report called 'A Chance to Participate: The role of the cultural industries and the community arts in the regeneration of Kirklees'. The key impact of CIK was to move the argument about the arts away from an 'art for art's sake' agenda to one where culture was seen as a tool for achieving wider Council objectives. The interplay between the already entrepreneurial cultural section and outside agencies helped move cultural questions up the Council agenda. Arts initiatives were supporting others linked to health, environment and social services.

Kirklees' cultural policy, developed in 1994, was an important link with the Creative Town Initiative. Phil Wood and I worked together on developing its three strands: celebrating diversity, maintaining distinctiveness and harnessing creativity. As principles it stated:

- Local cultural identity and pride are an essential pre-condition of achieving economic, community and environmental regeneration.
- Imagination and creativity are essential elements in achieving both local identity and personal development.
- Diversity of lifestyle, livelihood, culture and habitat is an asset and through the understanding and celebrating of this a tolerant society can be developed.
- Local distinctiveness takes centuries to develop but can be lost overnight and so must be defended and nurtured.

- Local culture is dynamic, not static, and therefore change and development are an essential partner to protection and conservation.
- Through investment, empowerment and education the creative abilities which exist in all citizens can be released for the good of the individual, the community and the economy.

Huddersfield's and Kirklees' passage from follower to trend-setter raises problems that the Creative Town Initiative will have to address as it progresses, such as sustaining the creative dynamic as new people come to take charge. Both Harman and Hughes left their posts in 1998 and a new generation of change agents has emerged. Will they be equally successful? The combined qualities of the two previous incumbents – the capacity to think at a high strategic level, tenacity, goodness and ruthlessness – might be hard to replicate. What is clear is that the priorities will change. The ideas of partnership and delegation do not need reinforcing. The next stage involves three key issues. First, the development of a form of social capital, so that individuals are willing to subordinate their self-interest to broader objectives; in this way partnership becomes more than lip-service. Secondly, a deepening understanding of the creative process at all levels within all sectors. Thirdly, more high-visibility manifestations of what the creative city means in terms of buildings, landscaping, traffic management, signposting, information centres and cultural facilities.

## HELSINKI: UNCOVERING A HIDDEN RESOURCE

Leading the urban life means living with contradictions. Helsinki is a city which seems to have achieved a successful balance of priorities between men and women, between the wish for safety and the need for cultural stimulation, in part by providing the unexpected within a secure framework. It has balanced its awareness of its own history with the desire for modernity and innovation. There are also more basic polarities which form an integral part of Helsinki's culture: it embraces both heat and cold – snow and sauna; solitude and Finnish tango; light and dark; land and sea. It is a modern urban culture, yet it has its roots in rural society – it is a culture rooted in the natural world. Helsinki's ability to master these seeming contradictions is an asset to be harnessed. The images entertained by foreigners are still stereotypical. Helsinki is thought of as 'cold', 'distant', 'unknown', 'gloomy' and 'mysterious'. But when visitors come to the city their perceptions change radically for the better. Helsinki is less cold than they thought, there are unexpected things to do even in the cold, there is passion and a 'wildness'. Helsinki has flourished despite an administrative practice which depends overmuch on historical precedent, an excessively compartmentalized approach to development and a fear of organizational change. The unpredicted and the unexpected have nonetheless found their place.

## The Forces of Light – Valon Voimat

In seeking to explore how the specific cultural resources of Helsinki could be further developed by building upon the city's existing innovative traditions, I was struck by the frequent references to SAD (seasonal affective disorder), the light deprivation syndrome which can lead to depression and in extreme cases to suicide. Yet when the snowflakes fall one experiences the mystic beauty of the Finnish winter. As the aurora borealis lights up the northern sky, life in the city changes too. Children skate where they swam in the summer, and people ski where in the summer they picked berries. The long five-month winter is illuminated by snow and lights. The extremes of light and dark and joy and tristesse had already been noticeable earlier. The wild turning point of Vappu in early May had signalled the escape from the long dark winter, and the summer wildness celebrated the joy of light. That vibrancy gave way to the gloomier atmosphere of November as the days closed in and there was as yet no snow to reflect back the brief hours of light.

I explored light in all its guises, rapidly noticing such traditions as candles burning in windows in the pre-Christmas period, the Lucia candle parade, the placing of candles on graves, and the lights that mark Independence Day. I noticed too that whilst Finnish lighting design was at the cutting edge, it was not as well-known as that of the Italians. It seemed to me that a winter Festival of Light, conceived as a two-week event, could turn the weakness of the dark into a strength. It was an idea, too, that went with the flow of tradition. The first festival was staged in November and December 1995 and it has been an annual event ever since. Starting initially on a small scale with funding of £30,000 it has grown ten-fold since then in unexpected ways.

Valon Voimat – the Forces of Light – plays on the contradiction of light and dark and is part of an idea to project Helsinki as a city for all seasons. It is both a celebration of light in darkness, with installations which sometimes become permanent, and a clarion call to take urban lighting seriously. The original concept saw lights fanning out from the central station square, and involved lantern projects and parades spreading in from the suburbs to link, through the symbolism of light, the different parts of the city.

Valon Voimat is an integrated development, in which a variety of factors come together: economic, environmental, social and cultural – and is at once an example of the concept of cultural planning in action, a tourist attraction and a holistic approach to light. Almost any setting serves as a venue for the festival, from shops and galleries to streets, parks and museums, even factories and construction sites. Today the festival not only generates a whole series of local projects, but also attracts international collaboration – latterly from Budapest, London, Istanbul, Aarhus and Barcelona – as well as acting as a brand-name for Helsinki.

Visitors arriving in late November are able to inspect new lighting at trade events and hear seminars covering issues of light and lighting. Innovations such as Skanno's 'Light Box', a domestic lighting installation that counteracts the effects of SAD, are showcased, as are examples of environmental lighting. This is the festival's economic dimension. Buildings, public spaces and islands are lit up and change colour in ways reminiscent of Hong Kong at New Year. In 1996 some art students came up with the idea of a dark tram to tour the streets unlit, allowing the passengers to look out onto an illuminated city. 'Forces of Light', with its complex outreach in terms of tourism, culture and image-making, gives the city a different perspective. The Festival director, Isse Karsten, fosters inclusiveness and participation by people from all walks of life. Whilst the organizing team puts together a core programme with some of the world's leading lighting artists, Karsten welcomes ideas from locals – the residents of Puistola, for example, animated the courtyard of their flats with candleholders made of ice. The educational and social dimension is further reflected in a schools programme which encourages children to make lighting of all kinds, especially on the suburban estates.

Initially sponsored by Phillips, the project has become a public/private partnership, unusual for Helsinki at the time of its establishment, but prefiguring the many arts events which were to be funded in that way in the following years.

Light is a new Helsinki brand-name; the festival is a fixture in the yearly calendar and was a central component of Helsinki's

European City of Culture programme in 2000. It has encouraged city officials and private businesses to think about light, its power and impact in innovative ways.

With hindsight, the use of light as a resource may seem obvious, since it is a key element in the Finnish tradition, yet the conceptual breakthrough was the creation of a framework within which this asset could be exploited. This framework – that of a particular kind of festival, with both economic and cultural dimensions – is flexible enough to create openings through which others can pass, pursuing their own paths.

## INNOVATION IN A NON-INNOVATIVE SETTING: EMSCHER PARK

The IBA–Emscher Park project in the middle of the Ruhr area – Germany's most industrialized zone – is one of the most dramatic, innovative and comprehensively thought-through urban regeneration projects. The Emscher is an area 70 km long, comprising 800 sq km straddling the river of that name, in which 2 million inhabitants live in 17 cities. Lying at the heart of the Ruhr, a dense urban agglomeration of 5.3 million people and one of Europe's most heavily urbanized and industrialized areas, it includes the principal cities of Essen, Dortmund, Bochum, Gelsenkirchen and Duisburg. The Emscher has been a crucible of intense economic and social development in both the past and current industrial revolutions.

The Ruhr's development was driven by massive, locally based industrial corporations such as Krupps and Thyssen. The environmental legacy that industrialization left on the Ruhr landscape cannot be overstated – extreme degradation, a polluted landscape, mountainous slagheaps, chimneys reaching to the sky, blast furnaces (many now inoperative) and towering gasholders. The Emscher itself had become an open sewer, as extensive mining activities had provoked subsidence, causing the collapse of sewage channels. The stench and smell on a bad day could be unbearable.

Over 600,000 jobs have been lost in the area in the closing decades of the 20th century and unemployment, at 13 per cent, is amongst the highest in Germany. The dominance of the large corporations had a debilitating effect on entrepreneurialism and small scale enterprise, and the Ruhrgebiet was steeped in the semi-feudal mentality of the old corporatism. Within the Ruhrgebiet restructuring process, the wholesale reconstitution and 'renaturing' of the river Emscher took on a symbolic significance. The idea of turning an open sewer channelled in concrete into a river where fish would swim and children play verged on the heroic.

New legislation in the 1980s brought large industrial polluters to account. By the late 1990s over 50,000 people were employed in the Emscher area in restorative and preventative technologies. Developed with state support, numbers of new companies were emerging, employing the latest techniques in quality assurance testing or environmental technology. Degradation had been used as an opportunity to create new products and services and markets, while stringent standard setting and legislation helped to drive the innovative process. The Ruhrgebiet's headstart in this matter over other old industrial regions led to the opening up of export markets.

The power house of this structural renewal (and a further array of over 100 innovative projects) was the Internationale Bauausstellung Emscher Park (IBA) – the International Building Exhibition. It opened in 1989 and closed ten years later. Its purpose was to serve as a think-tank for the regeneration of Emscher Park ecologically, socially, economically and culturally. It had no models to follow and provided a framework within which ideas and concepts could be thrashed out, tested and explored with experts, and with the local population, in a context of seminars, competitions, media discussions, special events and participatory activities. The regeneration process had to do more than refurbish buildings and restore a tarnished landscape; it needed to renew the psyche of the region whose monoculture of coal and steel, and its decline at the end of the 20th century, had etched itself into the mindscape of the people. The dying industrial culture still affected and determined the economic, political, cultural and social milieu.

Without outside impulses, no innovative climate could develop to renew the culture, economy and ecology – the problem of innovating in a non-innovative milieu became the issue. Key dilemmas emerged: how to create a culture change without erasing memory; how to innovate, while at the same time maintaining consensus, given that democracy fosters a tendency to institutional immobility, whereas innovations with a long-term impact by definition overturn existing policies; whether to initiate many individual, dispersed projects and thus reduce the need for consensus, or to mobilize support by focusing on landmark initiatives with their advantage of spectacular visibility. The IBA straddled these tensions and its director, Karl Ganser, coined the phrase 'incrementalism with perspective', providing a framework within which isolated decentralized projects could be chosen and could progress.

The IBA's sub-title, 'A Workshop for the Future of Old Industrial Areas', encapsulates the core concepts of innovation, mutual experiential learning, and the role of the public sector in putting conclusions into practice. The hundred-plus projects are grouped around five themes:

1   The ecological regeneration of the Emscher river system – the complete rebuilding and 'renaturation' of 350 km of polluted watercourses over a 30-year period.
2   Working in the Park – the creation of a chain of 22 science and technology centres on old industrial sites.
3   The refurbishment or building of 6000 new properties according to high ecological and aesthetic standards.
4   The finding of radical new uses for former mines, steelworks or factories, as opposed to demolition.
5   The creation of an Emscher landscape park and a series of seven green corridors to separate major urban centres from each other.

A review, undertaken after five years, shifted the focus to cultural issues, as part of a strategy designed to foster events, tourism and image-making; importance was also given to the creation of a new culture of work.

Over the decade more than 4,500 people have been involved over one hundred projects. Over £1 billion of public investment on the construction and related sectors has created jobs for over 30,000 people, while public funds have elicited many times that amount from private sources. Yet the real value and the long-term gain lie in the impetus given to the development of new forms of living and working, which have grown from the ecologically and culturally based renewal of the economic structure.

## From the Mundane to the Spectacular

The range of projects runs from the spectacular, awe-inspiring and monumental to the everyday and the invisible. Each project is seen as a learning initiative which may present a model for replication. The small housing estate design by women in Bergkamen has already impacted on the style of the local police headquarters nearby, while the self-build initiative is getting new groups into the housing market as well as creating new social bonds. The 10 acre healing park, Quellenbosch in Bottrop, located near the hospital, is consciously using plants to create a design that allows for new 'sensual experiences'; it is intended to serve and support general health care, outpatient rehabilitation, aftercare and self-help health groups. Europe's largest gasholder in Oberhausen was transformed into an exhibition centre. Zeche Zollverein, a massive coal mine became a conference, leisure and industrial design centre, and the steel works in Duisburg–Meiderich a landscape park.

The objective is the integration of innovative objectives within wider projects. Almost every project has a cultural dimension; the ecological element is highlighted through the use of new materials and building methods and the recycling of resources; lastly the project itself serves as a training and job generation initiative.

As examples of architectural innovation stand the Tetrahedron monument crowning a mountain of slag in Bottrop, and the futuristic glass facade of the Wissenschaftspark Rheinelbe in Gelsenkirchen, which has the largest solar panel system in Europe. Leading the technological field are the ecology business park in Hamm, and the Centre of the Future, which conducts advanced research into the re-use of industrial areas.

## How the IBA Works

The IBA, led by Professor Karl Ganser and an advisory structure, was a small, catalytic organization with approximately 30 staff. Quality standards and benchmarks involving organizational, social, environmental, design and aesthetic criteria defined its mission. It set strict deadlines in order to generate momentum and action. Its fundamental purpose was to mobilize expectations through the propaganda of the good creative example and the persuasive power of good solutions – a long-term, indirect process which takes time. It did not involve itself directly in projects, seeking instead to act as a catalyst, steering clear of highly contentious areas, like traffic control, and hoping that the example of good models would cross boundaries and thereby 'decrust the old system'; it served as a branding device and a benchmark of quality control. The IBA was a private company owned by the Land – 'part of, but not part of the public structures' – an attempt to keep it above and out of politics. The 'institutional immobilism' generated by the many layers of political authority in the region had long acted as a block to innovation and progress.

The IBA helped to develop ideas and initiatives through brain-storming, workshops, publications and feasibility studies, as well as competitions. Each of the 100 plus projects is autonomous, self-managed and responsible for raising its own finance. The IBA was not an agency or a plan in the traditional sense, but a perspective on development. It had neither money nor legal powers. All IBA projects follow normal procedures with regard to planning and finance; there was no special fund or development area status. It used indirect leverage: its political status and its label conferred prestige, as did the active support of local communities. The carrot it offered was access to resources under certain conditions, especially to the Land of Nord-Rhein Westfalen or the European Union.

A key theme was to see problems as potential and a crisis as an opportunity – the fact that, for example, the process of dealing with Emscher's problems gave birth to an export industry.

The IBA had to deal with contradictions. Old industrial areas by definition have little creative potential, otherwise they would have already escaped from their incipient decline. Restrictive attitudes and practices, acquired through cultural attitudes or power groupings such as trade unions, are ingrained. They thus need impulses from outside and from above. What the IBA gained in influence and independence from remaining outside political structures is today at risk. Now that it is closed, can we be sure the ethos for change is sufficiently embedded? Critics argue that the IBA should have relied less on the 'lighthouse effect' of its projects and worked more on the ground with the modernizers. Today, in its absence, the worry is that the old guard, still partly in place, will simply revert to former practices. The relative weakness of grassroots participation is also a concern. The IBA started with the intention of initiating many smaller participative social schemes, but this proved too complex, time-consuming and lacking in visible results; under pressure to deliver, the organization fell back increasingly on material infrastructure projects.

An industrial culture does not easily make the transition to a post-industrial culture. A workforce brought up passively under the wing of monolithic conglomerates does not overnight – or even in 10 years – change to being enterprising and self-reliant. So one of the strongest calling cards of the IBA has been its re-use of redundant industrial sites. The local working class have not seen their heritage simply fall into dereliction and nor has their collective memory been erased.

## Emscher, Where Next?

Inspired by the IBA, a new tourism and image masterplan for the Ruhr is being put into effect. The strategy has three key elements: industrial culture; modern entertainment and unusual cultural events. A 'Route of industrial culture' will highlight 18 symbolically significant anchor points as a means of binding the region together. Each of these 'points' acts also as a signpost to a theme, be it workers' housing, environmental improvement, social history or the re-use of industrial buildings. The masterplan has a vision of the Ruhr as the world's largest national industrial culture park. Other urban parks, such as Castlefield in Manchester with 4.5 million visitors or Lowell with 3 million, will be dwarfed. This symbolic park will be a living entity. Its objective is to bring into focus the challenges faced by the past in creating an industrial society, and to turn a spotlight on urban structural change and ways in which industrial society might develop in the future.

### What has the IBA Achieved?

The Emscher Park IBA, while not perfect, has yet proved very creative; the criticism from the academic community concerning participation and embedding may be valid, yet a truer, deeper judgement about the real impact of the IBA will unfold as time goes by.

The IBA had a strategic vision, in the sense that each designated project took its place in a greater whole, and its integration of ecological, economic, social and cultural dimensions amounted to a philosophy which acted as a spur to lateral thinking and to finding solutions which cut across existing boundaries. Seeing sustainability as an integrated concept covering cultural, economic and social life as well as ecology was another essential part of this thinking. Unconventional couplings and unusual mixes, such as the idea of working in a park or in coal mines, which had been turned into modern design centres, served also as triggers for lateral thinking. These unlikely associations found an echo in the idea of weakness as a source of strength, exemplified in treating environmental degradation problems as an opportunity to explore new products. The development of the Emscher project was greatly facilitated by the setting up of universities in the area in the 1960s, where theories could be tested out: the skills and expertise they generated provided a significant pre-condition for regional growth. Furthermore, the stringent environmental standards gave momentum to economic development by forcing companies to come up with solutions. Revaluing as assets such negative items as industrial detritus, unleashed potential while preserving the past in peoples' memories: industrial landmarks were thus transformed into sources of civic pride. In these ways the IBA was an urban R&D zone and without it projects, such as the estate in Bergkamen designed by women, might not have come into existence. They now have credibility and are replicable.

Much of the IBA's value lies in the power of its brand; IBA-branded projects attracted attention and gave access to funding and it is essential that the quality of the brand continues to be maintained in the future. The IBA brand embodies an ethos and has a symbolic resonance witnessed to by projects such as the nightly light show put on by the steel factory at Duisburg Nord Landscape Park. Brand is linked to the power of symbols – designating the Emscher concept as a park was symbolic, as was also the concept of 'living and working in the park'. Projects such as these continually contrast old and new, past and future, creating an interplay which fosters debate. The juxtaposition of the iconic and the everyday, of a giant gasometer and a self-build housing project, gave to the vision as a whole a significance greater than that invested in any of its parts.

The power of personality and leadership qualities of the director, Karl Ganser, were essential in driving the IBA vision forward: '60 per cent of the credit goes to him', noted one interviewee. The balance between the Land government bureaucracy and the leadership of the IBA was significant: Ganser's relative freedom was unusual and stemmed from the fact that he had previously been part of the Land structure and understood its workings. By contrast he was not able to manipulate the local authority in the same way. The use of key personnel to champion and replicate different projects played an important part in coordinating and pushing forward a decentralized programme. These correspondents have crucial roles as unofficial ambassadors, disciples and 'multiplicators' whose long-term effectiveness as guardians of the idea are likely to emerge in unexpected ways in the years to come.

## Have there been Spin-offs?

The Emscher programme was conceived as a number of interrelated projects within an overall plan, and it is the synergy between them which makes the whole achievement greater than the sum of the parts. This outstanding characteristic of the IBA was quickly recognized. Within the region professional support for the Emscher approach has grown from a few dozen people, planners for the most part, to several hundred in a variety of professions across the public and private sectors. The impact of these multipicators will only become apparent over time. Many industrial developments would not have taken place without the IBA. The large-scale demonstration solar panelling and research centre for photovoltaic technology in the Wissenschaftpark Rheinelbe in Gelsenkirchen led to the setting up of a solar panel factory in the city. The Centre for Applied Production Techniques in Gladbeck attracted as a tenant a medical instrument maker with 15 employees; they now have their own building next door and employ 150 people. Private sector attitudes are changing. Initially the IBA's quality thresholds were seen as increasing costs. Now companies, especially the younger and smaller ones, recognize their economic and social value in increasing expectations and aspirations. The Land's follow up 'Regionale' initiative has taken key elements of the IBA approach to encourage further innovative urban development projects within the Land as a whole. 'Regionale' is a two-year competitive programme for which regions or sub-regions within North-Rhine Wesphalia can bid, and the competition for the period starting in 2002 already has eight entrants. The powerful political interests from within the Land government, which supported the IBA to such good effect, have thus found new channels. The tourism development strategy springs directly from the IBA. Finally, Karl Ganser's former deputy, who left the IBA in 1996, did so in order to set up a similar organization in Sachsen–Anhalt in the former East Germany. Since nurturing memory through development is one of IBA's greatest legacies, the necessary longer term cultural changes may perhaps be brought to birth there with less rupture and insecurity.

## Three Icons of Emscher Park

The Emscher Park re-uses of industrial architecture are particularly emblematic. The conversion of Europe's largest gasholder in Oberhausen, 120 metres high and 67 metres wide, into an exhibition centre was completed in 1994. This icon is a landmark for the region. The first exhibition in 1994/1995, 'Feuer und Flamme' – Fire and Flame – attracted 500,000 visitors; it was oriented principally towards the region's past, whereas the second, on film and media, pointed towards the future. The search for a new use for this landmark led to the development of Germany's largest shopping centre, CentrO, next door.

The second significant change was the conversion of Europe's biggest coal mine, Zeche Zollverein, an area of 200 acres and 20 buildings, into a conference, leisure and industrial design centre. This last, designed by Norman Foster, integrated old structures into the new – even incorporating in many areas the grime of the past and abandoned tools left lying around since the mine's closure. One of the region's most popular restaurants owes its cachet to the old boiler house into which it has been inserted. The former coal works are themselves a visitor attraction.

The third of these transformations is that of the steel works in Duisburg–Meiderich into a landscape park: Duisburg Nord. The light show projected each evening in slow motion on the old industrial structures is unforgettable. Designed by Jonathan Park of Pink Floyd, it turns the area of the factory formerly out of bounds into a nightly spectacular for visitors clambering up the steel structures in the dark. The largest alpine club in North Germany has its base in the park and uses the factory walls as cliff faces, while the local diving association learns rescue techniques in the water-filled gas-holders into which old trucks and other wreckage have been thrown. An evening concert takes place in one of the sheds. In the daytime families wander through this industrial landscape as they might through any other park. The natural habitat has been restored after extensive consultation with citizens' groups, culminating in a competition in which five internationally renowned landscape planning teams put forward different proposals. In 1991 a committee determined the prize-winners and recommended further development under five headings: 'new wildlife', 'industrial museum', 'adventure playground', 'Volkspark' (or people's park), and the 'forum for culture'.

## SEEDING INNOVATION: THE URBAN PILOT PROGRAMME

### *The Programme in Action*

The Urban Pilot Programme competition was the most richly funded and the only structured multinational programme to foster urban innovations. It was launched in 1990 by the European Commission and during the period 1990–96 a total of 33 Urban Pilot Projects (UPP) were initiated and completed, with the support of funds totalling $108 million, representing nearly 50 per cent of the projects' costs. In July 1997 the Commission approved a second round of 26 projects, to be completed by the year 2000, after receiving 503 proposals to be supported by funding of $70 million representing nearly 40 per cent of project costs. Projects have been undertaken in 14 of the 15 European member states, Luxembourg being the exception.

The programme was designed to explore and illustrate new ways in which the economic potential of cities, together with their problems arising from social exclusion, industrial decay, environmental degradation and pollution, could be tackled and the lessons shared throughout Europe. Its aim was to support innovative strategies for urban regeneration. The criteria for selection were wide-ranging and encompassed plans for the better use of land and for tackling functional obsolescence; imaginative solutions to social and economic deprivation; the revitalization of neglected historical centres; schemes to combat environmental deterioration and the lack of eco-awareness; new forms of integrated transport; ways of maximizing the cultural, geographical and historical advantages of medium-sized cities, of overcoming the poor links between research and development activities and SMEs, of finding new uses for derelict industrial land, of using new technology to improve the functioning of cities and to tackle the institutional and legal issues necessary for realizing innovative schemes. The main emphasis was on integrated solutions which enhanced competitiveness, combated social exclusion and fostered sustainable development.

## Instances of the Integrated Approach

In Copenhagen an attempt was made to combine eco-technology with urban renewal. It focused on the conversion of Øksnehallen, a former market-hall in the run-down district of Vesterbro, where, out of a population of 45,000, almost half live on benefits. The building became a Centre for Urban Eco-Technology, featuring demonstrations of recycling processes and eco-building as well as a training and employment project. Further job opportunities emerged for locals as Øksnehallen became a catalyst for the future development of the market area.

In Porto in Portugal the programme funded the regeneration of Bairo da Se, one of the city's most historic and deprived districts. The main objective was to revitalize the area physically and economically, while remaining sensitive to its heritage and local culture. The renovation of buildings, landscaping and lighting improvements are linked to a series of economic and social measures, such as special services for the elderly and the young and the promotion of commercial, tourist and cultural activities. Management of the area is being rethought, with a coordination and information centre promoting direct links with residents – a new departure in that context. Porto's designation as a World Heritage Site both helped the project and was helped by it.

Another focus was urban competitiveness. The English town of Stoke saw the establishment of the Centre for Ceramic Design, known as the Hothouse and located in an old school. Building on the city's tradition in ceramics manufacturing, this vibrant new design quarter stimulates links between the cultural industries, the museums and the traditional ceramics industry. Venice, by contrast, needed to move from traditional, declining industries into new, sustainable, employment-generating economic activities, and set out to achieve this through the creation of a Marine Technology Service Centre. The conversion of 16,000 sq metres of the old Arsenal into a scientific and technological regional park includes not only this complex, but also a research centre for new materials, restoration and the environment.

In Rotterdam, the aim of the Inner Cities Programme was to encourage a 'social return' to the Kop van Zuid Area, to be triggered by an economic regeneration programme. Local employment opportunities were improved through training schemes, as well as by the creation of neighbourhood services companies, such as those involved in cleaning and upgrading the shopping centre. In addition, district teams to maintain and supervise housing and improve street safety were set up to enhance the area's image and attract people in.

The Neunkirchen project in Germany demonstrates how ecological and cultural considerations can stimulate job creation, local identity and sustainability. A former iron foundry which was reclaimed and refurbished is today a symbol of the city's social history; the old riding hall within its purlieus is now a cultural centre, while another building houses the museum's archives, as part of a wider commitment to document the industrial history of both city and region, and thus ensure that memory is not erased. The environmental improvements in the industrial wasteland resulted in a changed and de-contaminated landscape. A new infrastructure has been set up to attract companies, which are then located in the natural setting created by using the waste left by the coal and other industries.

Whereas both phases were directed at improving the material environment by integrated methods, in the second UPP tranche 'softer' issues, such as community participation, training and employment measures and social inclusion, came strongly to the fore. In addition the potential of culture as a catalyst for renewal, and the positive role of information technology in urban regeneration, were more widely recognized. In Huddersfield, Helsinki, Randers in Denmark and Friedrichshain in Berlin, culture was used as a regenerative trigger, especially to create more inclusive urban strategies to deal with the problems of a multi-cultural society. Helsinki's Lasipalatsi (The Glass Palace) – a media centre project – combines the twin themes of culture and technology in its programme to make the Internet and digital media a socially inclusive experience. Telephone kiosks, for example, where the visitor is faced with a screen, a web camera and a microphone, offer a digital version of Speaker's Corner in Hyde Park, enabling people to broadcast what they want to anyone in the world prepared to watch or listen on the Internet. Another kiosk allows passers by to create their own web page for $3. It was necessary to create new management structures, and for most of the projects new and experimental forms of partnership have been set up.

At European Union level there is no urban policy as such, but the Framework for Action proposed in Vienna in late 1998 was influenced by the UPP experience, and urban issues, as a result, moved higher up the agenda of member states. The lessons and thinking of UPP have been incorporated into the Union's funding support mechanism and, on a larger scale, into URBAN, a successor programme, which has been allocated an $800 million budget for 2001–2006.

## Weighing up

On the credit side, the public recognition by an organization of the European Union's standing of the value of innovation, and the decision to fund it, gave legitimacy and credibility to imaginative urban initiatives. The tangible gesture of acknowledging risk-taking and making exceptions to the normal funding regimes sent out a significant signal to local authorities in Europe, giving many their first direct link to the Union's bureaucracy – the Commission – as well as the increased status that went with it. The influence of UPP was greater in smaller urban contexts (where projects were more visible), than, say, in national capitals. The involvement of political decision-makers further heightened the impact.

Another notable feature, especially in the second tranche, was collective learning. Making the 26 projects aware of themselves as a special group by twice-yearly meetings and by the production of a website, newsletters and one to one exchanges has fostered an *esprit de corps* and a sense of their having embarked together on a pioneering journey. Should questions arise that nobody can answer, there is the consciousness that a support group exists within the network. Even the experienced have learnt from simpler projects, taught by the need to define and communicate their own knowledge. Know-how acquired by Randers, while integrating multi-cultural groups in its project known as 'The Wonder', was transferred to a similar project in Friedrichhain, Berlin, and there was a two-way exchange of lessons between Leicester's eco-initiative and Turin's 'Living not Leaving' project.

Validating holistic programmes which linked different regeneration strategies, ranging from the communal to the commercial, together with the emphasis on partnership, bore fruit in countries such as Greece, Portugal or Spain as interdisciplinary approaches were at that time uncommon and therefore harder to put into effect.

The pressure to complete time-dated programmes influenced management and usually accelerated the innovation process. Further positive features included the emphasis on forward planning, with an exit strategy established from the outset, as well as the need to align projects with other longer term policies and embed the ideas into a network of local institutions, thereby ensuring that projects would survive local political change.

Lastly and most importantly, schemes were pushed through that would otherwise have evolved more slowly, if at all. The Creative Town Initiative is one example, 'The Wonder' project to upgrade the Undervaerket marketplace at Randers, with, as its key factor, the encouragement of multi-cultural businesses, is another.

On the negative side, the whole process was far too slow. Second round applications for funds had to be submitted in April 1996 and the winners were not announced until July 1997. Later revisions to bids were not allowed, but circumstances change, and the refusal to recognize this was unrealistic. In consequence, amendments had to be made while projects were in progress, and this in turn caused bureaucratic chaos and interminable delays. As someone noted: 'A decision can take a year, there is an incredible process of dotting the I's and crossing the T's.' In the meantime those responsible for the projects had to make commitments, sign contracts and make payments. The lucky ones were helped over the acute cash flow crises by their councils, but this was not always possible for NGOs.

Furthermore, although the projects were innovative, reporting procedures were as bureaucratic as for mainstream programmes. Monthly reports, covering in minute detail every category and item of income and expenditure (all of which had to be related to the then changing exchange rate for the euro), were the norm. This chore took an inordinate amount of administrative time.

One has to ask whether an institution such as the European Commission is capable of fostering partnerships, interaction and mutual learning. Its structures tend to be rigid and its personnel not renowned for imagination. Such an institution is not quick-footed, has little experience of animating and lacks the necessary celebratory spirit that fosters inventiveness. The innovative nature of UPP did not seem to influence the inner workings of the institution itself, even though commission members saw creative projects on the ground which affected them at a personal level. There was a tendency to shy away from risks even within a programme about innovation. There was, for instance, an unspoken rule that there had to be a balance of projects from the different member states, even though this might militate against creativity (conversely, of course, that criterion spread opportunity more widely). 'Implementability' was a key criterion that eliminated a number of the 503 bids in advance – those, for example, where land ownership or management issues were unclear, since timing was important, despite the Commission's own tardiness in decision-making. Traditional as well as bureaucratic in its thinking, it chose the organizational structures that it recognized, and few initiatives focusing on fresh organizational forms got through, apart from public/private partnerships – common today in most contexts and certainly no longer novel. There was a preference for tried and tested experiments, such as 'integrated renewal', which in Germany and The Netherlands had been current practice for 15 years. The rules governing funding had a restricting effect on the range of projects found acceptable (housing and health were excluded). There was also a bias towards building-based initiatives and away from the more innovative schemes which today focus on empowering, networking or skills enhancement processes. Despite the fact that a three-year completion period was too short, renewal of the material environment was always the Commission's first choice, as it offers a visible proof of intervention.

Further details on the Urban Pilot Projects Programme are available from the Technical Assistance Office at ECOTEC Research and Consulting Ltd, 13b Avenue de Tervueren, 1040 Brussels. Belgium (Fax: +32 2 732 71 11 E-mail: upp@ecotec.com)

# 5

# Foundations of the Creative City

## EMBEDDING CREATIVITY INTO THE GENETIC CODE: THE PRECONDITIONS

There are a number of preconditions for a city to be truly creative and if creativity is to embed itself into the organizational fabric of a city. They start with various personal and collective factors, such as a stimulating environment, security, freedom from disturbance and anxiety. These and other factors are necessary to allow for creative thought, the incubation of ideas and objective testing. It is useful here to distinguish between concrete factors, such as the presence of educational institutions, and more intangible aspects such as value systems, lifestyles, and people's identification with their city. There are at least seven groups of factors, and a series of indicators can be developed for each:

1 personal qualities;
2 will and leadership;
3 human diversity and access to varied talent;
4 organizational culture;
5 local identity; — *is this threatened by cc.*
6 urban spaces and facilities;
7 networking dynamics.

The validity of any precondition can be tested by asking whether a city could be creative without it. Cities can be creative with some of these, but will operate at their best when all are present. The lack of key factors – like political will or an appropriate organizational culture – can put the creative process in jeopardy, and in itself raises further creative challenges. Urban creativity is difficult to achieve since it means bringing together a varied mix of actors, agents and interest groups with varying backgrounds, aspirations, potentials and cultures. The creative city has aspects which distinguish it from personal or even organizational creativity, with far greater emphasis on relationships, joint visioning processes and networking dynamics.

## Recognize Crisis and Challenge

Creative capacity is not generated in isolation. Innovative responses are sparked by recognizing that a situation is causing problems or is otherwise inadequate: it is much more difficult to generate innovation where everything is seen to be satisfactory. A self-conscious recognition that a city has a crisis or challenge that needs to be addressed is the starting point for considering creative solutions; without this no political will or sense of urgency can be generated to drive creativity. Sustaining innovation in successful situations is especially difficult, which is why business has developed concepts such as total quality management (TQM), centred on the notion of continuous improvement as a means of generating challenges internally; cities could adapt this model to their needs.

It is hard to say which types of crises may generate a creative response. Even acknowledging a crisis is harder for places which have been successful, which tend to look back to past glories and ways of doing things. Some crises are so deep-seated that they threaten to overwhelm cities: this was Glasgow's situation, when after a sustained period of creativity in the 18th and 19th centuries it experienced a period of decline and allowed nearly 70 years to pass before offering any kind of response, and even then only with external incentives, expertise and additional resources. Successful cities by contrast need to anticipate problems and generate their own challenges, in order to avoid falling into decline. The threat of competition can provide a spur to establish focus, to set new targets and challenges; new benchmarks of effectiveness can become targets for achievement.

If city stakeholders understand the paradigm shifts affecting them, they may be more ready to begin a reflective process. Addressing the concept of sustainability has forced decision-makers in many places to rethink resource use, with implications for every aspect of urban life – it provides an historic break at every level and has created a flow of innovations. But this is only a start. Indicators that can measure a city's understanding of its situation include the existence of self-critical strategic planning, public long-term forecasting data and trend analysis or the widespread use of TQM style systems.

## Personal Qualities

There can be no creative organizations or cities without creative individuals, people who think resourcefully, openly and flexibly, who are willing to take intellectual risks, to think problems afresh and to be reflexive. Their learning style fosters a virtuous cycle of creation and re-creation which opens up some possibilities and invigorates others. They can prioritize effectively and ensure that the routine demands are never allowed to smother the time for innovation.

The creative individuals need to be brought into play at strategic points because, though not everyone in the creative city needs to be creative, it depends on a critical mass of open-minded, courageous and fresh thinkers. A handful of strategically placed creative people can transform a city if they are in the right positions of influence – not necessarily of power. Barcelona, Glasgow and Emscher probably started with fewer than a dozen such individuals.

### *Mixing Imaginative Qualities*

If creative people are the motor of the creative city, they can achieve nothing without others, perhaps less obviously creative, who can test, pilot, adapt, deploy and explain – people, in short, who can implement and exploit their ideas. Creative thinkers are not always practical, consistent or easy to follow. But we should not fall into the trap, highlighted by Tudor Rickards, of seeing innovation as a process beginning with a creative idea and ending with its implementation, at which point execution becomes routine. Rickards argues that 'this separation of a "creative" stage and a "non-creative" stage has had significant real-world consequences. ... It allocates to some individuals the status of "thinkers and creators", while reducing the status of others to "pairs of hands" or at best the inferior status implied in the terminology "support-staff".' This view denies the possibility of organization-wide innovation cultures of empowered individuals; we need to recognize the different types of creativity involved in having an idea and using it (Rickards, 1996).

Different roles will be catalytic in different circumstances. It may take the form of a person running an area regeneration project, a director of a local football club, a social entrepreneur, a mother who sets up a victim support group or a business alliance that identifies a new investment opportunity. Creative action can express itself in myriad forms and emerge from any source, but its impact depends on the imagination of public, private and community leadership. Creative people within the city also need to recognize each others' existence to work on common agendas, develop synergies and provide mutual support.

## WILL AND LEADERSHIP

### The Qualities of Will

The creative city needs people with the will not just to be creative but to find success in change, as undirected, or uncooperative will can be dangerous. It can develop as a result of recognizing existing problems and concluding that new approaches are vital, so that individuals take on the city project, or a part of it, as their own responsibility. Will is cultivated when we identify with our city and visualize the goals to be achieved, and it can be produced methodically, by creating a vision and gaining strength from that visualization.

Assagoli describes seven qualities of latent will which can be triggered by belief. The creation of will involves appropriately harnessing energy, dynamism and intensity; discipline and control; concentration, focus and attention; resolve, readiness and a willingness to make decisions; patience, perseverance and tolerance; initiative and courage; and lastly the capacity to organize, integrate and synthesize. This coordination process generates the 'intelligent energy' necessary to make will effective (Assagoli, 1973).

But will is not enough on its own. It must be balanced by a degree of generosity, empathy and understanding. The use of 'good will', of using one's power and energy to maintain an open environment, has a self-reinforcing effect. Those concerned with changing their cities must guide and balance their will within the democratic and political structures of the city.

### The Qualities of Leadership

There are ordinary, innovative and visionary leaders. The first simply reflect the desires or needs of the group they lead. An innovative leader questions local circumstances to draw out the latent needs, bringing fresh insight to new areas. Visionary leaders, by contrast, harness the power of completely new ideas. A creative city has leaders of all kinds, in entrepreneurial and public, business and voluntary bodies. A key role for local government and other agencies is to create an inclusive vision to which local leadership can contribute in the pursuit of widespread change rather than sectional or personal interests.

Leadership is both quality and skill. In different circumstances different qualities will be called for – moral leadership to turn round corruption, intellectual leadership to identify original solutions, emotional leadership to inspire, or simply efficient leadership to build confidence. Leadership skills include the ability to understand what people want, even when they are not sure of it themselves, knowing when to push forward and when to retreat, exercising judgement and so on.

Successful leadership aligns will, resourcefulness and energy with vision and an understanding of the needs of a city and its people. It has coherent ideas appropriate to local circumstance and personal traits such as charisma, spirituality and what Gardner calls 'an enigmatic blend of ordinariness and extraordinariness'. Leaders are extraordinary in having self-belief, being willing to confront entrenched positions, and to take risks. They are ordinary in maintaining heterogenous contacts at many levels within and beyond the city.

Leaders must develop a story of what their creative city could be and how to get there. This story needs constant renewal through the interplay between it, local people and the wider circumstances. The creative urban leader will anticipate trends, appreciate feedback and will encourage debate about the problems and possibilities (see Gardner, 1996).

## Difficulties of Leadership

Leadership poses a continual problem. Debbie Jenkins (1998) believes there is a leadership vacuum: 'What we need is a clear direction', groups cry, whether they are middle managers, community workers, business leaders, or members of the public at various forums, 'why can't the people at the top get their act together/stop fighting/have some imagination/get some new ideas/be more creative/understand the problems/decide on a strategy to sort this out'. People often feel disappointed that their commitment to their city, to the organization for which they work, to the field to which they are devoted, or to issues about which they feel passionate are let down by people in power.

We have mixed emotions about people with vision and will; there is a simultaneous desire for strong, clear, even dogmatic leaders and for caring, nurturing leaders who can see different points of view and even admit that they don't know all the answers. Visionaries have enemies as well as followers. 'There is a demand for a new type of leadership, one that can cope with the new and increasing complexities and delicacies of contemporary urban life, dispense with the wearying conventions of hype and bluster that seem to be inherent in so many forms of traditional urban leadership, and weave into its fabric the many people capable of creating a shared vision, rather than depending on a few individuals to carry the burden of leadership alone' (Jenkins, 1998, p2). A desire for this new approach is very marked among the middle managers and implementers who stand between urban society and its leadership in all kinds of arenas. There are many people who 'have an expertise and a great deal of experience, a certain amount of decision-making power and who are still in touch both with policymakers and with people near the bottom of their particular pyramid'(Jenkins, 1998, p3). They believe increasingly that they have something to offer to the city as a whole, and want to contribute to a clear shared vision for where they live and work, yet feel unable to participate because existing representational mechanisms are inadequate and insufficiently open.

Many potentially high-calibre leaders have also rejected local authorities, impatient with systems and introspective politics, seeking out instead more rewarding leadership positions in the Third Sector or the cutting edge of business. One solution is Common Purpose, which runs annual programmes in over 30 British cities to bring together operational managers from health, education, retailing, the arts, media, local government, business and charities. The aim is to create a common understanding of the city's challenges and so to build a leadership network with broad and common understanding. Many innovative initiatives have occurred, such as in Milton Keynes where health care professionals have rethought patient rehabilitation with artists.

# HUMAN DIVERSITY AND ACCESS TO VARIED TALENT: MIXING PEOPLE

## *Diversities*

Social and demographic conditions can affect a city's creative capacity as when social and cultural diversity fosters understanding and learning rather than leading to xenophobia. A lively civil society usually depends on a history of tolerance, a commitment to accessibility with ladders of opportunity and a broad sense of security. These increase vitality, raising levels of use, participation, transaction and interaction to thresholds which allow activity to take off. By contrast, cities with single, homogenous populations often find it more difficult to be widely creative. They may find novel solutions within their own perspectives, but are less likely to find the mix of imaginations required for the emerging complexities of urban life.

## *Outsiders*

Throughout history outsiders and immigrants, from within the same country or abroad, have been key to establishing creative cities. In an environment where their contribution is allowed to flourish, rather than be feared, their different skills, talents and cultural values lead to new ideas and opportunities. Historical studies of the innovative capacity of places as diverse as Constantinople, Amsterdam, Antwerp, Paris, London, Berlin and Vienna show how minority groups have helped invigorate communities – economically, culturally and intellectually.

London, one of the most cosmopolitan cities of the world, has 33 different national groups with over 10,000 members. Waves of immigrants have passed through, including Huguenots, Jews, Irish, Russians, Chinese, people from the Indian sub-continent and most recently Somalis. They brought with them trades, skills, crafts and talents that have helped underpin London's position as a world city. There is evidence everywhere – in historic buildings, craft forms, food, traditions and cultural expressions, such as the jewellers in Hatton Garden, Little Italy in Clerkenwell, the textile trades in Spitalfields, the furniture makers in Shoreditch, pottery in Southwark and the City of London's financial and banking power. These contributions continue today: Asians in Britain have helped sustain and regenerate its traditional textile industries and even revive the traditional cornershop.

Outsider talent often has to be deliberately imported because most cities discuss their problems within the habits, traditions and cultures of a place – the insider looking inwards, with an occasional glance at the world beyond. The outsider – whether as new resident, business investor, consultant, mediator or decision-maker – is, initially at least, more free from institutional pressures and constraints. They can bring the virtues of freshness to a city, and their first impressions are often very revealing and quickly able to identify new potentials. Some traditional ways of running an organization or a city might not make sense to the outsider. This independence of the outside agent, perhaps a consultant, advisor or investor, also offers new connections and new insights.

## Insiders

Outsiders are important, but they are not a complete answer: it is also vital to harness endogenous intelligence, creativity and learning potential to motivate people and create local self-reliance and ownership. It fosters responsibility, generates an ideas bank and harnesses resources at all levels. Self-reliance is central to the culture of voluntary groups where, for example, many of the most creative solutions in dealing with social problems have occurred. Finding the right balance between insider and outsider knowledge is a key leadership task. At its best the outsider offers freshness and clarity and the insider deep knowledge; at their worst the outsider is ignorant and the insider stale.

Indicators to assess how a city is doing in these respects might include: What percentage of significant decision-makers have been brought in from other contexts or disciplines? What percentage of employees are on project-based contracts and at what level in the hierarchy? How many new organizations have been formed in a given time period?

## ORGANIZATIONAL CULTURE

Huddersfield's shifts in organizational culture describe well the changes necessary for more creative solutions and an innovative milieu to emerge. Organizations that do not innovate tend to be hierarchical, over-departmentalized and internally focused; the bureaucracy they engender are places where 'the end result is not important, but the procedure is' and which 'makes you lose

> ## SHIFTING TOWARDS A CREATIVE ORGANIZATION:
> ### KEY FACTORS
>
> Huddersfield in its experience of becoming a more innovative city noted a series of shifts that occurred in their organizational culture, which apply generally.
>
> | *Centralism* | – | *Devolution* |
> | --- | --- | --- |
> | Isolation | – | Partnership |
> | Control | – | Influence |
> | Leading | – | Enabling |
> | Information | – | Participation |
> | Quantity | – | Quality |
> | Uniformity | – | Diversity |
> | Low risk | – | High risk |
> | High blame | – | Low blame |
> | Conformity | – | Creativity |
> | Failure | – | Success |

perspective so that you can't tell the big things from the small' and where 'everything is forbidden unless it is specifically allowed' (Landry, 1998b).

## Learning through Empowerment

The organizational culture of the creative organization, by contrast, is a less rigid, more trusting one where most aspects of its work is turned into a 'learning experience by encouraging managers to swap jobs, putting together horizontal project teams and learning sets, routinely disseminating and sharing development ideas and training with sister organizations' (Leadbetter and Goss, 1998). Managers in such organizations, especially public ones, need to constantly expose themselves and other people in their organizations to new ideas and then 'to find opportunities to digest them, test them, and find ways to develop them in practice ... mostly by experiential and action learning. ... Managers can learn from each other through benchmarking clubs, shared problem-solving groups, buddying and mentoring systems. Perhaps the most important and least used source of ideas are the public and service users, ... generating a fund of ideas that training would find it difficult to match'(Leadbetter and Goss, 1998). Cities can measure and monitor how many of these ideas are in operation.

Allowing individuals to learn through empowerment requires a supporting framework where experimenting, learning and 'creative and innovative deviance' is positively sanctioned. It means changing the culture of most organizations with an emphasis on team work, empowering front-line staff, the devolution of authority and allowing individuals far greater scope to initiate and implement strategic projects. This more open structure allows people to communicate with each other in new ways where normal debating routes and hierarchies are put on hold to generate discussion about possibilities and problems, enabling younger personnel, often with on the ground and day to day contact with clients, to make a contribution.

Whilst all organizations once they have reached a certain size struggle with bureaucratic tendencies, public institutions probably find it hardest to address them as there is less outside pressure to force change. Commercial pressures often expose the inefficiencies of bureaucracy in business and lack of resources can make non-profit organizations more fleet footed. Thus traditional local authority structures find it most difficult to provide open contexts and are not able to simplify bureaucratic procedures, to shorten decision-making cycles, and to develop an attitude where opportunities rather than obstacles are highlighted. For this reason a raft of new organizational structures are being attempted, essentially involving various forms of public–private partnership. This is a way of harnessing the respective benefits of the private sector, with its greater capacity to implement projects and the public sector, with its concern with the broader public good and questions of accountability.

## Breaking Rules

The need to allow for learning may seem obvious yet most environments, including, ironically, universities, provide obstacles to learning, thus the capacity to break established rules and procedures is essential. Most obstacles are generated by organizational and bureaucratic mentalities as well as the rigid frameworks of professional disciplines. Bureaucracy, creativity and learning do not mix easily. Rules are essentially about containment and creativity about expanding possibilities. City governments need to regulate economic and social life to ensure peaceful, civilized coexistence of often divergent and competing interests and to protect and enhance the common good. This takes the form of complex rules, regulations and controls such as planning permissions, licences, by-laws and traffic restrictions. Bureaucratic systems necessary for the administration of controls and regulations have often been fixed for a long time, yet are not fundamentally reviewed and adapted sufficiently to changing circumstances. Bureaucratic culture tends to pervade and imbue all of large organizations. Then the life of the institution becomes more important than what it does. Indicators would be the amount of pilot projects or departments with overarching remits or levels of cross-departmental working, as these would challenge traditional ways of working.

## The Virtues of Failure

Attitudes to risk and failure need to change in the creatively learning city. Intelligent, innovative, imaginative responses to varied demands involve risk and the possibility of failure. In most organizations, especially public ones, risk is frowned upon and failure not sanctioned. Officially failure rarely exists and is infrequently openly discussed. Yet possibilities for experimentation and for failure need to be provided to renew institutions and test out new initiatives. Failure may contain the seeds of future success if analysed and not automatically punished. Reflecting on failure can be more beneficial as success can lead to complacency. As such, failure becomes a learning device – failure is rarely total and elements of a failure may be useful for future projects. Importantly we need to distinguish between competent and incompetent failure. Aversion to risk taking can mean that an institution has no internal R&D mechanism to weed out future failure. This highlights the importance of pilot projects as each experiment can provide lessons, which if successful can be learnt and incorporated into the mainstream. Institutions thus need innovation budgets with few strings attached. Resources may be lost, but when effectively used can create a bank of ideas for the city as well as a climate of continuous learning. An urban measure might be: How many pilot programmes has the city instigated? How many have been adopted by the mainstream? Is research and development given a specific budget heading?

## Catalysts

Some resources from an innovations budget should be spent on catalyst events and catalyst organizations which are important ways of creating awareness that a creative learning concept exists as a strategy. Without an associated media focus it is likely to have difficulties. An event may be an annual festival to celebrate achievements, such as a 'festival of inventions' or 'a learning fair'. The catalyst organization may be the promotional wing of an organization seeking to increase imaginative action in the city; a university department; a common purpose as referred to earlier or a success story in the city that is celebrated.

Being innovative is risky and scary, thus approval and recognition devices are essential. Competitions, prizes and public acclamations are one way of achieving this objective. Cities must look inside and out. Good ideas can be garnered from national and international competitions, which currently are limited to architectural, urban design, garden festival and arts related projects. The range of competitions remains disappointingly narrow. There could, for example, be competitions on the best way to deal with crime or drug problems or other social experiments or for environmental and economic development purposes. Measures include: Are there events that celebrate innovations or visions of the city? How many competitions does the city instigate? How many competitions have individuals or institutions in the city won?

## Towards a Learning Organization

The creative organization needs to be a lifelong learner, moving on a never-ending development path. It needs to be an organization that builds personal capacity; is able to create a shared organizational vision; to apply mental models that are continually self-improving; to transform collective thinking so that the team is greater than the sum of the parts and to see the organization as part of a system in order to see and understand inter-relationships as a whole.

To secure future well-being, education and learning need to move centre-stage. Only if learning is placed at the centre of our daily experience can:

■ individuals continue to develop their skills and capacities;
■ organizations and institutions recognize how to harness the potential of their workforce and be able to respond flexibly and imaginatively to the opportunities and difficulties of this paradigmatic period of change we are living through;
■ cities act responsively and adapt flexibly to emerging needs;

■ societies understand that the diversity and differences between communities can become a source of enrichment, understanding and potential.

The challenge for policy-makers, therefore, is to promote the conditions in which a 'learning society' or a 'learning city' can unfold. A learning society is much more than a society whose members are simply well-educated; it goes far beyond merely learning in the classroom. It is a place or organization where the idea of learning infuses every tissue of its being; a place where individuals and organizations are encouraged to learn about the dynamics of where they live and how it is changing; a place which on that basis changes the way it learns, whether through schools or any other institution that can help foster understanding and knowledge; a place in which all its members are encouraged to learn; finally and perhaps most importantly a place that can learn to change the conditions of its learning – democratically (Cara et al, 1999).

## Organizational Capacity

Organizational capacity and open governance arrangements are perhaps the precondition of preconditions for a creative city. Within a city at every level from individual to institution an appropriate handling and implementation-oriented capacity needs to be developed, so that innovative ideas can be absorbed, learnt and applied. This means that elements of creativity and innovation need to run throughout the city's decision-making processes, be that public, private or voluntary institutions or be they actors in the economic, social, cultural or environmental field. Organizational capacity acts like a multiplier of resources and potential identified and can be maximized through creative thinking, reflecting and learning.

Organizational capacity is an overarching skill. It involves the capacity to lead, to be technically competent and up to date, to identify strategic issues and priorities, to take a long-term view, to listen to and consult with others, to command loyalty and trust and to inspire and enthuse other decision-makers, to create a supportive team with a strong corporate identity, to create a consensus on key issues by establishing a shared vision, to raise confidence, to find positive uses of conflict, to overcome sectional interests, to form partnerships with a diversity of interest groups, to take responsibility and yet to delegate, make difficult decisions rapidly and efficiently and stick to an agreed course of action in the face of opposition and difficulties. This implies rethinking urban management. Creativity without solid organizational capacity is not sufficient to make the most of a city's resources.

## FOSTERING STRONG LOCAL IDENTITY

Strong identity has positive impacts and creates the preconditions for establishing civic pride, community spirit and the necessary caring for the urban environment. A city may be made up of diverse identities, sometimes rooted in different parts of the city, that express themselves in varied lifestyles, so tolerance is a key aspect to harnessing identities so they contribute to overall vitality and do not cause conflict and fragmentation.

### Cultural Identity

Establishing cultural identity is crucial as celebrating distinctiveness in a homogenizing world marks out one place from the next. Making the specific symbols of the city and its neighbourhoods visible through food, songs, manufacturing or any other tradition are assets from which value added can be created. Equally important is creating new traditions and images so the city's images are not frozen in the past. Historic cities have in-built advantages, they have textured layers of history and built remains to work with in projecting their uniqueness and specialness. This is more difficult for newer cities, unless they can create other forms of buzz. Beyond a certain level once basic services, shops and facilities have been provided, these differences are ways of adding value to what a city is about.

### The Ambiguity of History

History is complex and whether it is a trigger for creativity, learning and innovation is open to question. An historical track record in generating creativity and learning capacity can both hold back or push forward. At times it inspires at others it becomes a burden or weight. At its best it generates chains of innovation which rely on the historical precedent of a 'master' passing on skills to apprentices, of educational institutions developing reputations and expertise to reinforce a self-sustaining process of confidence, invention and collaboration. At its worst historical success can create arrogance, stasis and resistance to change along the lines of: 'We have seen it all before.'

Beautiful as Florence is, many regard the city today as a place that merely reflects, reinforces or reinvents its past glories. Self-satisfaction and arrogance, it is argued, over-ride everything, generating a sense of closure to outsiders and a lack of new ideas. Industrial Prato nearby, by contrast without the weight of history and expectation, has developed many recent innovations in the Italian context, related to new forms of business alliance to project the city or the contemporary arts.

Identity and distinctiveness provide the anchor and roots for a city necessary to select what is central or peripheral in the tide of available information and ideas. It can provide a bond between people with different institutional interests cooperating for the common good of the city. However, when identity and distinctiveness degenerate into parochialism, introversion, chauvinism and antagonism to the outside world they may destroy the foundations of a creative milieu and create a sense of claustrophobia and threat.

## URBAN SPACES AND FACILITIES

## Public Space

Public space, sometimes known as the public sphere or realm, is a multi-faceted concept at the heart of the innovative milieu. It is both a physical setting as well as an arena where exchange can occur through the variety of forms of communication from physical interaction to newspapers to cyberspace. It includes meeting spaces and occasions from the informal to more formal such as seminars. The public realm helps develop creativity because it allows people to go beyond their own circle of family, professional and social relations. The idea of the public realm is bound up with the ideas of discovery, of expanding one's horizons, of the unknown, of surprise, of experiment and of adventure.

### Physical Public Space

The classic Italian 'piazza' or public square like the Campo in Sienna, usually located at the city's core, is the physical embodiment of public space. Its four corners symbolically represent the essence and interaction of a city's power and aspiration. Typically at one corner there is a church representing spiritual power; at another a museum, library or university representing learning, knowledge and culture; at a third the town hall or castle epitomizing worldly power and at the fourth a market hall or trade outlets expressing commercial power. The square in the middle is their point of exchange for face to face encounters, news, gossip, the exchange of ideas and development of new projects. This idea is reflected throughout European urbanism, so in Helsinki's classic Senate Square, looking from below, one can see the cathedral dominating the landscape; at its right is the president's palace; at its left the headquarters of the university and opposite formerly there was the headquarters of the police – important at the time as it was built when Finland was controlled by a repressive Russian Czarist state. In moving with the times, this now houses a row of cafes and small shops.

## Urban Centres as Neutral Territory

The city centre or urban sub-centres potentially represent places for commonality, where some form of common identity and spirit of place can be created – counteracting the dangers of spatial segregation by social class – and where people of different ages, social classes, ethnic and racial groups and lifestyles can mix and mingle in informal and unplanned ways, more easily than in the suburbs or in outer areas, which are frequently highly differentiated and socially stratified.

City centres or public space as 'neutral territory' help creative ideas, because they are areas where people feel comfortably relaxed and simultaneously stimulated and challenged by contact with an environment that is more socially heterogeneous than normally experienced. At their best they function as showcases for creative ideas and activities generated in all parts of the city and places where the majority of public facilities agglomerate – ranging from museums to cafes, public squares, cinemas, pubs, restaurants, theatres and libraries. They are key locations for the public realm.

This conception of the city as an arena of public space and exchange of ideas is threatened by recent trends towards the privatization of public space, enclosure of shopping malls and self-contained, inward-looking buildings.

## Meeting Places: The Virtual and the Real

A sense of public space can be created in manifold ways and the city of imagination needs to tap into all of them. Meeting places are public spaces whether a conference or public lecture venue, a seminar facility; a cafe, bar or club; an open associative network such as the new trend towards discussion salons. For example, a dining and debating club boom has emerged in a number of large cities like London and Paris. In London a number of clubs have been founded in recent years – the Boisdale, the Maverick, the Asylum and in Paris the philosopher cafes are on the rise again. They are a reinvention of the Parisian salon, somewhere between a dinner party and a think-tank offering the intellectual formality of the lecture with the informality of the pub chat. Traditional clubs were for people who agreed with each other, the new clubs tend to be for the opposite reason. The idea is not to win arguments, but to stimulate debate. 'The trick of the new dining clubs is to combine enough structure to distinguish themselves from a night down the pub, with sufficient informality to distinguish themselves from traditional clubs' (Jan MacVarish from the Maverick Club, London).

The Internet age with its chat rooms, fora and interactive possibilities creates a new form of public cyberspace. In spite of endless opportunities new technology provides for exchange and telecommuting – the computer proves how much we need face to face contact. 'Despite the bits and bytes that we produce, we are still comprised of atoms ... we still need face time' (Andy Pratt – unpublished paper given at DCMS conference: 'A Working Culture', September 1998). The challenge for the creative city is to provide flexible settings for interaction, which incorporate the virtues of the physical and static with possibilities to operate in a cyberworld. Cybercafes are merely a start. The development of office formats to rent for an hour or a day are another. What are needed are envi-

---

### UTOPIAN NIGHTS, LONDON, UK

This represents a mixture of workplace and culture space, of seminar, food event, and exhibition, of the rebirth and recasting of the salon and the campfire. Ten years ago an English design firm, Interbrand Newell and Sorrell, started a programme of bringing in a variety of people to speak to their staff about a passion they felt for some activity. This was transformed into a public event, with an invited guest list of 200 from a variety of 'stations in life'. It has become one of the most desirable invitations in London. The programmes happen five times a year and are keyed to an in-house exhibition and a party with food linked to the guest's talk. School teachers and cabinet ministers mingle in a community that has come to build its own dynamic. The unapologetic goal of the evenings is 'inspiration'.

ronments, combining the two, which encourage an *esprit de corps* for the itinerant cyber-worker to feel both at home and part of a wider world.

## Public Facilities

The quantity, quality, variety and accessibility of a combination of facilities and amenities are crucial for encouraging creative processes in a city. Whilst amenities like the beauty of a city, health, transport, shopping facilities, cleanliness and parks are important, three factors stand out: research capacity, information resources and cultural facilities.

### Research and Education

The intellectual underpinning of a potentially creative city is a differentiated and comprehensive research and educational system, ranging from primary schooling to technical and humanistic universities as well as research capacity in universities, government agencies and private organizations. The possibility of transferring theoretical knowledge into practical applications is key. Science parks, especially linked to universities, or incubator units are important. They are key components in retaining and attracting skilled personnel and thereby giving them opportunities to further their personal development.

### Communication Channels

A sophisticated information and communication system from libraries, advice centres or communications media are needed to back up educational resources. The greater the information 'density' and exchange the easier it is for the creative individuals and institutions to keep abreast of events and best practice developments, both within the city and outside of it. The communication capacity of a city depends on whether it is the production base or houses the headquarters of local, regional and national newspapers, radio or TV stations and other media industries. Yet information increasingly important in 'post-industrial' cities is garnered not only in institutions, but through cyberspace, meetings and conferences and thus active international networking strategies are key.

The broader the spectrum of research and development activities in a locality the greater the chances of sustaining and renewing the economic strength of a city. This requires logistical, financial and material support from both public and private institutions (see Landry et al, 1996).

## Cultural Facilities

Cultural facilities and activities are significant factors in generating inspiration, self-confidence, debate or ideas exchange as well as the creation of a city's image. They help attract skilled and talented personnel, as well as provide opportunities for residents. Consuming high-profile arts and cultural activities has less strong transformative effects on individuals than direct participation, whose impact is greater in terms of human development and tapping creative potential.

### Creative Spaces at Affordable Prices

Creative people and projects need to be based somewhere. A creative city requires land and buildings at affordable prices especially for younger businesses or social entrepreneurs. These are likely to be available on the urban fringes and in areas where uses are changing, such as former port and industrial zones. Cheap spaces that can be innovatively adapted to reduce financial risk and encourage experiment, even at the most banal level of opening a new type of restaurant or a shop. Recycling older industrial buildings is now a cliché of urban regeneration, but does not make it less worthwhile. Typically they can be re-used as incubator units for new business start-ups, as headquarters for cutting edge companies, as artist studios, or as centres for design and new media.

Examples abound: the cable factory in Helsinki, formerly Nokia's cable production centre houses over 600 people from micro-businesses to museums; perhaps the largest centre of its type in Europe. The Centre for Media Technology and the Arts housed in an old off-centre munitions factory in Karlsruhe has new forms of exhibitions spaces for electronic media, research facilities for sound and visual arts as well as space for renting out; also attached is the arts college thus fostering synergies. Perhaps the world's largest arts space is the Massachusetts Museum of Contemporary Art (MASS MoCA), a 13-acre spread of renovated 19th-century factory buildings. The Tramway in Glasgow is a huge cultural centre housed in an old bus and tram depot a few miles from the centre. Bristol's Watershed Media Centre and Arnolfini Gallery housed in former warehouses on the river front just off the city centre have now become hubs of the city. These establishments generate new creative infrastructures and instigate other innovative, developmental chain reactions – most obviously relating to night life and property investment in surrounding buildings where higher values can be achieved.

## Artists as Regenerators

This creativity can establish interesting milieu, leading to spill-overs which encourage imaginative activities in other spheres. This dynamic, often created by artists, usually leads to the dispersal of those artists who set the regeneration process in motion in the first place. London is a good example. Artists are now dispersed throughout the capital with a tendency to agglomerate in cheap yet interesting areas as near as possible to the centre. Over the last 40 years there have been a number of waves. London's Soho was once an area where artists lived and worked, yet that time has long since passed – with increased property values artists were pushed outwards to lower value locations. Taking their place are the more successful new media companies. Camden Town is another area where a similar process has occurred. Now it is the East End where the UK's largest collection of artists live and work – in Wapping, Tower Hamlets around Brick Lane or Hackney and Hoxton Square.

---

### RECYCLING SPACES FOR CREATIVE CONNECTIONS: ZENTRUM FÜR KUNST UND MEDIENTECHNOLOGIE, KARLSRUHE, GERMANY

ZKM is an institution that has no exact parallel in the world, the Ars Electronica Centre, Linz, Austria and the Intercommunication Center, Tokyo are somewhat related. Founded in 1989 and opened to the public in October, 1997, the ZKM has more than 48,000 square yards of usable space. It houses in addition to a Media Museum, an Institute for Visual Media, an Institute of Media and Acoustics, a media library, a media theatre, a Museum for Contemporary Art and, under different direction, the State Academy of Design and the Municipal Gallery of the City of Karlsruhe. 'Touring the Media Museum is like roaming an electronic theme park, a futuristic playground for grown-ups where miniature theatres, videos and oversize images morph, dance, respond to questions and urge visitors along on fictive journeys. ... Though many of the installations ask hard questions about serious issues, the museum simply brushes aside the barrier between art and entertainment. ... Artists are invited to establish long-term residence in the labs ... experimenting in sound as well as the visual context. ... the media arts have created the first global arts scene ... just about everyone in the field knows everyone else' (*New York Times*, 14 February 1999).

Classically artists agglomerate in interesting yet run down areas, often subject to potential redevelopment pressures, but where the process has not yet started. The artist in effect is the explorer and the regenerator kick-starting a gentrification process, bringing life to run-down areas and generating the development of support structures such as cafes, restaurants and some shops. They then attract a more middle-class clientele who would not have risked being the first, either through fear, the dislike of run-down areas or pressure from peer groups. Only when the 'grottiness' has been tamed and made safe by the artist will this second group arrive.

From the planning point of view the key issue is how to maintain low value uses, that may have broader 'public good' benefits. In the cultural quarter of Temple Bar in Dublin, the city authority has given artists long-term leases in city-owned property, which has been designated for artists' use. The spin-offs that accrue to the wider area justify this.

## NETWORKING AND ASSOCIATIVE STRUCTURES

Networking has two aspects: networking within a city and networking internationally. Cities have always been centres of networking and communication, but the nature of networking is

### MASS MoCA (MASSACHUSETTS MUSEUM OF CONTEMPORARY ART)

A 13-acre spread of renovated 19th-century factory buildings in a poor rural mill town has been recast as the US's and perhaps the world's largest centre for contemporary and visual arts. Opened in May 1999, it spans the fields of sculpture, dance, theatre, film, digital media and music. 'Museums are a reliquary,' says the director. 'This is not a reliquary. This is a place for seeing art and directly relating to it.' Since visitors can see art works in the process of creation, it has been described by a reporter as 'the equivalent of a Hollywood studio back lot.' The museum will have no contemporary collection. It commissions on occasion pieces 'that resonate with the building, for example the Berlin artist Christina Kubisch has placed carillon bells on the mill's clock tower to ring compositions whose tones are dictated by the motion and brightness of the sun.'

changing as communities become more mobile and technically connected. A bird's eye view of cities reveals a series of overlapping communities and networks criss-crossing the city and well beyond, creating a form of invisible glue that holds the city together, generates multiple interactions, but also creates loyalty and connection far beyond the reach of the city. Each network sees the city in a different way – some are intensely local, others more global.

Networking and creativity are intrinsically symbiotic, as the greater the number of nodes in a system the greater its capacity for reflexive learning and innovation. To maximize benefits, networking needs to become even more intense and with new configurations. Many traditional networks contribute nothing special to urban creativity. They are simply part of what makes community, which is based on needing to communicate and cooperate to solve common problems and to socialize. Social homogeneity and immobility were dominant as was a far smaller geographic reach – conditions that no longer apply in a world of mobility, ethnic or lifestyle diversity and which has seen the erosion of geographically based communities.

The rise of partnership models for urban development are interesting in this regard. Public, private and voluntary partnerships have brought together people, each perhaps a member of the great and the good in their sub-sector, but previously unknown to each other. The process has eroded the primacy and power of local politicians and brought in new actors. The long-term impact of new urban cyber-communities remain to be seen. The 'virtual city' movement including Virtual Helsinki, Copenhagen, Amsterdam or Manchester provide not only information and marketing services for their own city, but a much wider function too. Several thousand ex-Mancunians from as far afield as Canada and Australia regularly hook up to keep in touch with Manchester, creating discussion fora with locals – this is a community too.

Connecting urban communities both to themselves and other places is such a crucial issue that it is time for local authority departments concerned with 'connectedness' and networking to be brought into being. Their primary aim would be to bring people together physically or virtually, focusing on communicating in the city. This might include urban information services like libraries or a council's own PR department encouraging internationally oriented networking – for officials, local businesses, schools or old-age pensioners – as competition and comparison with other cities provides stimulus and benchmarking. The brokering of new connections and new economic, scientific and cultural collaborations is key for future urban prosperity.

To maximize learning potential international networking between cities needs to change and move away from:

- networking based on ceremony to substance – less a focus on local authority 'junkets' which provide no practical outcome;
- friendship initiatives to projects which achieve tangible and monitorable results;
- amateurism to professionalism to ensure ideas and projects are carried through;
- community friendship links to the involvement of a wide range of stakeholders;
- general all-purpose initiatives to targeted activities involving real transfer of expertise, say dealing with degraded land or business start-ups;
- incidental to systematic technical collaboration to ensure that the benefits of working together can be maximized (see Gilbert et al, 1996).

Measures of connectedness could include: densities of communication such as availability of mobiles or Internet access; number of project-specific partnerships within the city and externally; or range of meeting places from bars to restaurants.

## Deeply Embedded Networking

Recent managerial literature stresses the importance of networked organization – within firms, between firms, within similar sectors and across sectors as well as between universities, the public sector and commercial companies.

Importantly though, Putnam's highly influential work has added a new dimension by emphasizing – especially in the European context – that these networking capacities are rooted in social structures that are very difficult to replicate in the short-term, yet are vital for innovation to spread (Putnam, 1993). This is especially important for innovations related to sustainable development, implying as they do behavioural change. Using a comparison between the development of northern and southern Italy over the centuries, Putnam shows how mutual aid structures, the strength of voluntary and community organizations which are deeply embedded in the social structure have helped foster in northern Italy an

industrial, financial and social structure that has encouraged collaborative working even in intensely competitive environments. This
emphasis on collaboration is contrasted to the 'failed' development
of southern Italy where a feudal, more hierarchical structure is seen
to have stifled progress.

These insights have cast some doubt on strategies such as the
Japanese technopolis programme which seeks to promote innovative milieu in regions that did not previously have these capacities
(Hall and Castells, 1994). It is interesting to speculate on the extent
to which this general schema applies to countries as diverse as
Russia, Peru, Finland, Egypt or China and whether their cultures
foster or deter a networking and partnership-based approach to
urban development, which lies at the heart of a creative milieu. As
an interviewee in Helsinki noted: 'A networking culture is not easy
in Finland – it might sound like a cliché, but it is the stubbornness,
envy and independence.' Or: 'You must remember that everybody
knows each other and until recently everybody lived near the rural
forests and was defensive.'

Nevertheless, while this networking capacity has been achieved
in some successful commercial organizations, especially in high-
tech and cultural industrial companies, it is infinitely more difficult
to achieve in the urban context as a whole. These companies share
a number of features that foster networking, and indeed are dependent on it. They tend to be project-based with changing groupings
agglomerating around specific time-dated tasks: the development
of a piece of software; the production of a play; the creation of a
CD; the production of a film. Their products embody intellectual
copyright such as the rights on a software program, a record or
logo. Intensely creative products are increasingly difficult, if not
impossible, to produce within hermetically sealed large companies
based on full-time employed personnel. Each product is unique and
needs a unique mix of people to make it happen and the economics
of production essentially tend to work better with sub-contracted
staff. Furthermore the key drivers of product development – the
'artist' or 'innovative technologist' – are often themselves stars
seeking to retain control, but in turn needing others to work with.
Business does not necessarily come in a regular flow and each
member of the process increases their capacity for survival by their
level of 'connectedness' or networking. Networking is based on
need not desire.

## *The City and Inter-organizational Networking*

Creating a felt, urgent need to network is much more difficult for a city given its amalgam of actors – public, private, voluntary – each with its own organizational culture and agenda. So, whilst organizations within a sector, like new technology, might be creative, networked and collaborative, the key issue is how they can be creative with others and find a reason to be creative together. If that reason can be found a culture of creativity can be embedded into the 'genetic code' of a city.

It is easier to understand why industrial firms might network together for collaborative advantage where skill sharing and knowledge exchange is mutually beneficial. But what is the rationale, especially for the smaller firm without a national reputation, to make the leap to network with city authorities on issues which do not necessarily generate an immediate short-term gain? The same is true for links say between voluntaries and business. One common

---

### ARTS NETWORKING IN COLOGNE

The rise of Cologne as an arts city was helped by the power of networking. Kurt Hackenburg, the city's director of culture, (1955–79), was the centre of a city-wide network of arts and music. He supported a range of spectacular events in the 1960s linked to the Happening and Fluxus arts movements. This in turn attracted more artists, gallerists and collectors, who between them developed a chain of initiatives, such as the Cologne Art Fair. A similar process occurred with electronic music, where the Studio für Elektronische Musik set up in 1951 became the focal point for modern composers who used the studio for experimentation. This attracted further composers to settle there, who have created what is known as the Cologne School of Modern Music. One of the achievements of these continuous sets of activities is not only that members of the group generate a stream of new projects, but also that the audiences for ultra modern art forms have increased, making Cologne a place, in the arts at least, where the acceptance of artistic creativity has become part of the established norm. The network between composers, artists, art galleries, collectors, etc has created not only advantages for the participants and financial benefits, but has also created an economic sector for the city as well as the image of Cologne as an 'arts city'.

---

### HELSINKI: THE INCLUSIVELY NETWORKED CITY

Helsinki is poised to take the lead by making the Internet an inclusive, citizen-oriented experience. Already 65 per cent of Finns own mobile phones and in the under-25 group nearly 90 per cent. Not to own one is to be excluded. The Lasipalatsi (Glass Palace) was opened in 1999 as a media centre with distinctive features: in a phone box you are faced with a screen, a web camera and a microphone – a digital speakers' corner, where people are encouraged to broadcast what is on their mind to politicians or anyone else prepared to watch or listen on the Internet; the public cyber-library has free access to the Internet; you can download difficult-to-order books that are delivered bound as well as self-publish; you can make films and transmit these costing no more than £2,000 on the Internet. The Arena 2000 project gives fast broadband access to the Internet to most of its citizens. This means the capacity to transmit live video as well as to receive it. Helsinki is well advanced in creating a virtual Helsinki on the Internet enabling people to follow buses and taxis, to order food; for parents to track children; for doctors to have face to face discussions with patients, for students to follow lectures, to share watching television with friends although they are in separate locations. It is a 3-D model of the city allowing residents to move down virtual streets to go shopping and to be part of the city from home.

*Source:* Keegan, *The Guardian*, 16 September 1999

---

way of generating a reason for joint action is through urban visioning, a process of scaling up the business plan concept from the level of the firm to the level of the urban area or city. To get people around the table to develop new potentially creative ideas in the first place is the most difficult part. Civic responsibility does not come naturally; thus crisis is an important trigger. It may be capital and educated people who have moved out, those whom the firm needs as staff otherwise its competitive position is weakened. Or public action can be seen as a way of increasing the value of a firm's assets. That self-interest may then broaden once the interconnections are understood. Yet keeping the commitment going remains difficult even once an urban vision has been agreed.

## Best Practice Benchmarking and Beyond

Encouraging a reflexive learning process is a key objective of a creative city: benchmarking spreads information about good practice and innovations so as to encourage, inspire and foster replication and to benchmark itself. Benchmarking is a means of establishing baselines for measuring current and future performance. The concept of best practice is a means of developing a 'culture of excellence within cities', whereby the idea of a best practice, that might be replicated, acts as a driver towards continuous improvement. This is similar to the idea of TQM prevalent in the business sphere. The notion of 'best practice' has in part been contentious, especially the idea of what is 'best'; a consensus is emerging that best practice essentially means 'good projects, that have worked elsewhere, and that may be replicable in my city'. Importantly there is an increased understanding that best practice is about learning, not ranking; and, in that context, going beyond the mere fact of knowing that a good project exists, to discovering how it came about and what were the conditions for its success. The most significant learning occurs through doing something oneself; thus, knowledge about an innovative project – however good the description – can only ever be a starting point.

The challenge for the creative city is to get beyond best practice and operate at the cutting edge. Adopting a best practice reduces the learning curve, but there is a danger of simply imitating tried and tested formulae without assessing what is relevant for the city given its peculiarities. The task is to assess when imitation takes a city forward and often this means applying the principles of a project rather than its details and when complete invention is appropriate. Measures might be: Has your city got benchmarking programmes? Is keeping up with best practice integral to the planning of organizations?

# 6

# The Creative Milieu

## Origins of Interest

The origins of interest in urban creative and innovative milieux lies in the marked success some cities and regions over the world have had in the past and recent present by using non-traditional, creative approaches to their urban and regional development, effectively embedding creativity into their city's 'genetic code'. Organizational culture; leadership and certain qualities in their environment were instrumental. Of relevance here are highly networked, non-hierarchical innovative regions such as Silicon Valley and the so-called Third Italy around Emilia–Romagna in which individual firms, often quite small, flourish in a milieu of constant technical improvement and the presence of specialized support services. Today the notion of necessary support services has broadened from the presence of venture capitalists or distribution chains to embrace the need for cultural facilities, urban buzz often created by cultural industry entrepreneurs or arts types, social activities and more generally amenities linked to quality of life, including good housing, transport and health facilities. Urban milieux need to provide networking opportunities in non-work settings or between firms. This might include the capacity for a chance meeting in a cafe, a concert, a health club or school. What is important is discovering which types of urban environment encourage such interaction.

Public intervention through regulation, incentives regimes and changes in organizational culture can help foster such a milieu. Much of the initial emphasis was initially focused on creating a climate for small firms to flourish through fiscal breaks or grants programmes. As quality of life issues have come into play other tools for intervention have been assessed. At one extreme they include the creation of hard infrastructure such as public transport or refurbishing and reusing old industrial structures, at the other issues like the licensing of restaurants or cafes to allow a more active social life to take place. Seattle, increasingly cited as a new innovative milieu, had a recent debate over a citizens' action which forced city authorities to accede to the building of a city-wide monorail system – the first in the US. The argument put forward was that increasingly the city's quality of life, guaranteed through public transport, was necessary to maintain the city's economic position.

## WHAT IS A CREATIVE MILIEU?

A creative milieu is a place – either a cluster of buildings, a part of a city, a city as a whole or a region – that contains the necessary preconditions in terms of 'hard' and 'soft' infrastructure to generate a flow of ideas and inventions. Such a milieu is a physical setting where a critical mass of entrepreneurs, intellectuals, social activists, artists, administrators, power brokers or students can operate in an open-minded, cosmopolitan context and where face to face interaction creates new ideas, artefacts, products, services and institutions and as a consequence contributes to economic success.

'Hard' infrastructure is the nexus of buildings and institutions such as research institutes, educational establishments, cultural facilities and other meeting places as well as support services such as transport, health and amenities. 'Soft' infrastructure is the system of associative structures and social networks, connections and human interactions, that underpins and encourages the flow of ideas between individuals and institutions. This occurs either face to face or through information technology that enables wider networks of communication to develop, so helping the trade of goods and services. These networks may include social ones such as clubs, regular meetings in bars or informal associations; common interest networks such as business clubs or marketing consortia; or public–private partnerships involving (say) financial support structures and devices whereby public and private resources and ideas people can be creatively brought together and their creativity harnessed.

The network capacity that lies at the heart of the creative milieu requires flexible organizations working with a high degree of trust, self-responsibility and strong, often unwritten, principles. These include a willingness to share and to contribute to the success of the network for the greater good. The health and prosperity of the creative network largely determines the prosperity of each individual company. Unless the milieu thrives, the inspirational flow that comes from being part of it dries up. Pure self-interest causes the milieu to atrophy. Trust is a central feature of the way a creative milieu operates, which can lead to chains of creative ideas and innovations which through their spread and acceptance can generate a further virtuous circle of inventions. The rules of such a system are strong on principle, such as that the network is more important than individual needs, and flexible in application.

The creative milieu requires easy movement between and within job categories and firms. This is very difficult where labour market rigidities persist, say dividing blue, white collar and research workers, leading to a loss of potential that comes from communication. Equally prejudices between sectors such as the private sector and public domain or xenophobia have an inefficiency effect. A culture of collaborative competition is a precondition for such a milieu to thrive.

## Creative Milieux through History

Historically cities have been creative in a number of ways: culturally, intellectually; technologically and organizationally and have established milieux to match. Since the industrial revolution at the end of the 18th century, the latter two have become progressively more important. In addition during the 20th century cultural and technological creativity and innovation has tended to merge, given the rise of the cultural industries. These links help to develop new synergies that may evolve into new products and services demanding new organizational, economic and political forms. Peter Hall summarizes their dynamics well in Cities in Civilization.

Intellectual and cultural vitality in cities, such as Athens, Rome, Florence, London, Vienna or Berlin at their highpoints depended on rapid and radical economic and social transformation; where excess wealth became important in fostering and investing in new ideas and especially artistic creativity. 'Invariably wracked by tension between conservative and radical forces' (Hall, 1998), which played themselves out on the intellectual arena, these radical forces felt themselves to be locked out of the established system, because they were young, provincial or foreign. Accepting 'outsiders' or radicals was essential, as was the ability to connect to the mainstream established order so as to have access to the wider society.

The democratic constitution developed by Cleisthenes in 500 BC in Athens was a socio-political innovation contributing to the city's vibrancy and success. It brought a voice and influence to larger groups of people as well as help expand an empire which resulted in an increase of new products, commodities, ideas and inspiration. Yet additional contact with the periphery of the Greek empire also caused instability resulting in greater influence for philosophers and personalities in cultural life. The creative turn of Florence between 1270 and 1330 was caused by ongoing power conflicts across generations, competition between families and other cities. The growth of a literary and artistic milieu in 18th-century England was linked to a changing balance of political and economic power between the court and developing middle-classes within an emerging commercial society. Crucial was the 'free constitution' which allowed the development of new forms of literature and performing arts. As a consequence London became the fastest growing city in Europe, a magnet attracting artists and musicians in a self-sustaining cycle. Vienna in the period 1880–1914 became a centre of creativity as the instability of the declining empire caused disequilibrium in the social, institutional and political structure. It led to rethinking in a variety of unrelated areas from economics, medicine, philosophy, to psychiatry, the expressive and visual arts, urban planning and architecture. Conflicts and generational clashes between culturally creative groups and old social institutions lay at the core of this febrile activity contributing to a 'positive' instability.

Out of this conjuncture came the rise of the cafe culture – a common feature from that period onwards in Central Europe in places as diverse as Berlin, Vienna, Munich, Prague and Zürich. Since then, the café culture has become a significant feature of creative milieux worldwide. Cafes provided daily points of contact for intellectuals, journalists, artists, scientists and even business people. They formed tightly knit networks where ideas, knowledge and technical expertise were circulated. Cafes were melting pots where distinctions between class and rank could be overcome.

Technologically innovative cities have a shorter history and are places where 'the innovators were outsiders living in outsider cities' – marginalized cities like Manchester, Glasgow or Detroit. Not totally distant; they were less bound by old ways of doing things; willing to take a risk; they mostly had egalitarian structures; an ethos of self-reliance, self-achievement and open educational structures. Grounded in technological skills and less involved in primary innovation and more downstream innovations they were attuned to the market. Los Angeles and its subsequent dominance of the film and entertainment industries is an example that combines the merger of cultural and technological creativity. Originally considered an upstart place, distant from traditional centres of power and wealth, it linked innovations to a mass market, in particular through the marriage of popular culture and technology.

Technological–organizational urban innovations occur in cities that need to solve the problems of growth and development that cities themselves have generated – from the need to create new sewage systems, to waste, public transport to new building techniques to the provision of housing to financial innovations to pay for emerging infrastructures. Cities from ancient Rome, to London, New York and modern Stockholm have been leaders in this field. The debate on urban sustainability has created a new drive to encourage such innovations. One idea has taken hold based on recent work from the Club of Rome called *Factor Four: Doubling Wealth, Halving Resource Use* (von Weizsäcker et al, 1998) which suggests that at least four times as much wealth can be extracted from the resources currently used by employing the 'doing more with less' principle. The notion is particularly attractive in appealing to businesses' own self-interest to become more sustainable, because it is potentially profitable. The success, again of this sustainability-driven creativity will depend on how battles between environmentalists and free marketers pan out.

This trajectory towards conflict is confirmed in much of my work in Comedia. We found deep-seated frictions and gaps in understanding often not related to age, but to a perspective on life in Helsinki, Huddersfield, Mantua and Adelaide, where generational ideas and values did not align. The change-makers had an implicit congruence of ideas and approach and, as a group, embodied a generational shift in terms of mentality, values and philosophy. In some cases even the languages used by different parties were so different that there was no common ground for communication. As Hall notes 'creative cities are not stable or comfortable places, but they must not be in total disorder. They are places in which the established order is under prolonged threat by new creative groups' (Hall, 1998).

The next innovative wave will naturally be linked to the implications of innovations in information technology and the fusion of telecommunications – television and computing into multimedia. Crucially their powerful drive will only be maximized if they are allied to social and political innovations which act as a lubricant and catalyst to increase their impact. In principle this allows for the end of the 'tyranny of distance' and the development of telecommuting. Yet because of agglomeration and clustering effects it is likely, ironically, to produce a cultural renaissance for cities, which, having got rid of dirty industry, will retain their attraction for activities that require face to face contact. These revitalized places are often called 'cultural quarters' and are being transformed by artists and new media businesses.

## Cultural Industry Quarters

The 'booming economy of bits and bytes' has made the idea of production-based cultural quarters or creative industries quarters fashionable the world over at the end of the 20th century: they range from London's Tower Hamlets Brick Lane, to Tilburg' Pop Cluster, from Berlin's Hackische Höfe to Johannesburg's Newtown, Silicon Alley in New York or Rundle Street East in Adelaide. The term is so popular that any coincidental proximity of cultural facilities are now being called 'cultural quarters' as a branding device from Amsterdam's Museumsplein to Baltimore's Inner Harbour, although here culture is consumed rather than produced.

The cultural industries in the US have just overtaken aircraft as the biggest export earner and employ over 10 per cent of the population – some say even up to 20 per cent (Pratt, 1998). In Europe the figure is around 5 per cent. In the case of Britain, music exports were larger than those of engineering from the start of the 1980s. These industries comprise music; publishing; the audio visual and multimedia sector; the performing and visual arts and crafts. They include sectors where the creative input is a secondary but crucial means of enhancing the value of other products whose marketability and effectiveness would otherwise be lessened, such as design, industrial design, graphics and fashion. The convergence of artistically based industries with computer communications and their cross-fertilization through digitalization has made them the drivers of the new economy. The image of this industry attracts business relocators and tourist flows, adding indirect economic benefits. Digitalization is the key force for change: images, sound and text are converted into a binary code language which can then be infinitely manipulated, blended – and very cheaply reproduced and transmitted.

This new digital media economy could work in telecommuting mode, but instead is flourishing largely without public intervention in characterful urban quarters where old industrial buildings can be recycled. Even in the US, the world's most wired society, software and multimedia companies are being drawn to areas such as 'Multimedia Gulch', a warehouse/factory district in San Francisco until recently completely run down; the same is true in New York's Silicon Alley and London's Hackney and Hoxton. Sheffield, by contrast, was public sector led, starting in 1980 with the opening of the Leadmill Arts Centre, followed by Red Tape, Britain's first municipal rehearsal, recording and sound training facility. Their ownership of a cluster of older industrial buildings allowed them to open an Audio-Visual Enterprise Centre, a complex called the Workstation and the Wired Workspace and most recently the National Centre for Popular Music. In Sheffield the creative industries have led to an astonishing physical renewal as well as the creation of an industrial sector in an unlikely location. The key issue is whether the public sector can intervene to create such quarters. Throughout the developed world authorities are looking for cultural and digital clusters in the hope of 'bringing a sparkle to rust belts' and that 'the 'digerati will see themselves not as dreamy artists, but more as driven, export-orientated entrepreneurs' (quote from Rob Brown in article 'Everybody needs face time' at rbrown@indigo.ie).

These 'creative milieu' are places where culturally alert 'techies' can collaborate with other cultural workers as well as have the 'face time' to spark off people in the same field of work. Multimedia, the supreme example of the 'weightless economy', embeds itself spatially through social networks, the presence of organizations and institutions as well as the proximity of its market and inter-trading with suppliers. In what circumstances is it useful for policy-makers to brand an area as a cultural quarter and when not to for the benefit of the city depends on a broader judgement of a city's overall prospects. At times, focusing resources on one area leads others into decline. In places that have less critical mass or are less well-known, encouraging clustering and branding is likely to be more beneficial.

### Implications of the Historical Detour
Four significant conclusions emerge:

1   To remain at the cutting edge cities in the future need to be creative and innovative in all the dimensions noted above –  intellectually, culturally, technologically and organizationally – and not merely focus on one type. The merger between cultural

and technological creativity as witnessed in multimedia allied to urban innovations to enhance urban sustainability will be key, with sustainability defined as an overarching concept with environmental, economic, social and cultural dimensions.

2   In the urban context creativity and innovation need to be seen as an holistic, integrated process covering every aspect of urban life from the economic, political, cultural, environmental and social-multiple innovativeness. Only then can the city deal with the strains and stresses of global transformations and remain efficient and effective.

3   An emphasis on new 'softer' forms of creativity and innovation is necessary, reinforcing the role of cities as tolerant, open-minded places. Solving issues of social cohesion, social fragmentation and inter-cultural understanding are perhaps the central issues. Mutual understanding between groups within cities, countries and between cultures will become central in the context of globalization, rapid movements of capital, mass movements of population triggered by the new world production order. Bosnia, East Timor and Rwanda are stark reminders of the consequences of not addressing these issues in a thoughtful and consistent way. Societies will inevitably become more multi-cultural. This can be taken positively or negatively. The way forward is to treat the issue as an opportunity not a threat – easy to say, but difficult to do.

4   The new raft of creative and innovative cities, such as Seattle, Portland, Vancouver, Melbourne, Zürich or Freiburg focus strongly on generating a high quality of life. They seek to connect issues of economic inventiveness, with sustainability and community empowerment combined with rigorous benchmarking programmes to drive their urban development. A high quality of life is used as a competitive tool, which reinforces their economic and social dynamic. It is noticeable that these groupings do not represent the central cities which are drivers of their wider region (San Francisco, Los Angeles and Sydney respectively) and as 'secondary' cities try to find new niches.

There is certainly more than one way of establishing a creative milieu and such milieux are increasingly not exclusively technologically driven. In all cases networking between the diversity of urban actors is central, such as links between universities and industries. History shows that great metropolitan cities remain outstanding creative milieux, especially if the focus is on economic innovation – simply because they multiply the capacity for networking. What is new, however, is the recognition of 'softer', more subtle conditions which allow innovations to occur.

## THE QUALITIES OF A CREATIVE MILIEU

Urban thinkers, such as Andersson, Hall, Toernqvist, Aydalot consider the main characteristics of a creative milieu to be:

- a place with a level of original and deep knowledge coupled with a ready supply of skills, competence and people who have the need and capacity to communicate with each other;
- to have a sound financial basis, adequate to allow room for experimentation without tight regulation;
- where an imbalance between the perceived needs of decision-makers, business people, artists, scientists, and social critics and actual opportunities exists;
- where the capacity exists to deal with complexity and uncertainty about future changes in cultural, scientific and technological fields;
- good possibilities for informal and spontaneous communication internally and externally; an environment catering for diversity and variety;
- a multidisciplinary and dynamically synergistic environment which especially links developments in science and the arts;
- and finally, structural instability. At times, indeed, structural instabilities need to be launched within a controlled context, such as when the environmental movement in its demands creates an imbalance between what is and what could be.

### Anchoring the Local

Even in a cyberworld there is the renewed importance of locality resting mostly on a set of 'untraded' interdependences (Storper, 1997) that are built at local level leading to a combination of organizational, technological and individual learning that happens by agglomerating activities tightly in a location. Thus globalization and localization do not exclude each other. Why certain localities become 'hot spots' depends on the dynamics of disintegration and inter-linkage in specific places. What is crucial is continual new firm formation as well as a great deal of entrepreneurial activity, with a reserve of experienced individuals able to capture the advantages of new technological and business opportunities as in the new media industries. This not only induces clustering at particular sites, but also creates the conditions for useful patterns of social and community development. The triggers for clustering can range from cheap buildings in need of refurbishment, the proximity of government research institutes, major universities, a high proportion of engineers, scientists or culturally aware people in the local population or the availability of venture capital.

Anchoring is helped through 'institutional thickness' (Amin and Thrift, 1994) – an interesting concept and a means 'of holding down the local' in the global. It involves a combination of elements such as: strong interaction between institutions, a culture of collective representation at the political level, the development of a sense of common industrial purpose and shared cultural norms and values. The mere presence of a network of local institutions is not enough to support the success of a place. It is the social atmosphere and the processes of institution-building that help to create this atmosphere. This 'thickness' is what continues to stimulate entrepreneurship and consolidates the local embeddedness of industry while at the same time fostering relations of trust, exchange of information and urban 'buzz'.

A degree of institutional flexibility is another outcome of institutional thickness evident in the ability of the organizations of a creative milieu to learn and change much faster than elsewhere. Multimedia companies which operate according to the 'new economy' logic are currently an innovating force and will remain so for a decade or more, transmitting new techniques and breaking historical labour relations patterns. Because the electronic engineers are constantly driven to meet new technical challenges they set off long chains of innovation. As in the industrial revolution, for example Glasgow's shipbuilding industry, key heroic figures serve as 'masters', instructing a host of 'apprentices' who in turn break away to establish their own careers, building on what they have learned and trying to improve upon it.

## Maintaining the Virtuous Cycle

In an era of growth the elements act in a mutually reinforcing way to produce a kind of culmination of confidence and achievement, and in a phase of decline a pattern of mutually sustaining circum-

---

### FOREVER CREATIVE?

'Perhaps no city, anywhere or at any time, has managed to remain continuously innovative for very long ... The pages of history are littered with examples: in the cultural sphere, places like fifth-century-BC Athens, fifteenth-century Florence, eighteenth-century Vienna; in the technological sphere, places like eighteenth-century Manchester, nineteenth-century Berlin and early twentieth-century Detroit are all places where the light of creativity seems to have been later expunged, sometimes for centuries. Indeed, counter-examples are rare: great European capital cities, such as London and Paris, and great American cities like New York and Los Angeles, seem to have retained some kind of creative potential over a sustained period often by attracting talent from elsewhere; or through their central role in administration and government, which means they effectively have a monopoly position in attracting that kind of talent.'

*Source:* Hall, 1998

---

stances generates cumulative problems in reverse. Virtuous cycles can become vicious ones. The openness and collaboration can become closure, defensiveness and competition. When a city is in survival and retrenchment mode it is difficult to maintain creative momentum. Creative milieux are uncomfortable places, both responding to and creating instability that need to combine the requisite balance between tension and comfort; collaboration and competition. The urban strategist's task is to read these waves like an investment analyst watching the markets.

## HARNESSING THE TRIGGERS OF CREATIVITY

Many triggers can set the creative process in motion, born of necessity, sparked off by using conscious techniques or resulting from complex processes: a more detailed examination may be helpful.

## Inescapable Pressures

### Necessity

We know that necessity is the mother of invention: two examples illustrate the point. The discovery of mineral resources in Arctic Scandinavia led to the development of ways of living in these extreme conditions. The need for new heat-retention technology has helped make Partek in Helsinki one of the world's largest construction and insulation material companies. At the other extreme, Cooper Pedy in Central Australia is so hot that people seek comfort by living underground, as they did in the past: nearly 1,500 years ago, a community of up to 9,000 lived in a 10-storey underground city at Demayurtuku in Turkey. This old form of living is now being revived by alternative communities and architects as 'earth sheltering'.

### Scarcity

In search of space New Yorkers built upwards, developing new building and project management techniques in the process. Japanese companies are investigating the construction of buildings up to 1km high, provided they can solve problems of wind-resistance. In Amsterdam, parking space is limited and water abundant – the solution is the floating car parks. The spiralling cost of energy has driven investment in renewable energy from solar, wind and wave sources: in Lykovrussi, a suburban workers settlement 18km north of Athens, solar power is delivered to 435 apartments. Energy efficient building and solar energy provides 80 per cent of all energy requirements at lower cost.

### Obsolescence

The need to replace techniques, equipment or buildings creates space for reconsideration. Environmentally unfriendly coking equipment in Emscher Park has been replaced with new technology that recycles excess heat to create new energy. The unwanted structures of declining industries provide new forms of living and working in converted mills, factories or light industrial spaces. Our sense of the shape of work and living spaces has been transformed through ideas like loft living, along with our aesthetic values and lifestyles.

## The Unexpected and the Unpredictable

### Discovery

In some ways the impact of discovery is obvious, but the chains of innovation which they sometimes unleash are less predictable. The discovers of electricity could not have foreseen the cascade of subsequent invention from radio to computers: its invisibility obscures how it pervades every crevice of modern life. By contrast the discovery of the negative effects of asbestos has changed construction dramatically. The apparently trivial innovation of plastic bags has created a series of social innovations fundamental to consumerism, from packaging, to shopping and waste disposal. The accidental discovery of gold in Syvankyla in Northern Finland led to many creative ideas in urban living, such as heat-insulating turfed roof housing.

## Luck

If the traditional explanations of how creativity occurs – inspired acts of genius or a sudden awakening in consciousness – are largely discredited, they do sometimes occur. Countless anecdotes exist of urban leaders coming across situations which enable them to see their city through new eyes. Britain's former Environment Minister, Michael Heseltine, had such a revelation when visiting the aftermath of rioting in Liverpool: the result was a substantial commitment to urban regeneration leading to the City Challenge initiative which, for the UK, had innovative features such as requiring partnership between the public, private and voluntary sectors. James Wolfensohn, the president of the World Bank was touched by a young boy in Uzbekistan who gave him money as a traditional custom in spite of his abject poverty. The importance of culture and custom was reinforced deeply and led to a re-assessment of culture's role in development – a difficult innovation for a bank to absorb into its operations. At a more trivial level, Percy Shaw from Halifax in 1934 invented 'cats eyes' on roads having realized 'in a flash' how using reflective glass glows back at you when you shine light at it. They cost practically nothing and have changed how we are guided in cities at night.

## Ambition and Aspiration

### Opportunism, Entrepreneurialism and the Search for Profit

Competitive action is one of the most fundamental creative triggers, whether it leads to success or failure. Clive Sinclair, one of the pioneers of microcomputers in the late 1970s, tried to create a powered urban bicycle: the C5. Its notorious failure has not discouraged numerous other attempts at the same project, one of which, one day, will work. The cultural quarters emerging in down-at-heel inner urban areas from Digbeth in Birmingham to Newtown in Johannesburg are driven by the combined energies of innovative property developers and the ideas of artists and designers working in new media, often with a commercial agenda of their own. Their lively ambience itself creates further synergies and downstream innovations, as these production hubs often become centres of new retailing. The entrepreneurial application of new social 'technologies' such as Harrison Owen's 'Open Space' – a means of rapidly involving several hundred people in participatory decision-making – can have urban impacts as is illustrated in South African townships and American cities alike.

### Competitive Pressures

The progress of cities is shaped by urban competition and creativity is essential to cities competing for investment, skilled labour, international events or tourists. In securing inward investment many factors count. The cost of labour is most obvious, but skills and flexibility are becoming increasingly significant. For those not in the world league or key secondary cities like Singapore or Sydney, there is intense competition to show distinctiveness. Beyond the cultural and business facilities expected of every large city, the task is to show difference. This has led cities to re-assess their resources and potential and the way Barcelona or Bilbao have been brought to world attention illustrates the value of creativity. It has been most obvious in architecture – Bilbao's Guggenheim Museum by Frank Gehry, or Barcelona's brave public realm interventions with artists such as Serra, Pollock, Ellsworth and Miro. In the UK, Sheffield chose one of the most zany architects it could find – Nigel Coates – for its National Popular Music Centre. But grandiose statements alone cannot suffice. Creativity is found from business life to social affairs dealing with the intractables of urban living, often unseen and unacknowledged.

# Participation and Ideas Gathering

### Debate

Despite its limitations – notably in excluding women – the Athenian culture of debate fostered a high degree of urban creativity: expounding, pondering, contesting and wrangling over opposing viewpoints contributed to the development of urban society. The democracy 'invented' by Cleisthenes in 510 BC was a creative social innovation with sufficient life, development potential and adaptability to remain central two and a half millennia later. A contemporary, more technical example of this debating culture is Silicon Valley where continual discussion and exchange is fostered to generate new products and is seen as a competitive element of the creative milieu.

## Urban Visioning

A vision is equivalent to a city's mission statement or business plan; from its origins in 1970s America, visioning has since become common. Unlike a local structure plan, which replaces aspiration with regulations, the urban vision is an attempt to generate momentum for change. Visioning opens space between current reality and expectations and so stimulates creative responses. A core element for success is to develop a widespread culture of institutionalized leadership to promote continual self-improvement. In this way visioning becomes a change agent, which has to manage public participation, generate flagship ideas, establish benchmarks for success and trigger goal setting.

# Learning from Others

## Centres of Excellence

Freiburg, a small city of 220,000 inhabitants in Southern Germany, now has a world reputation for ecologically focused urban development. The existence in Freiburg of the Fraunhofer Institute, an internationally oriented renewable energy institute, has attracted other innovative bodies such as the Öko-Institute and the International Centre for Local Environmental Initiatives (ICLEI), which produces a database on environmental urban best practices. This cluster reinforces Freiburg's position as a pilot eco-city – it has the oldest solar-powered demonstration house in Germany (dating from 1978) and strong municipal environmental policies for energy saving through public transport, cycling and use of building materials. Thus a virtuous cycle is set up involving technical demonstration, awareness raising, public participation in eco-living, paralleled with a commitment from the municipality. Freiburg is projected to the outside world as an innovator in the field attracting again more talent, ideas and resources to itself.

The University of Lapland's Arctic Centre in Rovaniemi plays a similar experimental role as a means of identifying a niche for this city on the Arctic circle – aside from Rovaniemi calling itself the 'home of Santa Claus'. Coping with cold and distance have become their selling point from heat retention in buildings and clothes to communication technologies. Research resources spread throughout industrial sectors, but geographically clustered, force-fed creativity through personal interaction, job rotation and concentration of skill. Silicon Valley, originally spawned by its proximity to Stanford University and public research expenditure in defence is one example. Similar clusters of public/private coalitions account for the rise of Los Angeles, the Bay Area and route 128 around Boston as foci of the new multimedia industries which have changed their urban fabric, ambience and reputation. A string of innovations were built deriving from within the defence industry that were later adapted for civilian use, including, most importantly, the Internet itself.

## Inspiration from Outside

The creativity of others is often an effective means of sparking creativity in oneself, especially in shared experience. Retreats, study trips, seminars that build first name familiarity and personal bonds foster collaboration and are powerful spurs to change. A Comedia study of innovation among Swedish urban librarians found that joint study trips abroad to visit other creative libraries was the most effective activity. In the mid-1980s a group of 60 Chattanooga decision-makers went to Indianapolis to look at its urban regeneration process and how it depoliticized critical issues. In the process of learning about Indianapolis they learnt about one another, and laid the foundations for Chattanooga Venturer, and then Re-vision 2000: Chattanooga won one of 12 Habitat World Best Practice awards in Istanbul in 1996.

## Unexpected Connections

Bringing together disparate disciplines or people can widen horizons and generate new forms of creativity. The Wellcome Trust SCI-ART competition – of which the author was a judge – has successfully brought the insights of science and art closer together with over 400 joint proposals in two years. An evaluation of the first year's competition concluded that the process of collaboration between a scientist and an artist stimulates 'a new kind of creativity, creating something which is a synthesis out of the scientific and artistic mind' (from the evaluation of SCI-ART by Dr Claire Cohen, Brunel University, 1997). Bringing an artist into urban regeneration can have equally unexpected results. In Batley (West Yorkshire) Lesley Fallais worked with tenants of a degraded housing estate; her projects involved residents, housing officers, planners, architects, community leaders and the police, and resulted in environmental improvements to buildings and play areas, as well

---

### CAR SHARING IN BERLIN

From its beginnings in 1990, the private initiative STATTAUTO – its name a German pun on 'city-car' and 'instead-of car' – has become the largest car-sharing company in Germany with 4,000 members. One hundred and forty vehicles are stationed at forty distribution points spread over the city, concentrated in densely populated inner city districts; the average distance to a distribution point is ten minutes. STATTAUTO achieved a reduction of 510,000 car kilometres in 1996, resulting in an annual decrease in $CO_2$ emissions of 80.32 tonnes. A shared STATTAUTO car is driven 30,000 km per year compared to a national average for private cars of 14,500 km per year, and carries an average of two persons compared to the 1.3 national average.

---

as activities such as puppet plays and festivals with positive impacts on local self-respect, social cohesion and liveliness.

## Exceptional Circumstances

### Political Change

Politically contested situations and socio-political change can be fertile ground for creative experimentation as well as stagnation. Berlin's post-war status and then its re-emergence as a unified city created an opportunity to think afresh. The socio-political transformation process, whilst rushed and seen by some as a takeover by the West of the East, has created a climate receptive to new ideas in public and private spheres. Seen as a kind of pilot urban project, social and economic well-being has been linked to environmental consciousness. For instance, unemployed people were taken on to conduct city-wide energy audits; when the scheme lost public funding it was able to set up a specialist business. In Kreuzberg's 'Block 103' former squatters were given space they had occupied and trained to convert houses to modern ecological buildings. In Hellersdorf, in the former East, apartments have been retrofitted to high environmental standards.

### Political Crisis

Conflict, as in Belfast, Beirut or Sarajevo, can sometimes create incidental innovations. In Belfast, ossified local government structures were suspended to allow new partnership structures to emerge and develop their own organizational and governance procedures. Another innovation is the proposed university for Belfast's disadvantaged in Springvale, championed by the former vice-chancellor of the University of Ulster, Trevor Smith. It straddles the dividing line between Catholic and Protestant communities of west Belfast, and in overcoming immense hurdles, it has been continually redefined. Finally accepted as the first 'lifelong learning' college, it will experiment, for instance by adopting a lifelong learning credit system allowing students to achieve their qualifications in stages. This structured alternative to university entrance exams will enable the 70 per cent who fail entrance exams to build up credits over life. More tragically the troubles created other innovations, as Belfast surgeons have now become world-renowned for dealing with violent injuries.

## Changing Leadership

### Clearing the Decks

Change can have dramatic effects and unleash unrecognized talent as Huddersfield's experience has shown. Regarded in the 1980s as one of the worst performing municipalities in the UK, a decade later it was an urban leader thanks to a recognition that its urban management had to change fundamentally. The newly-appointed Council leader and chief executive immediately dealt with the entrenched and self-focused divisional baronies seen to have been at the heart of the problem. A small layer of personnel was 'encouraged' to leave. Changes then regarded as creative have now been mainstreamed elsewhere, such as developing corporate working and separating strategy formation and overview thinking from operational management. An open door policy and a training agenda including mentoring to encourage personal growth was catalytic. Creativity did not exist as an isolated attribute: the initial trigger to institute the changes required qualities such as courage, tenacity, persuasiveness and political skill. Once started the benefits cascaded downwards, involving a series of best practice management techniques that secured commitment and talent. It increased the professionalism of staff, cross-departmental working and a more open style of management. It filtered down through the organization. As a secretary noted after giving her forthright opinions to some sections heads: 'Five years ago I would have been afraid to say this for fear of losing my job.'

## Celebrating Local Distinctiveness

### Local Constraints

Some local traditions, especially when they are reflected in planning law can draw out creative responses as religious, symbolic or historical factors over-ride 'rational' decision-making processes. A Melbourne by-law requiring that the Anzac Memorial should always be visible has led to some unusual designs of several city centre skyscrapers. Another by-law, passed to preserve the Victorian skyline has led to imaginative use of space in the courtyards behind existing buildings. As a result Melbourne combines a distinctive cosmopolitan appearance with intimate, walkable Victorian spaces.

## Conceptual Breakthroughs

### Changing the Thinking

Redefining a problem can reveal its potential for innovative action. Seeing waste as a resource rather than a liability opens endless possibilities. Sharnhorst (Dortmund, Germany) has involved unemployed youth in collecting waste for resale. In Oeiras, Portugal, the response has been a backyard composting scheme, while in Italy waste has been used as a building material in Parma and in agriculture in Rimini. Thinking about accessibility instead of mobility draws our attention away from the private car as the primary means of transport. Accessibility encompasses mobility, but also highlights proximity and the placing of facilities or social networks and how people communicate. Looking at the accessibility of services draws attention to issues such as opening hours and a spectrum of transport possibilities including shared cars, buses, trains and walking.

*Factor Four: Doubling Wealth, Halving Resource Use* (von Weizsäcker et al, 1998) is a simple concept based on 50 real-life examples. Since the industrial revolution progress has been defined by an increase in labour productivity aided by technology: Factor Four delivers sustainable urban development by redefining progress as 'resource productivity', showing that four times as much wealth can be extracted from current resources if regulatory and incentives structures reward resource efficiency. Many examples represent insufficiently known best practice such as the role of electronic trade in reducing travel costs, superwindows, integrating building design, daylighting and energy systems as in the Darmstadt Passivhaus, reducing the energy use of appliances, changing organi-

# From rags to riches, Belo Horizonte, Brazil

Professional scavengers have never been popular among local authorities in Belo Horizonte, a city located in south-eastern Brazil. But for many, recycling materials from waste heaps near homes, offices and shops is a livelihood. Now, an annual parade is held to help change people's perceptions of street scavengers and waste.

Maria das Gracas Margal spent her childhood as a waste picker in Belo Horizonte. She recalls the hostility of police and pedestrians. Since then, things have changed. In 1990 she helped form the Street Scavengers' Association (ASMARE) that oversaw the construction of a large warehouse where waste pickers could sort through their materials and keep them for market. In December 1992, the government and the association signed an agreement to guarantee funds for its maintenance. Storage space was later expanded, and ASMARE equipped workers with carts to facilitate waste collection and developed training workshops. The waste pickers are now earning a more regular income. Revenue is distributed proportionately according to how much each waste picker collects and sells. Each associate receives a 20 per cent productivity incentive at the end of every month based on his or her monthly production, and surplus revenues are distributed annually. The occupation still carries a huge health risk; disease is common. A recent international workshop on waste disposal sponsored by multilateral and bilateral organizations held in Belo Horizonte determined that much more research is needed on waste picking activities. There is a serious lack of information about health conditions, income levels, involvement of children, and the actual number of waste pickers.

Since 1994, the association has held the annual street scavengers carnival parade where scavengers and street sweepers dress in colourful, recyclable materials. Its purpose is to change peoples' traditional perception of waste from something that is useless to something that is valuable. It gives the waste collectors an opportunity to socialize amongst themselves and with the partners involved in the programme. The programme has given a sense of hope to local people who now take pride in what was once deemed a dirty and useless occupation. They feel empowered and recognize the importance of their work, both as a means of making a living and as an opportunity to draw people's attention to their environment.

*Source:* Information from Gabriela Boyer, environmental consultant at the World Bank. For more information contact: Sonia Maria Dias, Rua Tenente Garro, 118–19 Andar, Santa Efigenia, Belo Horizonte, 30240–360, Brazil, tel: 55-31-277-9373

zational purchasing policies to demand very efficient equipment and so on. Regulatory mechanisms demand slight shifts in perspective, such as providing density bonuses to reward the co-location of houses and workplaces or rewarding proximity to public transport or rebate structures for efficient uses of energy.

A relatively simple change, like taxing labour less and resource use more, can produce wide benefits. Industrial development is driven by increasing labour productivity, even if more natural resources are used. 'Businesses should sack their unproductive kilowatt hours, tonnes and litres rather than their workforce'. Entrenched ways of operating hold the professions in a 'vice-like grip': architects, for example, are 'paid according to what they spend, not what they save, so efficiency can directly reduce their profits by making them work harder for a smaller fee' (von Weisäcker et al, 1998).

Factor Four is innovative because it can create a profitable, sustainable eco-capitalism involving all actors in a city business, local authorities and consumers. The shift from labour productivity to energy productivity will be revolutionary as its implications cascade down into innovations in the economic, social and lifestyle structure. The key is to create a regulatory framework that calculates true ecological costs, which would deny firms damaging the environment with the competitive advantages they now have.

## Learning from Failure

Failure can be an unexpected teacher of the imagination, sometimes a more powerful catalyst for change than success, which may cause reflection and a tendency to listen to the decline, allowing complacency to fill the gap. The result may be a reactive response that is tried and tested but inappropriate to current needs. The expansion of airports to meet growing demand seems an obvious solution in Los Angeles or London Heathrow, but increased travel and handling times may give a competitive edge to trains for shorter journeys. Although failure is seen as negative and overwhelming, the distinction noted between competent and incompetent failure is useful. Incompetent failure is the result of thoughtlessnesss – eg trying to reduce crime by copying zero tolerance policies, without understanding the local circumstances, the causes of its effectiveness or the drawbacks. Incompetence repeats acknowledged failures like building housing estates next to motorways and cutting them off from their surroundings. The consequences for social cohesion and crime are known, yet the practice persists.

Competent failure by contrast arises even though every aspect has been considered according to best practice and available knowledge. But best practice may have unpredictable weaknesses or cease to be appropriate as circumstances change: a guarded shopping centre may lead to increases in crime and fear of crime in surrounding areas. Failure, handled well, can lead to open-minded and systematic analysis of its causes and the learning for follow-up initiatives. It is important to anticipate a degree of failure within the course of innovative urban practice, and even to legitimate it. The issue should not be who fails, but how we respond to inevitable failures.

## Symbolic Triggers

### The Statement of Intent

A charter, declaration, or manifesto can act as a rallying point, campaign or benchmark to stimulate action and innovation even when they are not legally binding like conventions. The launch of the Montreal Protocol on the ozone layer in 1990 raised awareness of the need for environmental consciousness and research into measuring rates of depletion. In 1972 the Unesco Convention concerning the protection of world culture and natural heritage was signed. Since then 555 places have been inscribed as World Heritage Sites, including over 100 World Heritage Cities. They include places as different as Sana'a (Yemen), Djennè (Mali), Quebec, St Petersburg, Split (Croatia), Cartagena (Columbia), Brasilia, Isfahan (Iran) and Bath (UK). The designations have helped galvanize action, which have led to a dual impetus to revive traditional building skills and develop innovative techniques to slow deterioration processes, to stabilize foundations or even speed up the making of mud bricks. Many such techniques have enhanced knowledge of building in general.

### Place Marketing

Cities increasingly use branding devices such as the 'Intelligent', 'Educated', 'Green' or 'Creative' City. These marketing slogans raise expectations and can be mechanisms to focus strategy on reducing the gap between hype and reality. Kakegawa in Japan, Edmonton in Canada and Adelaide in Australia all seek to project themselves as 'educated' cities and thus reality has to catch up with hype. Well-executed marketing campaigns, such as the now famous Glasgow's Miles Better, which successfully recreated awareness of a

---

### LEICESTER: ENVIRONMENT CITY

Leicester became Britain's first Environment City in 1990, a designation requiring a commitment towards sustainable urban development which demanded a creative response. The challenge of sustainability set in train a comprehensive rethinking of management and resource use. The Environment City idea led to the creation of cross-departmental think-tanks, drawing from the public, private, community and academic sectors, as well as the establishment of a Best Practice Research Unit. The Environment City has carried out environmental reviews and Council purchasing policies have been made eco-friendly; they have set up a showhouse – Ecohouse – assisted in cutting energy consumption in municipal buildings by 16 per cent in ten years and given greening grants to industry. They have installed low energy street lights and surveyed the contribution of 4,000 private gardens to city wildlife. They have raised money through Leicester's Asian community to re-forest a Hindu site in India and 'green accounts' have been made with 200 charities to help in the collection of recyclable waste throughout the city.

---

changing city, can have substantial multiplier effects. This campaign, with its associated culture and inward investment strategies, helped Glasgow to the crown of European City of Culture in 1990. That prize itself helped attract new talent to the city, creating a virtuous circle of creativity, which recently led to the city being designated 'City of Architecture and Design' in 1999. Within these events there has been an experimental programme projecting Glasgow as an innovative city, and broader work to develop the infrastructure for culture or generate a more internationally oriented design industry.

### Landmark Events

Landmark events, prizes and competitions – such as those associated with the UN Habitat Conference in Istanbul in 1996 or the Rio Summit on climate change in 1992 – can shift perceptions of problems and set innovation processes in motion. The Habitat/UNCHS (United Nations Centre for Human Settlements) event was the climax of various processes highlighting holistic, integrated approaches to municipal activity, the involvement of citizens' associations and NGOs in decision-making and sustainable urban development. Over 50 countries gathered to display their best practices: the showcasing and competitive element can be important for mutual learning and the exchange of experience. The database was built up by a call for best practice, which elicited 700 examples. Getting on to the database involved a two-stage process. In the first stage technical experts worked with host countries to draw up a shortlist from which an international jury made a selection: just 12 received global awards. This process continues and will create two tiers of databases, one developing a list of 500 global best practice awards, with a much bigger list running into several thousand examples.

### Branded Concepts

Concepts can be powerful catalytic agents. Local Agenda 21 – invented in 1992 after the UN Rio Summit on the Environment – has unleashed imagination and led to a mass of creative responses from the green discount card in The Hague to ways of measuring the state of local environments based on citizens' involvement. In one area, the decline in the frog population may be the key indicator of environmental decline; in another it may be the status of an orchid species or an insect. Local Agenda 21 is a rallying call to action, challenging city government to change and adopt ecological principles for sustainable development. By focusing on local issues and accountability it has shifted the sustainability debate towards local democracy and the sustainability of social networks.

## Strategic Clarity

### Creativity Policies

A self-conscious and comprehensive urban creativity and innovation policy is rare. Yet as the need for urban creativity becomes apparent cities are asking how they can actively encourage urban imagination. Cities have experience of industrial and technological strategies to encourage the innovative firms it needs, from start-up funds to science parks to marketing support. In the social arena strategies for citizen participation in planning and decision-making are becoming good practice: in over half the 515 case studies reported in *Innovative and Sustainable European Cities* (Hall and Landry, 1997) consultation procedures played an important part in project development. Although these processes demand a greater initial investment of time, effort and resources, the benefits of greater ownership, increased responsibility for results and enhanced motivation lead to significantly higher success rates. Huddersfield's Creative Town Initiative is so important because it is such a rare example of a city looking at creativity and innovation across the board. Although there is a huge amount to learn about integrated urban creativity and how it should be organized and implemented, it is clear that the process of developing policy is already producing valuable results.

## Structural Crisis

### Crisis

Crisis requires an urgent response which may help to overcome obstacles to innovation. Situations need immediate solutions and it is impossible to insist on old approaches if they are not immediately effective. Wartime has often allowed women to show their abilities – after their contribution in the First World War it became unsustainable to deny them the vote in Britain. In 1995 the Kobe earthquake revealed the inadequacy of the Japanese civil service to deal with a major disaster, and produced innovations in the management of central and local administrations. The 1982 riots in Brixton, London, led to increased investment and changed policing policies.

But crisis is not always a singular event: it can be the slow erosion of capacity and ability to respond. Years of corruption, inefficiency, the inability to maintain infrastructures or to adjust to new needs can create a loss of morale. Such crises are debilitating, because their causes are systemic, and creative responses require the power and will to act. Often things have to get worse before they can get better, as when the Emscher river sewage began seeping into the water supply, finally forcing the Nordrhein Westfalen Government to take action. Crises are not always as unexpected as they appear: the collapse of European and American steel and coal industries in the late 1970s was foreseeable to anyone concerned with longer trends given their high wage structures and effective new technologies in Japan and the Far East.

### Instability

Implicit in the concept of structural instability are many of the individual development triggers outlined so far – crisis, debate, conflict, declarations, manifestos. As cities evolve they experience power struggles between existing and emerging élites, ideologies and groups. 'Innovative cities at their zenith such as Athens, Florence, London, Weimar, Berlin were cities in transition, moving out of the known, into new still unknown modes of organisation' (Hall,

1998). This instability makes creative cities as uncomfortable as they are exciting. As noted in ancient Athens the new democratic constitution produced new ideas, inspirations and aspirations, giving greater influence to philosophers and others involved in cultural life. In Florence between 1270 and 1330, competition between leading families generated structural instability which led to the city's expansion. Turn of the century Vienna, in the dying days of the Habsburg Empire, combined deep pessimism with extraordinary creativity in psychiatry, philosophy, economics, literature, music, medicine, art and architecture. At different times, New York, London, Paris, Berlin and many other cities have benefited from similar creative instability.

Today a new form of 'structured instability' or 'controlled disruption' driven by urban competition, is being self-consciously developed. Urban leaders can mimic the conditions of crisis by creating desirable aspiration that does not match current reality, through visioning, triggered goal setting, or even by encouraging campaign groups to exert pressure. This, in part, lies behind the momentum within the cluster of cities in the region around Zürich, Basle, Karlsruhe and Freiburg which compete on a new terrain – a quality of life agenda driven by sustainable development. This generates what Parnes in describing creativity calls 'an exaggerated push for change' (Parnes, 1992). This region's vision is driven by a quest for continual ecological improvement. Continual idea exchanges, movement of personnel between the cities and urban competition have generated a new kind of creative milieu with a different focus from the more common reliance on new technology.

## CONCLUSION

For each spark of creativity there are examples. Which are most important and which explain most comprehensively the urban creative dynamic? Which factors are primary, which secondary? Which triggers generate chains of innovation that are sustainable over time? The creativities engendered through need, scarcity, obsolescence, the consequences of conflict, changes in leadership and socio-political change, and the emergence of paradigm shifts all point to crisis – in its core meaning of turning point – as the primary trigger. Yet crisis responses can be singular, related to a single event as when aid donations rise when there is a particular famine disaster.

This gives strength to the argument of 'structural instability' – a kind of permanent crisis which occurs when one enters a paradigm shift. Then old ways of working are inadequate. Endemic structural disorder involves change in multiple dimensions and the equilibrium in the economic, social, institutional and political structure has become unbalanced. A plant closure in one part of the world occurs because another area, say 10,000 km away, has a cheaper labour force. Globalization and local needs do not necessarily align, producing battles between central government and local, urban power. Movements of population create xenophobia before the idea of the benefits of cultural diversity can be absorbed. Dealing with such instability is more than a singular event, it requires a continuing process of adjustment before another balance can be created. This adjustment can generate healthy or negative creativity. Creativity can be a spur to deal with change, or turn inwards as a defensive shield. When lessons are learnt from previous mistakes and the trends of history are understood, change has more chance of being constructive, affirming and able to integrate difference.

## The source of creative responses

Where do the creative sparks in cities come from to cope with change? The private sector? The third sector? The public sector? Alliances and partnerships? Creativity can come and is needed from every source. In future hybrid combinations that break down the rigid divides between public, private, voluntary sectors may bear the most fruit. A private sector entrepreneur, perhaps working in social care in the voluntary sector; an environmental campaigner becoming head of transport in a local authority; a cultural worker heading up a property-led urban regeneration project (as happened for a period in the development of the Temple Bar Cultural Quarter in Dublin); a public official running a recycling scheme; the variations are endless.

The challenge for urban strategists is to recognize which creative triggers exist in their city and to judge which ones they need to help generate. The discipline of nurturing creative cities involves harnessing the innovative sparks in the right combination and assembling them in an effective order to lay the foundation for a creative urban milieu. Consider, for example: is there a crisis with a structural cause in the city, such as increasing youth unemployment caused by jobless growth brought about by new technology?

Is this creating downstream effects like crime, violence or graffiti? Has an inclusive vision for youth been charted? Is there a need for a youth manifesto? Has the youth problem been re-assessed as an opportunity? Can a new incentives structure for youth be developed? Is there a centre of expertise on youth in the city? Is there a multi-disciplinary team dealing with the problem? Can urban leaders identify a place elsewhere that has dealt with youth imaginatively? What elements are replicable?

Part Three

# A Conceptual Toolkit of Urban Creativity

# 7

# Getting Creativity Planning Started

## WHAT IS A CONCEPTUAL TOOLKIT?

A toolkit is a coordinated set of instruments and devices geared to solving a problem. A conceptual toolkit is a set of concepts, ideas, ways of thinking and intellectual notions to make understanding, exploring and acting upon a problem easier. The concepts discussed should be seen as the intellectual equivalent of a hammer, a saw and a screwdriver. They are a set of approaches, techniques and a box of tricks. Their aim is to generate a form of mental agility in thinking through city issues, to look at problems in a rounded way, from a multiple perspective and holistically. Holistic thinking is one step beyond thinking issues through from many angles or in an interdisciplinary way. It implies that seeing the sum of the parts, all in one, creates its own dynamic, achieving something greater and independent.

Focusing on concepts forces us to think from first principles, which is normally seen as too time-consuming and cumbersome. Expediency determines we take the more 'thoughtless', instinctive and acquired route – the route that seems to work. In this way we cope and respond to the myriad decisions taken by councillors, business people and officials, some planned and expected, many others out of control. How these actions turn out shapes the way we address subsequent problems. The resulting mindset formed by collective experience is our sense of how things work. Equally important as how we solve problems is how we divide them into various categories, such as: Is everything separate or connected?

Are activities static or dynamic? Are economic factors more important than social concerns? Are events inevitable, because of the 'nature' of people or is it how we nurture them? As real life solutions are rarely black and white, an ability to see the other side of the problem is vital.

The mindset that says 'that is the way we do things here' is often a disguise for simply accepting existing power configurations. The power constellation in cites determines how urban problems are addressed. Usually those individuals concerned with 'hard' infrastructure are at the top of the hierarchical tree – engineers, land use or transport planners. Any solution to a problem is seen through that prism. Mental pictures – concepts – drive what we do and how we do it. This group's concept of the city is as a machine, which leads them to find mechanical solutions. In contrast, those who see the city as a living organism would focus on the dynamic effects on the people who inhabit it.

Equally the name we give to an issue determines how it is treated. If a city's transport department were called the communications and connections or the accessibility department it simply could not be staffed by engineers alone. The movement of cars or public transport would become only one aspect – walking and talking would start to have far greater priority as would networking. The 'hard' infrastructure issues would become important secondary technical consequences once the human domain had been assessed. The same rethinking would happen if, instead of calling a division of the city administration the housing department, it were called the habitat section. Calling it habitat makes the house just one element, the surroundings become just as important as the shops, the amenities and the way people get on with each other (see Greenhalgh, 1999).

Finance and accounting divisions are also at the top of the hierarchy. Yet their view of efficiency, effectiveness and value for money is usually narrow. They all too rarely understand the true nature of economy, where indirect social impacts are just as important to efficiency, output and achievement. In order to create urban equilibrium wealth creation and social cohesion should be seen as two sides of the same coin. In current city hierarchies any sections dealing with feelings and emotions, such as social services, culture and leisure has lower status. This 'soft' infrastructure of human networks, connections, trust or a capacity to work together is often underplayed and yet the start of the 21st century is the time of the network society.

## Assumptions behind the Creative City Toolkit

My belief in the potential of harnessing creativity leads me to accen-
tuate the positive and move away from discussing cities exclusively
in terms of problems. In fact cities may provide the answer to issues
such as sustainability because they are more dense; or to wealth
creation, because they have a higher level of interaction.

I challenge the notion that the move to 'non-space urban
realms' is inevitable, or that it is simply luck of geography or proximity to resources that determines the fate of cities. Individuals or
governments can take decisive actions. The purpose of the toolkit
is to rethink how problems can be addressed, by re-examining the
underlying philosophies, principles and assumptions behind decision-making and to challenge the ways urban problems and
solutions are framed.

Creativity on its own does not provide the solution to urban
problems, but at least it gives decision-makers an ideas bank with
which to work and out of which innovations can emerge. In seeking
to encourage new ways of thinking about the city or to explore
new concepts and organizing principles the goal is to find interpretative 'keys' that improve our understanding of urban dynamics
and enable us to act on them. Crucially, a concept or organizing
principle is only as useful as its explanatory power and its power to
help decision-making and subsequent action.

Seven concepts are proposed, plus a series of techniques to help
creative thinking and planning. Some ideas may seem obvious, but
to my knowledge they have not self-consciously been used in the
city context and this is what makes them novel. The first 'civic
creativity' embodies a call for action. It stresses creativity in the
civic realm as a future priority. The 'cycle of urban creativity' by
contrast is an analytical or explanatory device. It breaks down
complex issues and explains flows and processes to allow an insight
into strategy making and priority setting. The notion of 'innovation and creativity lifecycles' highlights the need to be aware of
timing; it calls for the development of judgement and getting a feel
for when to be creative. The 'urban R&D' concept advocates an
approach to implementation, monitoring and evaluation that legit-
imizes creative action. The 'innovation matrix' is a benchmarking
device allowing decision-makers to assess how innovative a project
or class of projects is and whether the city is performing at its best.
The 'vitality and viability' indicators provide an example of a new
type of indicator. Finally, by conceptualizing 'urban literacy' we

seek to tie these concepts together with other ways of interpreting and understanding urban life and dynamics and creating a new competence. Over time it might emerge as a kind of 'meta-urban discipline' bringing together insights from cultural geography; urban economics and social affairs; psychology; history; cultural studies; urban planning; design and aesthetics.

The overall objective is to start developing and legitimizing a new language and set of tools within which urban affairs, policy and development can be discussed. The aspiration is that it will offer a richer array of interpretative possibilities, yet at the same time be practical. It will be a language that does not fall into the classic discipline of land use planning although it will have a bearing upon it.

## THE CREATIVE CITY STRATEGY METHOD

The planning and implementation of the Creative City idea involves four stages:

1   An overall five-step strategic planning process.
2   The application of a set of analytical tools, the most important of which is 'the cycle of urban creativity' concept.
3   A series of indicators to measure how relatively creative a city or project is.
4   A range of techniques that help creative thinking and planning.

Within the overall planning process, analytical tools, indicators and techniques are used as appropriate. The Creative City approach is a form of strategic planning undertaken within a specific perspective. Its characteristics include the idea that planning can only be effective and maximize its potential if certain preconditions are met, such as:

■   an acceptance that one's own way of approaching issues might be limited;
■   a conscious recognition that creative thinking is a serious input to any planning exercise;
■   a willingness to think from the point of view of other disciplines even if they seem to have little relevance to the issues at stake;
■   an appreciation that potential resources for planning are far more extensive than usually considered, and may include tangi-

ble assets such as: advantages due to the location; the availability of research institutes; the presence of companies or the skills base in a city; as well as intangible assets such as the confidence of citizens; the images and perceptions of a place; the potential that can be drawn from a city's history, traditions and values; or the lateral imagination of local communities.

Through these means an open-minded approach can be brought to bear on any task and traditionally useful techniques of planning such as SWOT analyses – a strengths, weaknesses, opportunities and threats assessment – are enriched. Indeed, as a form of strategic planning at a purely technical level, many of the techniques applied in developing a Creative City strategy are similar to those used in conventional strategy exercises. For example, any planning process needs to consider inputs and the operating environment, and requires procedures to judge performance, a process by which plans are implemented and a mechanism by which outputs and outcomes are assessed.

However the Creative City sets different priorities. It is aware of the multiple dimensions of creativity. and innovations and searches out the necessary and varied imaginative angles of any project. This could be in terms of an original concept that perhaps identifies and describes an issue in a new way, drawing a complex set of dilemmas in project and thus increasing the effectiveness of the proposed solution; it could be a new end product or service; it could lie in the technology used, the technique, procedure or process applied; it could be the implementation and management mechanism adopted. It might mean a project is internally managed differently, involving a new relationship towards staff or to outside stakeholders with novel decision-making procedures. The innovation could be how a problem is redefined; or in the way a new target audience or set of customers is addressed. It might be that relationships between city organizations and partners, stakeholders and customers are different. The innovation could lie in the project's capacity to have a behavioural impact, or be an innovation in a professional context. Thus, for instance, it would be innovative for planners to adopt participative approaches that are common currency amongst community development activists.

The Creative City method is different also because it highlights the significance of pilot projects and new kinds of indicators and introduces fresh ideas like a strategy of influence to open people's thinking. Creative City strategy-making differs in being holistic and valuing connections, in being people-centred rather than land use focused. This is because it is people's skills and creativity which drive urban development.

The over-arching Creative City strategy-making process has five components: planning; establishing indicators; execution; assessment; and reporting back. Within each phase there are key analytical tools including preparation and planning, assessing potential, devising indicators, execution, communicating and disseminating.

## Phase 1 – Preparation and Planning Phase

The first stage is to identify a problem, need or aspiration and assess which stakeholders and partners should be involved. This is followed by a process of awareness-raising, seeking to convince decision-makers of the value of thinking in Creative City terms – in effect developing an advocacy process. This will involve developing a strategy of influence or an assessment of the operating environment and how best to affect it. It requires drawing up a power and influence map of the city in order to look for points of leverage and actions that put creative city ideas on the agenda: a starting point could be to hold a talk at a university or on the premises of an innovative local business. As part of the strategy it will be necessary to gather case studies and examples of good practice where creative solutions to urban problems have been effective (the databases listed in the appendix will help). Better still – encourage decision-makers to visit creative sites and projects. In any survey of relevant, existing creative projects it will be important to examine how they came about and what the trigger was to their development, the obstacles that were encountered, the key ideas that contributed to the project's success, the costs and the lessons learnt.

Whilst a Creative City approach can be initiated by any source, its success depends on new partnerships – between departments and disciplines, between the public and private sectors and community organizations, between doers and thinkers. If the starting point of an awareness-raising exercise is within a local authority or government agency it may be best to work in a limited area to highlight the importance of creativity in urban development, and link professionals in planning, transport, environment services, economic and social provision with colleagues with cultural knowledge to think through ways in which their work may be enhanced. However, an initiative could equally start in the private sector, for example the re-use of old industrial buildings for arts and new media, such as in Birmingham's Custard Factory, London's Spitalfields market or Berlin's Hackische Höfe. A different approach achieving similar effects might be setting up a Creative City conference on the future of the city, bringing in as speakers people who have implemented successful projects. This preparatory work provides the platform for the next phase.

## Phase 2 – Assessment of Potential and Obstacles

The Creative City process can start in a building, a street, a neighbourhood or the city as a whole, but smaller projects will be easier to handle while people learn new approaches. Sometimes it is best to start with a small inspiring project that can be scaled up, at other times persuading key decision-makers to take the perspective on board is appropriate. Examples of both approaches abound, in many cases the two work simultaneously as activists working on the ground find a powerful ally, or a decision-maker meets someone innovating in a way that supports their own goals.

An audit of local resources is key to the Creative City strategy process and how this is approached determines future success. If the audit is undertaken in a narrowly focused and unchallenging way it may be useless. The objective is an assessment of the potential of change and whether applying creative solutions to existing and emerging problems is helpful. There is no place for defensiveness and territorialism in a process which demands listening and respect.

The Creative City auditing process is not a free-for-all, but a focused, wide-ranging and imaginative endeavour with a particular perspective, involving people with diverse viewpoints and knowledge. It audits resources from a cultural perspective: the skills, talents and ideas of different constituencies should be mapped as well as the physical fabric to identify possibilities for economic and social development. The mapping exercise should try to gauge people's feelings, ideas interpretations and dreams for the area, with reality checking mechanisms brought into play as late as possible to allow for a free flow of potential.

It may be necessary to use professionals with experience of creative urban developments to assist with the audit as insiders are often restricted by what they already know. These outsiders could contribute by leading seminars and similar events: for example the Urban Design Action Team or *charette* techniques have frequently been used to trigger intensive brainstorming. The audit should include an assessment of internal and external resources which might be brought into play, as well as precedents and models of success and failure of comparable projects in their country and elsewhere.

Perhaps the most important analytical tool at this stage of the Creative City process and later on is an assessment of the 'cycle of urban creativity' (described below). It provides an overview of all inventive projects in a city or district and assesses the potential to get ideas or projects off the ground, implemented and circulated so that new initiatives are generated. It helps the assessment of whether a city is a creative milieu or has the potential to be one. In the auditing process there should be an assessment as to whether it is strong or weak in any of the stages.

The next stage in the audit is a review of obstacles. Some of these may be generic and involve issues discussed under 'Preconditions for the Creative City'; they will need to be tackled case by case by side-stepping or confronting them, but other obstacles will fit into the cycle and it will be possible to make judgements about how to intervene.

The assessment of potential and obstacles allows one to dream and idealize forward and to plan backwards by devising an action plan focused on overcoming obstacles. This is the opposite of the traditional forward planning process. By not allowing oneself to be restricted at the outset it is possible to generate an ideas bank from which innovations can emerge. An innovation is a creative idea that has been made feasible and has passed some kind of reality check. A Creative City strategy is often concerned less with implementing imaginative projects, than with finding creative ways to persuade sceptics to believe in the idea and therefore support the vision.

The audit will facilitate a broad Creative City strategy identifying imaginative, achievable initiatives based on principles which the partners have agreed and which will guide its implementation. Some should be cheap and easy to implement quickly, both for their own value and to inspire confidence in the strategy and people's ability to deliver it. More costly and complex initiatives can be phased in as important future staging posts.

Visibility is important to a successful Creative City as results need to be seen – though landmark projects are not always the most effective regenerators: a group of a hundred newly confident and competent citizens may have far more impact on a city in the longer term. Thus a balance needs to be considered between capital developments, activity-based projects and human development. Other areas where balance should be sought are between focusing initiatives on the city centre and peripheral estates, large- and small-scale projects, between increasing the productive capacity of a place and providing incentives to consume, or between community and economic development. The strategy arising out of the audit should draw conclusions from these dilemmas.

## Phase 3 – Measuring Success and Failure

Once objectives are linked to identified aspirations and needs, and an audit of potential and a strategy to maximize it is in place, the Creative City team should decide how they will measure their success and failure. There might be a need for indicators of two types, the first to assess how far the city has gone in meeting the criteria of the 'cycle of urban creativity' – which will give a sense of how creative the city is – the second linked to the specific project goals of the strategy. In terms of the first, a number of indicators are proposed under 'Preconditions for the Creative City', 'Indicators for Vitality and Viability' and the 'Innovations Matrix'. The indicators are best decided by those directly involved at various levels of the project.

## Phase 4 – Execution

By this stage, everyone involved in the project will know what is being done, why, and how it is to be assessed, and will have given their consent to these. The work can be carried out, and monitored, by whatever method has been chosen as most appropriate. Two significant issues emerge at this stage: the first relates to pilot projects and the second to the organizational structure necessary to drive the creative city process forward.

Given that this is an innovative approach to urban development, bureaucratic structures like municipalities, development banks or complex partnerships are likely, initially at least, to play it safe. Pilot projects take on an extra significance as they will be the means through which innovation occurs. The challenge is for supporters to use the same creativity that got the project off the ground in the first place to help the mainstreaming process.

A decision also needs to be made as to whether a more formal high profile arrangement like a Creative City Initiative (CCI) should be set up or whether to proceed at a low key level with projects that happen to be creative. If there is a broader objective – to embed creativity into the genetic code of the city – a partnership forum will be essential to involve a wide cross-section of local interests and stakeholders, give credibility and accoutability to the initiative and agree and amend development proposals. The risk in setting up a high profile entity is that expectations are raised and this should be done only if it is certain the momentum can be maintained: not meeting expectations will discredit the creative city notion.

## Phase 5 – Communicating, Disseminating and Reflecting

Communicating results of the cycle of creativity is essential to its sustainability. On completion sufficient evidence should be available through monitoring to compare with the chosen indicators, to measure achievement, register problems, understand failures and communicate progress to others. This should take various formats from academic studies, to public events and exhibitions that discuss the future of the city. By these means the cycle of creative thinking, planning and acting can continue.

## Summary

The five stages set out above, as well as analytical tools like the cycle of urban creativity and innovations matrix are deliberately cyclical, returning the project teams not to the point where they began – since they have all developed and learnt since then – but to the starting point of the next project, where the process can be repeated, more effectively, by people who have gone through the procedure before.

In working through the process, analytical tools, indicators and techniques emerge as relevant. In the preparation and planning phase all may be alluded to and simple explanatory devices – eg breaking down creativity into creative thinking, creative planning and creative acting – may help understanding. Yet cultural resource mapping and the innovation matrix only come into their own fully in the audit of potential.

## CULTURE AND CREATIVITY

### *Culture as a Platform for Creative Action*

Consciousness of culture is an asset and a driving force in becoming a more imaginative city. 'The Creative City' approach is based on the idea that culture as values, insight, a way of life and form of creative expression, represents the soil from within which creativity emerges and grows, and therefore provides the momentum for development. Cultural resources are the raw materials and assets to get the process going. Cultural planning is the process of identifying projects, devising plans and managing implementation strategies based on cultural resources. It is not intended as 'the planning of culture' – an impossible, undesirable and dangerous undertaking – but rather as a cultural approach to any type of public policy.

The city expresses a people's culture: their likes and dislikes, their aspirations and fears. Culture is linked to tangible and intangible qualities. These include what is remembered, what is valued and their tangible manifestations in how a city is shaped. A living culture continually sorts out for itself the significance and quality of everything it does; building on its current position, making the most of available resources and assets, whether this is its favourable location, its local raw materials or the characteristics of its people. Over time the dynamic of culture begins to take on a life of its own, feeding off its past and responding to an unfolding future, with its foundations in a system of values which flow from the sorting process. When it uses an expanded and emancipatory notion of citizenship, potential is enhanced as it is closely linked to the grain of democratic sustainable development objectives. These guide the priorities and how city leaders and decision-makers shape and make their city. The result etches itself into the urban landscape and the city's sense of itself as: behaviour; a set of settled traditions, that are continually contested and reinvented; talent that moulds itself into characteristic skills from which products and services evolve; a particular built form.

Emerging out of this broad base of assumptions about city life and aspirations are cultural spaces which we consciously designate as special. Today visible manifestations are the cultural institutions like museums, galleries or theatres, where what a city cherishes is displayed or performed and where its culture is framed. In the past these special places were more commonly churches where God was represented, but God was also everywhere in the city. The same is true for culture. The culture of the city infuses everything: its industrial traditions; networks of mutual aid and the skills base of the population. Culture makes each place unique and so we can talk of a typical Roman, New Yorker, Muscovite or an individual from Mumbai or Buenos Aires. It is the cultural distinctiveness and special qualities of each city that provide the seedbed, foundation, raw materials and resources for urban development. It is the environment which nourishes the city. In a world where cities look and feel alike these cultural differences matter and add value. Importantly these can be positively or negatively moulded by creativity. Some cultures are inward-looking and defensive and use their imaginations to respond aggressively to new influences – closing in and erecting barriers. Others do the reverse.

Culture offers the platform for creative action, providing possibilities for a city to sustain itself across time and involves thinking through its panoply of influences and effects. Looked at so the resources of the past can help pre-figure, inspire and give confidence for the future. Enriched by a sensitivity to a city's culture policy-makers have at their disposal a pool of resources to help develop a city in an integrated way with each uncovered resource representing possibilities.

## Culture as a Resource

A cultural approach to urban strategy involves looking at each functional area culturally. For example, in the area of health we can ask: Are there indigenous health practices we can build on that might foster preventative care? In social affairs: Are there mutual aid traditions that can be adapted to provide support structures for drug users or lonely elderly people; or alternatively to kickstart the setting up of the increasingly popular local exchange trading schemes (LETS) where people barter skills and services? In terms of job creation we could undertake an audit of older craft skills in a city and assess how they can be attuned to the needs of the present. We could participate in the enthusiasms of the unemployed youth and see whether economically viable businesses can be created from their pastimes. To attract tourists we could scan history and traditions and seek to rediscover local cuisine or craft potential that could help brand the city. One could invent celebrations or congresses that chime well with a city's aspirations for the future, yet build from the soil of the past. Educational institutes can be looked at afresh to assess whether circumstances are providing triggers for action. Derry in Northern Ireland, for example, used the fact that it was a centre of the 'troubles' to create the world renowned Centre for Conflict Resolution. The style and design of a place, how people socialize or dress can itself be turned into value added either as a means of attracting outsiders to visit or to invest. Indeed, every facet of culture from history to contemporary events, a quirky circumstance or how a city has dealt with its topography can be seen as a resource to be turned into an opportunity. Some of these opportunities might be unexpected and can be explored by following some of the techniques discussed below.

Light might be the resource to focus on in Helsinki in order to turn it into a factor for social cohesion or economic advantage; a style of music or sound can be branded by a city, in order to transform its image or develop a cultural industry; a typical local food like the ham in Parma can be used to alter the fate of a city forever; a tradition of running a festival can be metamorphosed by using the core skill of organizing to become an all-year congress industry as in Adelaide. A political tradition can be drawn on and reinvented as happened in the Stroud area in the South Cotswolds. Alternative communities have existed for over 100 years, where core ideas have been recreated and have fostered new up to date experiments, such as the first UK electricity company using alternative energy sources and the development of perma-culture which has a strong following. Even one of the local petrol stations, the epitome of pollution, is part of a green shop.

The creative city approach, therefore, does not look at policy sectorally. Its purpose is to see how the pool of cultural resources identified can contribute to the integrated development of a locality. By placing cultural resources at the centre of policy-making, interactive and synergistic relationships are established between these resources and any type of public policy – in fields ranging from economic development to housing, health, education, social services, tourism, urban planning, architecture, townscape design, and cultural policy itself. Policy-makers in all fields should not simply be making an instrumental use of culture as a tool for achieving non-cultural goals. So specialists in place marketing should draw strength from the encounter with cultural knowledge by recognizing the richness and complexity of places. A place's overall stock of culture in turn is enriched by the fact that a more sophisticated form of place marketing exists in the public domain. Likewise an artist may contribute to innovation in a social services department; and a social worker might run the outreach service of a theatre; or an environmentalist might run the business development agency.

The key issue is not so much their specialism, but their core competences – the capacity to think open-mindedly, laterally across disciplines, entrepreneurially and to be managerially and organizationally competent.

Linking into and drawing on all aspects of culture forces synergies with other disciplines and helps create new ideas. The intrinsic connection-building, crossover and boundary-blurring process encourages innovation and creates an urban planning approach focused on local distinctiveness. Given the motivational power of working in tune with one's culture the overall effect is likely to be strong whether it has an economic or a social impact. My colleague Franco Bianchini (Bianchini and Ghilardi, 1997) summarizes well the attributes of thinking necessary to uncover and use cultural resources: holistic, flexible, lateral, networking and interdisciplinary; innovation-oriented, original, and experimental; critical, inquiring, challenging and questioning; people-centred, humanistic and non-deterministic; cultured, and critically aware of the cultural achievements of the past. To think like this policy-makers need practice and retraining. This will release the creativity of being able to synthesize; to see the connections between the natural, social, cultural, political and economic environments, and to grasp the importance not only of 'hard' but also of 'soft' urban infrastructures.

# GETTING THE IDEAS FACTORY GOING: CREATIVE TOOLS AND TECHNIQUES

## Debunking Myths

Some people think creatively quite naturally without help, others find it more difficult. Many people are frightened of trying to think creatively and assume it is a skill that others have. They might have the habit of convergent thinking, which is more logical and step by step, whereas they see creative thinking as more haphazard. Common too is the myth that creativity is about having the 'big idea', or that creative thoughts are plucked out of nowhere. Creativity needs to bed on some soil and before an idea turns into reality it needs a process of refinement. Other myths include the belief that people whose brains are dominated by the left hand side, like artists, are more creative than people for whom the right hand side is dominant, like scientists; or that marketing and advertising people, always alert to selling opportunities, are more creative than managers; or that lateral thinking is the sum of creativity. Yet lateral thinking is simply a way of getting 'out of the box' by conceiving ideas or addressing problems differently. It does not, for example, assist in implementing creative ideas. Creativity is not limited to a particular stage in a problem-solving process. You can be creative anywhere. At its simplest the brain has two modes of thought: an exploring, searching mode and one focused towards practical achievement. One can be creative in both. There is creative thinking, creative planning and creative acting. The main task is to look for those opportunities where creativity adds value and then to discern what kind of creativity adds most value. For example it may be at the concept or implementation stages where creativity is turned into an innovation.

Many ideas and techniques highlighted in this book are also likely to be debunked as myth in the future. They are current models and the best we have got at the time of writing. When people explore and apply these models themselves and make them their own, their ideas banks will develop. Starting with someone else's idea is a good beginning, but it is not sufficient. Developing one's own ideas in context is key as the examples from Huddersfield to Helsinki have shown. Finally attitude is crucial – a mindset that is willing to explore and to admit that it does not have all the answers is likely to come up with more answers than one that claims it already knows everything.

## Inventors of Creative Techniques

Many people have thought about creativity. In essence they say that there are tools for being creative. It is a skill that can be learnt, provided there is dedication and persistence. They encourage people to try being creative. Everybody is creative to some degree, they argue, and the challenge is to enhance and learn to use one's available creativity and encourage the belief that it can continue to grow as it is an incremental process.

Going through shelves of books on creativity, imagination and visioning can be confusing and a series of names and techniques turn up again and again. In their different ways they highlight visioning as creativity, which at its core is concerned with 'what could be'. All are making essentially three points: patterns of thought can change; ideas can be liberated through tools; and new solutions can be found. They do this by utilizing techniques to increase the number of ideas, to generate new ideas and reframe old ideas. There are a number of key people in the field. Edward De Bono is possibly the supreme popularizer and has written over 20 books on thinking. In 1967 he came up with the idea of lateral thinking – a way of generating new ideas – and has been developing variations on the theme and how to apply it ever since. Alex Osborne invented the idea of brainstorming in the 1950s and Tony Bazan is the inventor of mind mapping, a way of understanding, recording and reflecting on ideas in a holistic way. Roger van Oeck is the designer of the 'creative whack pack', a pack of cards on each of which is a statement or prompt for which van Oeck provides an example of how it might be looked at differently. William Gordon of Synectics focuses on the idea of metaphor and analogy as a means of exploring creative possibilities. Robert Fritz's book *Creating* focuses on the need to exploit the structural tension between where you are and where want to be to create solutions. The energy released by this structural tension is used to drive forward. Gareth Morgan's book *Images of Organization* reframed thinking about organization and management, and in *Imaginization* he provides a toolkit to mobilize imaginative capacity. Writers on Neuro-Linguistic Programming (NLP) show how, on a personal level, people can reframe their idea of themselves. Its essence is the search for excellence, getting people to model themselves on the best and improve on it. One imagines oneself being like a model person and by 'spotting the difference that makes the difference' takes on board those characteristics.

There are a mass of writers who summarize what creativity is or its future role, such as Andy Green in *Creativity in Public Relations* or *Best Practice Creativity* by Peter Cook and John Kao in *The Age of Creativity* and *Jamming*. For over 50 years people have pondered what the steps in the creative process are and how they work. However, they need not concern us in too much detail. For example Alex Osborne's seven-step process of: orientation; preparation; analysis; ideation, the piling up of alternative ideas; incubation; synthesis and evaluation. Maurice Stein has a three-phase model: hypothesis formation, hypothesis testing and the communication of results. Andy Green defines five I's: information, incubation, illumination, integration and illustration.

## Types of Techniques

There are three classes of creative techniques. The first helps to increase the number of ideas; the second helps to create new ideas and the third reframes how existing ideas are seen.

### Increasing the Number of Ideas

The simplest way to increase the number of ideas is to create a list; more advanced is the idea of *brainstorming* which involves writing down as many ideas as possible on a flipchart without allowing other participants to comment critically as this would halt the flow. *Brainwriting* is an elaboration, yet instead of writing on a public flipchart, you write on individual cards which are then passed around, allowing more chances for creating side-tracks and new connections.

Also within this category is visiting other places and looking at best practice databases to see what other people have done and effectively imitating or stealing someone else's idea.

### Creating New Ideas

Creating new ideas may involve originating completely new ideas or developing new ideas from old ones. *Association, analogy* and *metaphor* are ways of bringing together, by force, seemingly incompatible concepts; by making the familiar strange and the strange familiar. For example, an image survey we undertook in Helsinki was based on associative thinking to find a means of discussing the city in new terms. We asked what Helsinki would be in terms of 40 associations including: if Helsinki were a colour, a car, a fruit, a musical instrument or a song, what would it be. It came out as dark blue, a Volvo, a raspberry, a flute and the song 'Silence is Golden'. Looking at the meanings in the subsequent analysis helped to define a cultural strategy for the city based on the importance of light, inclusiveness and female strengths, which would not have come about through traditional thinking paths.

Other techniques range from day dreaming to visualization, to mind improvement packs to the Po-provocation and random word techniques as a means to learning to *think laterally* developed by De Bono. The concept Po is a provocation such as 'cows can fly' and is used in order to get people to jump out of habitual thought patterns. The random word technique is especially useful for product development. You look up a noun in a dictionary on a random page and, having hit on an everyday object, you then force the word to fit your problem. For example, if the problem discussed is the future of copiers and you hit upon 'nose' (which has nothing to do with copiers) you explore connections. Nose is related to smell and perhaps different smells could become fault indicators. In another case cigarettes were apparently linked to traffic lights leading to the 'signal, danger, stop' bands on cigarettes. As De Bono notes, since solutions are logical in hindsight we assume that logic is what got us there. This is completely untrue as most situations involve being in complex patterns whose logic cannot be decoded in advance. If everything were logical we would not need creative thinking.

### Reframing Devices

*Reframing* is changing the nature of something or a situation by looking at it from a different standpoint. For example: 'is the glass half full or half empty?' One's attitude and perception can be changed depending on the answer, because the context has been transformed not the ideas. Comedia uses many reframing devices including the notion of 'turning a weakness into a strength' as when Emscher Park decided to use its industrial degradation as a trigger to create an environmental protection industry using the degraded landscape as the experimentation zone.

Similarly the notion of *'seeing through the eyes of ...'* has a similar effect, such as planning the city through the eyes of women, the elderly or children. The children-as-planners initiatives in Kitee in Finland, or Rouen and Locarno, or women-as-planners projects in Emscher or Vienna, or senior citizen involvement in Utrecht have created innovative perspectives as to how cities should develop. Involving children not only gains a commitment to their own environment but has been instrumental in developing civic pride and ownership. Taking a woman's perspective has highlighted facilities traditional planning tends to 'forget'. Enhanced spaces for social interaction; a greater emphasis on play areas; better attention to lighting and safety issues; rethinking the interiors of apartments with a greater emphasis on kitchens as the central place in households. In terms of the elderly, similar priorities emerge with a particular recognition of frailty and how that affects the way buildings are put together.

The *survey of the senses* analyses the city through its sounds, its smells, its views and panoramas at different times of the day and night. It changes conventional ways of discovering possibilities and problems by attempting to get decision-makers to connect with their visceral experience of city life. In so doing it can become a spur to preventative action by directly experiencing a bad smell, high-pitched noise or an unsightly view. Awareness of the potential of good sounds, intoxicating smells and pleasant outlooks, as in healing gardens or comforting vistas, makes these senses a creative resource

Imagining and thinking forwards and planning backwards is a strategic planning tool involving *reverse thinking*. It differs from forward planning by being aspirational as it creates visions rather than merely extrapolating existing trends forward. When you take yourself to the place where you want to be and then look backwards the barriers appear. By visualizing the final hindrances from the future back to the present the tasks to be achieved unravel in an increasing array of options, like a reverse pyramid, as each obstacle is thought through. With analysis and a strategy of influence, an action plan unfolds as it is clear what needs to be done to overcome the obstacles. Usually it needs a one-, three- or ten-year horizon with options for achievable projects that range from the cheap, easy and short term to the expensive, difficult and long term, whilst orchestrating staging posts and markers of progress in between. Having explored options and obstacles both forwards and backwards in time it is simpler to be strategically opportunistic rather than opportunistically strategic. This is similar to the way indicators work where a measurable target is set and actions are geared to achieving them.

*Broadening* the meaning of *concepts* such as capital, sustainability or time equally acts as a reframing device by opening out possibilities for interpretation. For example, linking the word social to capital reconfigures how social affairs can be discussed and what is at stake by adding a hard-edged dimension that highlights value and costs.

## Applying Techniques

There are three levels at which techniques can be applied: the personal, the community and the city.

### Individual Level
Essentially individual techniques focus on getting people out of set patterns of thinking so they can make novel connections and gain insight. The website www.ozemail.com/~caveman/creative/content.xtm has over 20 individual techniques that can be applied

at an individual level and is an excellent summary of available tools. De Bono's *Teach your child how to think* is another. They both include lateral thinking, which De Bono defines as: 'escaping from established ideas and perceptions in order to find new ones'; or as 'trying harder with the same ideas and same approach may not solve the problem. You may need to move "laterally" to try new ideas and a new approach.' To develop lateral thinking the tools used include 'random word', Po and six thinking hats.

*Six hats* is a method of thinking in one way at a time so that conversation can move forward without getting bogged down by antagonistic dialogues veering between the negative and the positive. Each hat has a set of qualities that together encompass the range of characteristics needed for a rounded discussion. Each hat is given a turn to explore where it leads. The white hat considers facts and information and asks: 'What information do we need?' The red hat is about emotion and intuition and considers: 'How do we feel about the issue?' The black hat focuses on caution and judgement and asks: 'How does it fit the facts or will it work?' The yellow hat looks at the advantages: 'What benefits has the project got?' The green hat explores and looks for alternatives. The blue hat thinks about where we are and summarizes.

Another tool is the *questioning technique*: where in any problem-solving exercise the issue is analysed by asking: Who, what, why, where, when and how. An extension is not to forget the creative possibilities of asking a question with a supplementary attached, such as 'who else', 'what else', 'where else'. Other supplementary questions might be 'need'; such as 'what need', 'whose need', 'when is it needed'; the list is endless. (Thanks to Rob Lloyd-Owen for this techninque.)

## Community Level Techniques

Creative community-based techniques have the objective of empowering groups to feel confident to jointly design and create their futures. They incorporate tools for enhancing individual creativity and adding to them. Within a group framework a new set of priorities emerges for creative thinking centred on group dynamics, personality and networking. Attention is paid to how consensus and common ground is built as well as to the alliances and coalitions created. In a group setting communication skills become central and all techniques work well with the proper dialogue, especially 'Talkworks' – 'seeking to understand before seeking to be understood'. Experiencing the art of conversation involves skills such as: listening; sharing understanding; searching for clarity; bringing stories to life and controlling emotion. It requires awareness, for example that under 20 per cent of communication happens through speech and that body language is key. The essential creative process is the joint exercise where barriers are broken between individual and group. The key task in defining the resulting common ground after brainstorming is to reduce the mass of ideas to the ones most people think are important and then identifying solutions that all individuals in the room will be committed to taking further.

All the tools have a core logic which boils down to: reviewing and sharing a view on the past; exploring the present; creating ideal future scenarios; identifying a shared vision and making an action plan.

The models involve stakeholder partnerships and incorporate participative vision-making processes such as Future Search, Open Space, Planning for Real and stakeholder visioning, so popular in the US. The central point is not necessarily getting the vision right but providing the conditions for networking and allowing diverse groups to come together and interact. This often leads to the discovery of new, formerly hidden, leaders or project champions. The objective is to create a culture of collaboration by depersonalizing leadership, institutionalizing leadership and creating a climate for leadership. Done well this is a creative process because it harnesses 'the motivational power of the incongruity between what is and what might be' (Brunner quoted in Fryer, 1996). Examples have been tested from Saltsjöbaden near Stockholm; Pihalisto in Helsinki; Prenzlauer Berg and Hellersdorf in East Berlin to Stroud in the UK. Below are listed some examples taken from the excellent *Participation Works! 21 Techniques of Community Participation for the 21st Century* by the New Economics Foundation (1997).

'Future Search' generates action by building a shared vision among a diverse group of people. One of the first took place in 1995 in Hitchin in Hertfordshire which created a 'Whole Settlement Strategy' through Future Search. Sixty people spent two days getting the process started. Subsequently specialist groups have worked on particular projects, including developing a one-stop shop for council services and installing a town centre manager. Since 1995 over 35 urban future search conferences have taken place in the UK.

'Planning for Real' creates a large 3D model of a neighbourhood made and used by the people who live there. The model is taken around several venues for discussion. In the exercise a mass of illustrated suggestion cards are available covering health, housing, crime, transport and the local economy. Blank cards are available for people to make their own suggestions. These cards are shuffled around and the model can be adapted and in follow-up meetings suggestions taken forward. Using suggestion cards means ideas can be put forward without any need for the participant to be articulate. Planning for Real is used worldwide.

'Choices Method' is a systematic way of involving as many members of the local public as possible in developing an urban vision and inspiring them to act. Chattanooga, which won a Habitat best practices award in 1997, undertook ReVision 2000 in 1993 after the original exercise Vision 2000 had met most of its goals set in 1984. It took a year to plan and three months to implement. It has four steps: through a myriad of meetings people generate ideas that would make life better in the future. All ideas submitted are presented to vision workshops led by facilitators, they are then consolidated and clustered into goals by people interested in the subject. At a 'Vision Fair' people vote on which ideas interest them most and on which they would like to work. Action groups are formed to carry out the chosen ideas.

'Community Appraisal' as a survey of, by and for the community and an action list of recommendations for the community. Tetbury in Gloucestershire has a population of 5000. A questionnaire was distributed to over 2000 households; an open weekend held and service providers were invited to defend their past performance as perceived by local residents and to outline future actions. The appraisal has led to major redevelopment proposals orchestrated by local people, including for the railway sidings.

'Community Indicators' concerns the development of indicators by local communities of issues that really matter to them. Merton identified equal access as a key indicator. Volunteers from Merton Association for Independent Access (MAFIA), whose mobility is restricted, visited shops, banks, churches and post offices to see how accessible they were. With a long-term target of 100 per cent accessibility they found only 49 per cent of places were accessible. On this basis the local community and authority agreed that 60 per cent was an achievable interim target.

'Open Space' is an intensely democratic framework which enables an unlimited number of participants to create their own programme of discussions around a central theme. It is particularly effective in generating high-energy participation, learning and commitment to action. The UK Local Government Management Board now runs its annual forum for environment coordinators through Open Forum, as a response to fewer lectures, the desire for more networking and more say in what happens. A 120-page report on 'Achieving Sustainable Development using Local Agenda 21 processes in 21st century Britain' was delivered one day after the event.

The 'Imagine' technique seeks to understand and appreciate the best of the past as a basis for imagining what might be and then creating it. It has three phases. 'Imagine Chicago' was a pilot project initiated by Bliss Browne, a priest and banker. From 1991 onwards participants were asked to describe the most meaningful memories of Chicago and to compare these with what they experienced today. They then imagined what they wanted Chicago to be and what it could be a generation from now. In the final co-creation stage partnerships were formed between organizations interested in taking projects forward. From 1993 onwards many other pilots were created and 50 young people were trained as interviewers to generate ideas. Since 1995 over 100 community organizations, schools and cultural institutions have used the process for urban development and have created an Urban Imagination Network.

## City Level Techniques

Creativity at the city level does not involve a different class of technique from at the neighbourhood or individual level, but the application of creativity becomes more complex as the range of actors increases. The operating environment is broader and the extent of human and non-human resources in play are more diverse. Collaboration and competition between firms and with other cities is more obvious, as is public–private partnership. A feedback mechanism is vital as without it there can be no adjustment of direction. The inevitable complexity and unintended consequences requires support, coaching and facilitating styles of leadership. Creative communications are key. Through an increased understanding of communication, corporate strategy making has gained a new lease of life. Planning in the public gaze and thus being accountable was initially frightening for those preferring safer, internally focused contact. However, opening out to people at the receiving end was ultimately seen to be liberating, as planners could admit that they did not need to hold the answers – they are out there.

The rise of urban visioning is a response to a new spirit of collaborative, democratic leadership. Some cities are responding to previous leadership malaise, either by turning to consultants, by identifying weaknesses and by devising new structures and organizational cultures. Others are forming new coalitions with an increasing recognition of the need for openness and power-sharing, which often does not come easily to existing power structures.

Urban visioning is a relatively new phenomenon. The origins of shared visioning are in the heretics of the post-war period, like Kurt Lewin and the counterculture movement in the 1960s. It arose as a method, first in the US, to deal with the exacerbating crises of cities which the public sector on its own could not handle, because of lack of resources, curtailed powers and legitimacy or the power of interest groups. Traditionally it was assumed that municipalities or the government would deal with urban problems alone. It was not seen as the responsibility of businesses or individuals. Yet the increased recognition of the relative powerlessness of each actor – public, private, voluntary – has created a reason for joint action as did the increasing acknowledgement that businesses have social responsibilities. Organizations and individuals acting in their own self-interest left dire problems unattended, from drug abuse to general urban decay to missed opportunities for growth. So, whilst organizations might have been creative, networked and collaborative internally, they were not creative across the public/private divide.

Urban visioning involves scaling up the idea of the business plan from the level of the firm to the level of the urban area or city. Historically it has developed in cities under threat where capital and more educated people have moved out. Pulling together and partnering to reskill and regenerate was seen as a way of increasing the value of assets. It is now an integral tool in developing creative ideas and a commitment to action. Examples proliferate, from the Nordic countries, Germany, The Netherlands and Britain and even in Asia through organizations such as the Asia Pacific Forum. Good examples of visioning today tend to come from three types of city. Successful cities wishing to stay ahead in the urban game such as Barcelona or Frankfurt that were especially focused on a cultural vision. The underlying driver for Frankfurt was to become the finance capital of Europe; for Barcelona it was the Olympics and cultural independence as Catalonia – a real unifier. A second category contains crisis-ridden cities, most famously in the past: Baltimore, Pittsburgh, Cleveland and even Detroit. A key component providing moral force and partly driving the vision was the racial divide. They all shared the need to restructure across the board from manufacturing to service provision, as have St Petersburg, Budapest and Glasgow. The third type are opportunity makers, such as emerging gateway cities between east and west like Vienna or Helsinki. The latter brands itself as the city that has ended the 'tyranny of distance' through new technology.

Urban management is thus being radically adjusted in a wide number of American, European and Australian cities as well as more isolated examples in Asia, Africa and South America. The principles include: creating citizen participation to overcome exaggerated deference to bureaucracy; decreasing petty procedural control mechanisms and developing more citizen-responsive procedures; refocusing on outputs rather than inputs; instilling motivation in civil servants, and increasing the competitiveness of the public sector.

The challenge of creative empowerment is seen as moving up the scale from:

- Co-option – representatives are chosen, but have no real input or power, there is an element of tokenism and manipulation.
- Cooperation – tasks are assigned, with incentives, but outsiders decide the agenda and direct the process.
- Consultation – local opinions are asked for, outsiders analyse and decide on the course of action.
- Collaboration – local people work with outsiders to determine priorities; responsibility for directing the process, however, remains with the outsiders.
- Co-learning – local people and outsiders share their knowledge to create a new understanding and work together to form action plans, with outside facilitation.
- Collective Action – local people set their own agenda and mobilize to carry it out, using outsiders not as initiators/facilitators but as required by local people (Cornwall, 1995).

Long-term sustainability is generated by moving towards co-learning and collective action, as commitment to goals is greater. Apart from community led models there are four other popular styles of visioning. Commonplace techniques such as SWOT or PEST are used as a means of distinguishing the essential from the trivial. They assess the operating environment by reviewing strengths, weaknesses, opportunities and threats of the political, economic, social and technological context. But the really creative momentum in all approaches was always been brought about by two factors: mixing people and embedding evaluation as a continuous process, and it is this mix which has ensured that action has happened, making the techniques themselves secondary. Helped usually by facilitators when groups were mixed, the ideas factories started when, with common commitment, politicians, business people, officials and others talked, set goals and agreed corporate objectives.

## The Visionary and Charismatic Leader-led Model with Relatively Little Focus on Consultation

Charismatic leaders can enable communication and lead by example. They release personality resources rather than the typical bureaucratic response and therefore personality traits such as charm, persuasiveness and tenacity are key. Typically their middle management training programmes seek to create a wide-ranging pool of people with leadership potential and commitment to their urban area. The down side is that adversaries will regard such people as self-centred or autocratic. Examples include Jaime Lerner in Curitiba, Georges Frêche in Montpellier or Rob Hughes in Huddersfield, who have had long-term impacts on their cities.

## Municipality-led Models Based on Traditional Departmental Strategy

Many visioning exercises are led by municipalities through traditional departmental strategy-making processes and sometimes statutory consultation models involving sending out pre-prepared plans for comment. Often there is no concerted attempt to involve outsiders and get any commitment for real action. One example of this model is Glasgow, where external resources from the government-sponsored Glasgow Development Agency were guaranteed and the objective was long-term development. The funding gave the city the flexibility to think ahead and consider long-term strategy. Their momentum building techniques have been copied elsewhere. For example, how they conceived their explicit staging post strategy from the Garden Festival in 1988, to the European City of Culture in 1990 and the 1999 Year of Architecture.

Municipal models which incorporate more consultation often involve internal management change. The Tilburg Model, which won one of the Habitat Best Practice Awards and initiated in the late 1980s, incorporated into the City Programme agreed targets, worked out in collaboration with citizens and monitored these on an annual basis. The Duisburg modernization programme, has resulted in a City Business Plan which makes the city transparent and accountable for urban development. The Kirklees administrative reorganization programme in the UK has a similar philosophy. Brazil's Porto Alegre participatory budgeting techniques developed under major Tarso Genro or the similar initiative in Italy's Reggio Emilia are other examples. The Regies de Quartier, a neighbourhood management structure, is now operational in 60 French communities and has been replicated in The Netherlands in Opzoomeren and Stedenwijk in Rotterdam and at Schiedam.

### Business-led Models or Coalitions for Growth

Developed initially in the US the first example was in Pittsburgh starting in the 1940s and called the Allegheny Conference. Its initial concerns were with air and water. It later became the Urban Renewal Authority, which rebuilt the 'golden triangle' and went through a number of stages and is now involved in social renewal. Other instances of this model include the Baltimore coalition started in the 1950s, which developed the Charles River Centre office project, and subsequently the now famous inner harbour and arts facilities. In Melbourne commissioners were put in to run the city by-passing democratically elected structures. This parallels the urban development corporation model popular in the UK in the 1980s. More recent coalitions have used the technique of clearing out obstacles such as opening out planning laws or easing up on development controls to trigger activity.

### Partnership-led Models

The partnership-led model seeks from the outset to create a joint body made up of public/private and community sector partners to help implement an urban plan. Usually they have little direct authority to implement the plan, nor are they involved in day to day service provision. As a coalition of joint interests they usually influence major projects or strategic direction. An example is the Adelaide 21 project, which instead of by-passing the local authority attempted to give a voice to other stakeholders, such as educational institutions, the cultural, voluntary and business sectors. Three examples from the US include: Sioux Falls Tomorrow, which involved 60 stakeholders in a nine-month strategic planning process in South Dakota; the 18-month Lee's Summit in Missouri, which enabled 65 stakeholders to prepare a plan for the city's economic development, public services and quality of life; and Vision Indianapolis Tomorrow which engaged 90 representatives in developing a strategic plan to improve the city's quality of life. The key issue is whether there is true partnership. Examples from around the world suggest that sometimes there is collaboration without joint agenda setting, or if strategy is planned jointly, implementation can be problemetical, either in terms of budgets, resources, timing or authority handed over.

## CIVIC CREATIVITY

Public and private organizations should shift focus and reinvigorate their purposes and goals so as to shape what they can achieve. The 'civic creativity' agenda seeks to be a means and guiding principle for this. The 'civic' and the 'public' have come in for a battering over the closing decades of the 20th century. A string of negative connotations are associated with them: bureaucratic, red tape, hierarchical, inefficient, social welfarist, lacking in vision, machine-like. They are linked to under-achievement, lack of strategic focus and failure. Yet for most of the last century they stood for self-development, social improvement and modernization. Can these purposes be renewed within a 21st century framework? 'Private' by contrast is seen as alert, quick-footed, responsive, well-managed. The time has come to focus less exclusively on the need for city management restructuring, how public authorities can run themselves better and to get beyond intra-organizational issues, important as they remain in many places.

'Civic creativity' is defined as imaginative problem-solving applied to public good objectives. The aim is to generate a continual flow of innovative solutions to problems which have an impact on the public realm. 'Civic creativity' is the capacity for public officials and others oriented to the public good to effectively and instrumentally apply their imaginative faculties to achieving 'higher value within a framework of social and political values'. This may be translated into monetary terms or non-financial objectives that can be quantified through other indicators. Those applying civic creativity are able to negotiate commitment, ownership and credence for their ideas and actions so that the tendency to take risks, often at the boundaries of existing procedures and rules, is seen as accountable and full of probity. Its scope is the confluence point between individual self-interest and collective desires, where being 'me' and being 'us' at the same time is possible. It is a creativity that negotiates and balances a harmony between a diversity of conflicting interests and thus is always involved in some form of politics. It has so much potential as it deals in the arena of political power where many of the largest obstacles to progress are present and where gatekeepers can block opportunity. Being creative in a civic sense needs to be legitimized as a valid, praiseworthy activity. The particular context will determine what this might be. In one instance it may be the need to deal with urban violence innovatively, in another raising the income levels of the excluded, in a third creating a sense of beauty in urban design. The urgent issues of urban life will play themselves out in the public realm: how to behave in a civilized, tolerant way towards each other so we feel safe in cities or how the built environment inspires or deflates. Many solutions need inventing from new forms of incentives to make public transport work to successful social mixing within housing estates. This is the ambit of 'civic creativity'.

The concept may seem like a contradiction, yet it is its incongruity that gives 'civic creativity' power. The 'civic' is seen as worthy, necessary and publicly oriented and 'creativity' is seen as exciting, forward-looking and enterprising. By combining the two in tangible projects civic life can be revitalized.

'Civic creativity' has unique qualities centred on a passion and vision for the civic. It involves qualities well beyond management technique. In contrast to the creativity of the artist that might come across as selfish and inwardly focused, civic creativity is not egocentric. It encompasses: a capacity to listen; an imagination and antennae that can judge political mood; being a political animal in the positive sense and a desire to nurture and assemble political forces; an ability to defuse tensions creatively and to come up with ethical compromises; the skill to carry people along and to inspire disparate groups of people to do something that transcends their self-interest by persuading them that a course of action is better for everyone. This requires political skills and leadership qualities to achieve political consensus. In this way civic creativity can motivate and empower people to become self-starters and spread competence and confidence as well as 'reconfigure resources, often public and private to deliver better social outcomes, higher social value, and social capital' (Leadbeater and Goss, 1998) In this way creative persons operating in the civic realm perceive value, create value and add values. It is a precious resource to be nurtured.

Civic creativity is connected to public and social entrepreneurship, but is not the same. Social or communal action includes the civic realm, but is not exclusive to it. It is not driven by the formal mechanisms of power nor is it necessarily linked to governing bodies. Indeed social action often happens because civic action has failed. The good intentions of the civic are often thwarted by the risk averse, inward-looking culture of the civic. Civic creativity seeks to overcome this problem even though civic authority may fear it. Creativity is dangerous or unsettling, but not using it is even more dangerous. It seeks to re-inspire the culture of public policy-making organizations and bureaucratic operations as well as businesses to act in a more socially responsible way.

## Creating Value and Adding Values

There is no reason why the best of the cultures the words 'civic' and 'creative' embody cannot be combined to mutual benefit. It is possible to be creative in a public context or be a social entrepreneur whilst maintaining public good principles. Operating creatively and managing risk within the public realm is different from doing so in a private company or voluntary organization. Taking over private sector management techniques wholesale and applying them uncritically is inappropriate. The task is to identify those creative and entrepreneurial qualities associated with the business world that are useful in the public sphere without letting the means distract from the public ends. A civically creative or entrepreneurial approach to problem-solving is adept at identifying resources: money; novel ways of looking at a problem; an old cultural tradition that can be twisted to modern purposes; an asset represented by a submerged aspiration in the population that can be tapped, such as a deep desire for a cleaner environment. It is a managerial ethos that looks for and consistently exploits opportunities to achieve results beyond what an individual can do. Civic creativity can learn much from business and voluntary associations but has its own distinctive qualities. It can 'learn best from its own best practice' (Leadbeater and Goss, 1998). Also business can learn from how civic creativity operates as it increasingly needs to act with social responsibility in the communities where it operates. No sector has a monopoly over how to be creative. There are leads and lags in different sectors.

Merging two cultures can create dilemmas. The civic realm operates and gains credence through formal and informal rules, which provide stability, consistency and structure within a set of accountability mechanisms. Creative people, by contrast, continuously test rules and boundaries, questioning them and at times breaking them. Thus the more creative a person is within the public domain the stronger the principles, vision and incorruptible ethical framework must be. Otherwise there is a danger of slipping into opportunism.

## Generating Pressure to Perform

What drives civic creativity forward? There are two main processes: new measures to quantify the public good and public dialogue. Public bodies such as municipalities do not have competitive pressures to inexorably drive and push forward the innovation process. However, pressure is mounting as the concept of 'cities as corporations' with citizens as shareholders takes hold. These include: transparent accounting systems; a shift from input to output budgeting; outsourcing or the notion of 'best value'. Yet publicly inspired urban innovations do not necessarily seek to yield direct commercial returns, which are what pushes business creativity forward. What is the public sector equivalent of the profit motive, what are the criteria for success? For an elected official it may be re-election or praise for a job well done. What though for the civil servant or the organization as a whole? This will depend on objectives and indicators might include: reductions in resource use or pollution levels; the encouragement of social cohesion and a reduction in social fragmentation measured by decreases in vandalism or family breakdown; changing behaviour such as a move from private car use to public transport.

A different means of creating momentum is public dialogue on what constitutes the public good, founded on a common commitment that the public sector can again become a force for renewal of urban life embodied in an ethos linked to a vision and a set of targets. What the public good is will be continually negotiated. A minimalist definition, with elected representatives embodying the public good simply because they are elected, will not do. Elections give a mandate that is too generic. Further legitimation is required. Elected people might instruct officials to conduct further analysis of what might or might not constitute the public good in a policy arena. The methods include extensive use of focus groups, commissioning research or soliciting the opinion of external experts. This is a rather technocratic model which assumes this proceeds in an ideology-free way. Political parties tend not to commission research with an open agenda, it is usually directed towards validating an initial understanding of the public good. For political parties the

## WHERE THE PUBLIC CONTROLS THE PURSE STRINGS, PORTO ALEGRE, BRAZIL

Allowing people to make the decisions of government has taken deep root in Porto Alegre, Brazil. During his administration, Tarso Genro, mayor of the city from 1993 to 1997, challenged the traditional relationship between state and public providing the philosophical inspiration and practical impetus behind participatory budgeting. The hallmark of Genro's administration was putting into practice the concept of citizen control, allowing the public to make the decisions of government by getting local professional, business and advocacy groups to join community boards that set strategic, long-term policy directions for the city. 'The only fundamental reform of the state is one which reforms the relationship between government and society and ... the goal of reform is to combine representative democracy with control by society of public policy,' he says.

Initiated by Olivio Dutra, with whom he served as vice-mayor from 1989 to 1992, the system flourished under Genro as the public gained more experience in its unaccustomed role as decision-maker and because key tax reforms strengthened municipal finances. Participatory budgeting starts from the ground up. In Porto Alegre, the city is divided into 16 regions or districts each with a Popular Council made up of representatives of community associations, mother's club and other local groups. A city-wide organization of residents, the Council of Representatives, is formed with two representatives from each Popular Council who are elected in their district. Several city hall officials are assigned to act as permanent liaisons with these organizations.

The Council of Representatives sets the agenda for municipal spending as it puts together a list of priorities for public works. This is done in close coordination with delegates who each represent 30 residents and are elected by their neighbours. At the outset, the neighbourhood delegates compile the list of demands for projects like building schools or health centres, putting in sewerage systems or paving streets. Then, delegates and the Council of Representatives meet with city hall officials and together assign a weighting to each project request based on what percentage of the population and district lacks urban services priority projects set by the Councils of Representatives. In 1998 the priorities were sanitation, community paving and housing. So, a request to pave a street that runs in front of a school will get a higher weighting than a similar request for a street that has only a few homes. The final decisions on public spending are made in a three-way meeting that includes the officials from city hall, the Council of Representatives from the neighbourhoods and the Chamber of Councilmen who win their posts in the city-wide election. In a typical budget cycle, some 1,500 requests are made for public works, and slightly over 200 projects can be financed.

After selection, the community representatives begin supervising the progress of each project and monitoring how the funds are spent. It took time and a re-thinking of political philosophy to devise a system of participation that has drawn at least 1,000 community groups and 1,200 delegates into public spending decisions as initially people did not know how to participate.

The triangular relationship between City Hall, elected city councilmen and neighbourhood representatives evolved from an earlier notion that the Council of Representatives should make all decisions which was soon seen as anti-democratic because it reduced the importance of municipal elections. The reformed vision re-legitimizes the electoral process and combines citizen participation with organizations of representative democracy. The concepts of accountability and a public that takes hold of local affairs now run deep in Porto Alegre extending too to thematic councils to decide on long-term strategic plans for the city. As an outgrowth of the participatory budget, some residents formed a non-governmental organization called 'Eyes on the Budget' with the purpose of monitoring the use of public funds and providing critiques of the budget process.

The process is popular, with Genro's popularity rating at 75 per cent in 1997, and he turned over a solvent township to his successor. An opinion survey about participatory budgeting found that 85 per cent of city residents had either been active in the budget process or considered it positively. The success of the participatory budgeting process can now be quantified. Porto Alegre is the Brazilian state capital with the highest quality of life indices. Participatory budgeting is being replicated as in Belo Horizonte, the capital of Brazil's third most important state, and in some 50 other Brazilian cities. The system is being implemented in Buenos Aires and Rosario, Argentina and Montevideo, Uruguay.

*Source:* Lucy Conger, *Urban Age Magazine* World Bank, Spring 1999

limit of what they regard as the public good is often electoral popularity. The public good is not only a numbers game and in the real world the process of prioritizing and legitimizing is messy, decisions are never perfect, especially the balance between sectional issues which are to be defined as 'in the public interest'. For example slowing down cars in a city may save 10 lives yet 'lose' time for millions of people. The complexity of public goods is that they might not be popular.

Campaigning groups or charities, whilst at times over empha-sizing certain issues do this for good reason, and may sensationalize an issue, as green organizations have done, to get it debated on the political agenda. Private business, by making a profit, can act with public good intentions. One does not exclude the other. The civic creativity agenda needs to shift business towards objectives for the public good by getting them excited about its possibilities and providing innovative incentives for social housing, environmental improvement or entrepreneurship among the disempowered. Public good projects can be generated from any source, public or private.

Civic creativity can only occur in a changed organizational culture – one that is predisposed to risk taking. This requires a culture change for most public sector organizations, from local authorities to universities. Creativity cannot be a driving force unless the bureaucratic mindset is overcome, without this truly creative people cannot be retained. First, the atmosphere will deter creative people as they will immediately recognize that their ability to work productively will be limited. Secondly, they can usually earn more money elsewhere. Public sector organizations have two key problems. They find it difficult to provide sufficient financial incentives or to give autonomy to people to run programmes the way they want to. Thirdly, the lack of confidence generated by continuous concentration on shortcomings, as seen in the media coverage of social workers, teachers or public officials. The conse-quent demoralization leads to a loss of purpose and makes being creative the last thing on the agenda (see also Leadbeater and Goss, 1998).

# 8

# Rediscovering Urban Creativity

## THE URBAN INNOVATIONS MATRIX

By what criteria can we assess the relative creativity and innovativeness of urban projects? The innovations matrix provides a way for cities to situate themselves by asking: 'Where does my project stand?', 'How does it measure against best practices?' or 'What could I be doing?' Assessment and benchmarking against a comparative scale is useful to generate reflection, understanding and learning. Indeed the primary focus should always be on how a novel solution addresses a local need and its intrinsic creativity is thus a secondary issue.

The matrix originally developed in *Innovative and Sustainable European Cities* (Hall and Landry, 1997) describes what level of innovation a project embodies. It is a self-assessment tool and benchmarking device. It does not claim to represent the truth, but to sharpen thinking, aid judgement, and does not imply that a city has to be continuously innovative. A set of examples of how the taxonomy works are shown in subsequent graphs taking an overarching world perspective. Crucially a city can build up its own local or regional version and ask: 'What in our context is a paradigm shift in addressing a problem or creating an innovation?' The target for any city – in the north or south – should be to gear its performance at least to best practice.

The imaginative dimension of a project can enter at any stage, for example in terms of original concept, technology, technique, procedure or process applied, or the implementation and management mechanism adopted. Invariably innovations imply a process of creative thinking: the capacity to see a problem in a new way, perhaps even reformulating it as a quite different problem with a quite separate range of possible solutions. Sometimes this creative leap can be quite fundamental, as when it was suggested that mental illness could be better treated outside mental hospitals, or that traffic planning consisted not in changing the city for the car, but in restraining the car to maintain the environment of the city. Sometimes the leap is of a second order, not involving a fundamental paradigm shift, but nevertheless redefining the problem and thus opening up a different range of solutions. There is thus an entire spectrum or chain of innovative solutions; their number depends to some extent on the judgement of the observer, but it is useful to distinguish at least seven:

1   Meta-paradigm shift: a Paradigm Shift in the most trenchant and thorough sense as originally suggested by Thomas Kuhn (1962): a completely new way of ordering reality and conceptualizing the world. Such a shift straddles and informs a diversity of policy areas in a comprehensive and overarching way. Shifts of this order of impact happen rarely. The notion of sustainability – which reorients in principle the way we think of urban economics, the environment, social and cultural life – is perhaps the most obvious example from recent years. Central to it is the idea of holistic, integrated thinking and an attempt to understand how impacts of every kind and at every level are inextricably interconnected. It re-conceptualizes a city from a machine to a living organism incorporating the notion of metabolism.

2   Paradigm shift: a quite basic redefinition of a problem, say in a given policy area, or perhaps the discovery of a new problem or solution; whereby the objective of policy is itself changed. Often in these cases a problem is turned on its head and seen as an opportunity – such as when waste is seen as an asset – or involves complete rethinking as happened with the empowerment and social equity agendas in urban management. Examples, during the last 20 years, include the notion of traffic planning to restrain rather than facilitate vehicular traffic; and the concept of recycling urban economies from declining sectors, such as manufacturing, into expanding ones, such as services or tourism. The annual Finnish snow castle project in Kemi involves a paradigm shift: turning a weakness – coldness and snow and the closure of the paper mill – into a strength – a successful tourism project that now sustains the economy of

the town. Helping the homeless take their fate into their hands, as the *Big Issue* has done, is another example.

3   Basic innovation: once paradigm shifts in conceptualizing an issue have occurred a new way of achieving an objective. Almost invariably this includes an element of 'fine tuning' the problem definition. Examples are the idea that city centres can be pedestrianized (first in Essen, Germany, in 1904); or the idea of developing the 'festival marketplace' and associated urban tourism as a means of regenerating central and inner urban areas, with the re-use of old buildings formerly designed for the manufacturing or warehousing economy (as in Covent Garden, London, in the 1970s). Zero tolerance as a means of abating crime is another instance. Finally a more trivial example: New York Zoo was the first to use animal excrement to create a new marketable, commercial product, called 'zoopoo', as compost for gardens. This has been replicated in zoos throughout the world.

4   Best practice: an outstanding example of realization, generally regarded as unique. Examples are the pedestrianization of Munich in the 1970s, or the regeneration of the Barcelona waterfront in the 1990s – both, interestingly, associated with hosting the Olympic Games. In other spheres, best practice has been the adoption of new forms of combined economic and social accounting to assess the efficacy of urban regeneration projects; environmental auditing; self-help building projects; children-as-planners projects or citizen involvement in city budgeting.

5   Good practice: a realization that reaches a standard benchmark, replicated in a number of other cases, that may be easily described in codes of practice or good practice guides. Nowadays adopting consultation procedures within planning is an example, although at one stage the idea of consultation itself represented a paradigm shift and innovation. Other examples now include public/private partnerships to achieve area regeneration; the production of annual city reports; well-designed urban furniture; environmentally sustainable housing developments and energy efficient buildings; park and ride systems.

6   Bad practice: a continuation of a practice that has recognized weaknesses, such as urban motorways severing established residential areas or central shopping areas; creating social housing ghettos; wholesale demolition of old urban structures; neglecting the diversity of the ethnic make-up of cities. Such practices

invariably deny the possibility of sustainable development in the sense of fracturing communities and deepening social stress. Often they arise from ignorance and/or inertia. It is surprising how frequently bad practices continue in spite of the documented evidence of their negative effects.

7    Appalling practice: activities which consciously and deliberately work against the principle of creative, sustainable and equitable development, such as new property developments that totally neglect their urban context and raze traditional communities to the ground; ignoring the demands of the socially excluded and thus exacerbating cycles of decline; providing no consultation procedures for those affected by decisions. Again it is extraordinary how common such practices are.

Each phase, from paradigm shift to good practice, has its own life-cycle and is not etched infinitely in time. There is a kind of circular motion whereby new ideas lead to new practices, that are implemented well, then become common and may need reassessing again as they no longer cope with newly emerging tasks. Indeed a best practice may become a bad practice over time or be a bad practice from the outset in the wrong context. Paradigm shifts arise, because older ways of understanding or doing something are inadequate to the task at hand. For instance, the notion of sustainability arose as a concept and an aspiration in the face of growing dismay at the evidence of ecological mismanagement of the planet's resources triggered off by publications such as Rachel Carson's *Silent Spring* in 1962. Thus the sustainability paradigm took over from the previous 'growth at all costs' paradigm as the most appropriate means of organizing and ordering the world. Innovations like traffic calming, setting up cultural quarters to focus artistic activity in one place, electronic democracy, solar villages, etc were, over time, examples of best practice implementation and became merely a good practice as they popularized. Crucially, if the tried and tested continues too long in the face of new knowledge it becomes bad or even appalling practice.

In any city at any stage of development urban decision-makers need to ask whether a task can be more imaginatively executed in order to hit more targets, be cheaper or fulfil more complex objectives. There is a very long list of potential domains, topics or policy areas where creativity and innovativeness can be assessed through the taxonomy notion including: economic regeneration; addressing environmental issues; governance and evaluation, which are described below. Others are described in *Sustainable and Innovative Cities* including: social cohesion; communications and citizen involvement; transport – from traffic constraint to new ways of moving people around cities; urban infrastructure; how the building, financing and management of housing can be rethought and finally the role of culture to foster distinctiveness of place.

## Conceptual Issues

The taxonomy may be useful, but it also shows that classification is by no means simple or straightforward. A range of issues need to be considered and we will now discuss these in more detail in this section.

### Context, Time and Space Dependence

The most fundamental difficulty is that innovations appear, develop and are emulated, in specific contexts, at particular times and in certain geographic locations. Only a few, say the use of a technology like the Internet, diffuse seamlessly throughout the urban world, most others diffuse via networks of like-minded organizations in often erratic and unpredictable ways. Some countries, regions or cities tend to develop innovations earlier than others, because they are 'ready' for them. Objective factors are vital, such as a 'problem waiting to be solved' or the existence of a level of consciousness so decision-makers are ready to accept new ideas. As a consequence an innovation may diffuse quite widely, even though cities have barely begun to adopt the innovation. Germany for instance pioneered city centre pedestrianization, and it became standard in German cities in the mid-1970s, quite a long time before most other European countries. It was related to external factors, such as levels of car ownership and environmental awareness making traffic restraint an issue. More widely, the entire local resource base will determine the limits of the possible: the Finns developed the brilliantly innovative idea of a snow castle to generate tourism in the bitterly cold north, which would have been impossible in the south – but equally they could not have invented a solar village.

### Can Creativity and Innovation be Force Fed?

Innovations do not necessarily come singly and instead cluster in certain places at certain times, sometimes almost accidentally, sometimes as a matter of deliberate policy. Germany's Emscher project is one of the few examples of a deliberately planned cluster of innovative projects turning a weakness into a strength. An area left degraded by former industrialization became in essence a research and development zone to invent the solutions to degradation. Each project has interesting features, but what makes the scheme outstanding is the synergy between them making the whole achievement greater than the sum of the parts.

In assessing urban best practices throughout Europe the clusters we discovered around northern Switzerland, South Germany around Freiburg and Karlsruhe and in Alsace-Lorraine, as well as others in Emilia Romagna around Bologna and in Vienna were not self-consciously planned as in the case of Emscher Park. Crucially, they arose through competition, imitation and exchange of well-qualified personnel thus generating a creative milieu. The competition was not exclusively focused on economics narrowly defined, but rather on competition for a better quality of urban life in which culturally sustainable development was key and from which wealth has been generated. These range from progressive energy tariffs, designed to penalize profligate users, to innovations in the social domain, such as interesting ways of dealing with youth unemployment problems or illegal immigrants, as in Bologna.

## No Linear Progression

Innovations do not progress in a linear way. Urban creativity often involves daring to take the risk to go back into history and even repeat or reuse something from the past. The focus on recreating public squares rekindles the age old traditions of Italian medieval towns; the return to the local in part turns the clock back on globalization; the re-use of old industrial buildings recognizes their qualities in the use of fine materials that newer buildings find difficult to re-create. Perhaps most important of all the 'natural laws' of resource management adopted by indigenous peoples embed what we would call sustainability principles. For them to hear the West pontificate about culturally sustainable development appears to be returning to old truths. Their virtues were partly lost in time, falling back on them now appears imaginative and innovative, especially to those with shorter historical perspectives.

Thus innovation can frequently be cyclical: people return to ideas, approaches or projects, albeit at a different level of technology. The technologies or materials used to construct a square may change, but the core idea of creating a public realm remains the same.

## The Cultural Relativity of Innovativeness

Cultural factors often seen as intangible are key, which may mean a best practice in one case is bad practice in another. Liberal democratic attitudes are seen as an *a priori* good in the West, but not so in Singapore or the Islamic world. So the conceptual framework of the taxonomy itself is value laden, with a series of assumptions that need to be made explicit. The assumptions running throughout this book include the idea that creating ladders of opportunity to participate actively in economic, political and social life is an intrinsic good; that partnerships and linkages between diverse organizational types – public, private, voluntary – create interesting synergies; that culture itself, simplistically defined as 'who we are and what we believe in', is of over-riding importance in creating unique, distinctive urban environments. A single benchmark may be useful and possible for assessing innovations within Europe or within 'western society' more generally or within the Islamic world, but in many instances is unlikely to be applicable on a global basis.

This raises a fundamental question: are there principles of creative urban development that hold true, whatever the local circumstances? For example, are there urban design or urban vitality 'truths' that hold true throughout time and space, such as a 'golden mean' of spatial relationships in buildings or the collective 'truths' of Mumford, Lynch or Jacobs that may be applicable throughout urban history? Here again cultural factors come into play: the urban design principles of Islamic, Greek, Roman or Indian architecture have their own versions of what creates harmony or unity within buildings or how people 'should behave' in urban settings. Are these principles which derive from different cultural traditions compatible? At the most general level they often are in that they, for example, seek to ensure the right balance between private and public life or the relationship been outsiders and existing communities, but in detail there are substantial differences. In Islamic traditions it is essential that no outsider can see into someone else's home for fear of seeing a woman in inappropriate attire. Architecture has had to respond accordingly, such as higher boundary walls or the careful placing of windows.

Environmental sustainability principles, it appears, hold true throughout cultures, yet how they are implemented will differ. For example, mutual aid structures because of their collaborative principles, have a stronger rooting within some cultures, whereas others are more individualistic and may find such approaches go against the cultural grain. Not surprisingly American approaches to development are focused on incentives structures geared to market mechanisms and individual 'choices' as distinct from traditions that encourage collective action. Indeed, is an unfettered market useful and efficient in every cultural context?

## Replicability

Both cultural factors and level of development in a city can determine whether a project can be replicated. At first sight many projects seem replicable in principle, but in reality are not. Importantly an assessment of the causal mechanisms leading to the success of any project are crucial since the peculiarities of each situation will affect the outcome of any programme. As a consequence people are often disappointed that they cannot achieve the same results from a given programme. Thus replication of an innovative project, such as a *charette* – a form of visioning process – a cooperative housing scheme or recycling initiative, depends on the personalities, skills, experience of the people involved; the aims, agendas and relationships of project stakeholders; the location and social situation into which the project fits as well as level of resources available and time scale allowed.

## Unforeseen Weaknesses

Innovations or best practices can embody unforeseen or invisible weaknesses or begin to develop them over time. Pedestrianization may lead in some instances to dead streets at night, causing increases in crime and fear of crime. Thus as a response a mini-innovation, such as reversing the regime in the evening, may be necessary. Yet, even when such foreseen consequences emerge, they may themselves constitute an innovation: thus, empowering people through a charette may encourage them to undertake a different project in a novel way, as when Easterhouse residents in Glasgow set up their own betting shop to bypass the commercial providers, reasoning that since they were betting so much it might as well stay in local pockets. Thus creative solutions have within them both the seeds of possible reinventions as well as the seeds of their demise.

## Absolute and Relative Creativity

A project is rarely 'absolutely' creative in that it has never been thought of in that way. This would be a key innovation. It is more usual for projects to be relatively creative – creative in their circumstance or locality. Many urban decision-makers with little overview of the totality of innovative projects think their initiatives are creative even though a similar initiative might have taken place in a neighbouring country. There is nothing wrong with this in principle and it does not weaken a project, as long as they learn from the previous example. As noted it is ultimately not the absolute innovativeness that counts but whether a project deftly solves a problem. Indeed an innovation 'copied' into a more conservative environment may face as many problems in getting implemented as the original.

## Calculating the Cost of Best Practice

To our knowledge there has as yet been no city that has methodically calculated the financial, human resource, and organizational costs of applying a set of agreed and already established and learnt best practices across a number of fields. If the logic of the creative city holds together the commonly held opinions about best practices ranging from economic regeneration, to social development or environmental husbandry should place a city at a competitive advantage *vis-à-vis* others in the same position or maximize its potential. This is because a best practice is likely to contain a number of key features such as 'achieving more for less' by dealing with problems more effectively and efficiently. Creative best practices do not inevitably cost more, it is precisely in the nature of their creativity that they can save resources. The accounting procedures required to make such a cost assessment will need to be developmental and dynamic with wider criteria than the limited financial calculus normally applied, including estimates of direct and indirect social benefits, such as whether an initiative reduces crime in an area. The major problem is twofold – both an environment that fosters creativity as well as an insufficient number of people in any given city to carry out and follow through innovative ideas.

# LIFECYCLE THINKING

Every creative idea has a shelf life. Initiatives are launched, consolidated, mainstreamed, lead a useful life and then might need discarding. Lifecycle thinking sees the birth, fulfilment and decline process as natural and stands as a warning to complacency and rigid routinization. It gives a sense of evolutionary direction, the need for constant awareness of how well a project is performing and how intrinsically developmental urban creative ideas and innovations are. A 'lifecycle conscious' routine implies building in an innovations budget as well as embedding a monitoring or evalua-

**Table 8.1** *Economic regeneration*

|  | Example | Place and time |
|---|---|---|
| **Meta-paradigm** | Services as basis of wealth creation<br>– up to that point physical production had dominated | Boston, 1975 |
|  | Information and knowledge as driver of urban economy | Silicon Valley region, early 1990s |
| **Paradigm** | Urban Development Corporations<br>– giving special powers and autonomy to a lower authority to develop a part of a city<br>– opened up possibilities for the idea of public/private partnerships | New York, 1975 |
|  | Enterprise Zones<br>– special incentives and concessions to encourage the urban development process in either greenfield sites or deprived areas | London, 1981 |
| **Innovation** | Recycle old structures<br>– the prevalent approach until then had appeared like a 'slash and burn' policy<br>– recognition of how refurbishing the old fostered distinctiveness, identity and could generate money | Lowell, US, 1977 |
|  | Urban tourism and industrial tourism<br>– aside from key world cities such as Paris or London and cities with artistic treasures such as Florence, tourism had largely been associated with getting away from cities | mid-1970s |
| **Best practice** | Cultural cities<br>– using culture as a trigger for celebration, regeneration and marketing | Athens, started 1985 and continuing |
|  | European Union Cultural Capitals of Europe scheme | Barcelona, 1987 |
|  | Waterfront developments<br>– reintegrating older harbour areas into the urban fabric often leading to regeneration<br>– shipping activities shift from a trade focus to leisure | Baltimore, early 1980s |
| **Good practice** | Refurbishment of industrial buildings<br>– for multipurpose uses from offices, to arts centres or exhibition spaces to housing | 1980s onwards |
| **Bad practice** | Demolition of all old structures<br>– continuing practice that causes 'loss of memory' and social stress for existing communities as well as losing economic potential | Singapore, 1980s onwards |

Table 8.2 *Environment*

| | Example | Place and time |
|---|---|---|
| **Meta-paradigm** | Sustainable development | Oslo, 1987 and before (eg Club of Rome 1972 report *The Limits to Growth*) |
| **Paradigm** | Sustainable urbanism<br>Polluter pays principle<br>Regional sustainable development | Freiburg, early 1970s, 1980s<br><br>Emscher Park, 1991 onwards |
| **Innovation** | Sustainable transport | Amsterdam, early 1990s<br>Grenoble, Stockholm, 1997 |
| | Gas buses<br>Solar village<br>Air quality monitoring<br>Escalators as transport | Bristol, 1996<br>Near Athens, 1978<br>Strasbourg, 1971<br>Perugia, Orvieto, 1970s |
| **Best practice** | Environmental audit<br>Environment city<br>Autoplus | Mulhouse, 1991<br>eg Leicester, 1991<br>La Rochelle, 1991 |
| **Good practice** | Cycle network<br><br>Separated waste bins, backyard composting<br>Energy efficient building<br><br>Green railway strip | Montpellier, Amsterdam, 1970s<br>Oeiras, Portugal, 1993<br>Germany, early 1980s<br>Vienna, Hamburg, mid-1980s<br>Madrid, 1980s |
| **Bad practice** | Housing along heavily trafficked trunk roads | |

tion function allied to benchmarking to ensure adaptations and change are made when appropriate. This does not mean everything has to change continuously only that there is continual assessment. Some things will stay the same, the difference is they will have been reviewed to stay the same. Yet over the long-term most things will have changed. The creative city notion is an urban journey not a destination, it is a dynamic not a static endeavour. It requires an approach to problem-solving that feels a problem has never been completely dealt with. This is its internal driver. It does not imply restlessness, but awareness of notions such as total quality management where a continuous cycle of improvement is endemic.

**Table 8.3** *Governance*

|  | Example | Place and time |
|---|---|---|
| Meta-paradigm | Empowerment and social equity | 19th-century thinkers Skeffington report, UK, 1969 |
| Paradigm | Hierarchy to matrix plus other organizational structures | Management literature eg Morgan and Stenge, late 1980s |
|  | Participative design | eg Byker, Newcastle upon Tyne, 1970s |
|  | Development of the *charette* | US, 1975 |
| Innovation | Electronic democracy | 'Conversation with Oregon', 1989 Alaska Teleconference Network, 1990 |
|  | Public/private partnerships | US, late 1970s |
| Best practice | Internal restructuring towards openness | eg Kirklees, 1991 |
|  | Children's office | Unna, Germany or Neuchatel, early 1990s |
|  | Citizens' budgeting | Reggio Emilia, 1993 |
|  | Community ownership | Respond, Dublin, 1981 |
|  | Children as planners | Kitee, Finland, 1996 |
|  | Citizens' planning | Saltsjöbaden, 1992 |
|  | Women as planners | Örebro, 1992 |
| Good practice | Consultation procedures | |
|  | Voluntary groups as service providers | |
|  | Public/private partnering | Post-1990 |
| Bad practice | Ignoring community input | Frequent |

Lifecycle thinking provides a situational analysis and helps define whether a solution meets a need at hand. It helps decide when to innovate and when to leave things as they are, even those aspects of an organization that are already routinized. Every internal organizational element as well as external projects should be subject to review and potentially be innovated. A danger is that creative projects are developed at the margins without affecting or threatening the workings of the organizational core itself. They tend to become an add-on to solve a problem, when often, in fact, it is the core itself that is the cause of the problem. Creativity implies a new organizational and management ethos where adaptation and redesign are ever present. It suggests questions, such as: Have we

## Table 8.4 *Evaluation*

| | Example | Place and time |
|---|---|---|
| **Meta-paradigm** | Merger economic and social accounting | 1980s |
| **Paradigm** | Benchmarking | Xerox, 1975 |
| **Innovation** | Community Impact Evaluation | Nathaniel Lichfield, 1957 |
| | Social accounting | Social Audit movement, 1976 |
| | Urban visioning | US, early 1980s |
| | Oregon Benchmarks agreed via legislative process | Oregon, 1989 |
| **Best practice** | New indicators movement | ISEW, Stockholm and New Economics Foundation, 1980s onwards |
| **Good practice** | Annual city reports | early 1990s |
| | Public monitoring | ealry 1990s |
| **Bad practice** | No public feedback | |

built momentum? Does the project need consolidating? Has a particular creative project run its course? Does it need reconfiguring? Should it be diffused? In this way self-consciousness about the development process is achieved. The lifecycle idea provides an analytical framework to ask questions that act as a checklist for action and to assess progress. In assessing the situation of an innovation and how well it is doing, policy-makers can usefully break down the phases of a project and ask questions in the following areas.

- Launch issues: What was the purpose and origin of an innovation? What problem was being addressed? What is the nature and extent of the problem? How did the innovation come about, what was its conception? What made it possible? Who was involved, what interests and power machinations came into play? Who paid for it? How has it been dealt with before?
- Momentum building and consolidation issues: How has the innovation evolved? What experiments have been necessary? How is it being implemented? What stages and difficulties has the innovation gone through to reach its current form? Which aspects were predictable and which unexpected? What were the obstacles that blocked its progress and how did it affect the

evolution? How did the panoply of interests settle? What processes of monitoring and evaluation have been undertaken? Who supported the project and why? What have we learnt from the process?

■  Horizontal diffusion: How widely has the innovation been disseminated geographically? Throughout the city? By what process? A proliferation of pilot projects? Has it been mainstreamed into policy, if not why not? Has it been upscaled or replicated? What is its impact in new locations, did it need adapting? If so why? How was the innovation promoted and marketed?

■  Vertical diffusion: Has the innovation been incorporated into policy? Has it cascaded throughout structures into the heart of an organization? At what level – the neighbourhood, city, region, state? Was the innovation adapted as it entered policy? What was added, what was left out? Why? Did this strengthen or weaken it? What has the effect on its impact been as it was replicated? How is it being funded? Through what budget?

■  Problem redefinition/second-cycle innovations: Have the nature, purpose and goals of the innovation changed as it goes through the cycle of urban creativity? Has the original problem been solved or changed in the process? Has the innovation led to a chain of subsequent innovations? Has the innovation paradigmatically changed the issue at hand or has it only incrementally affected it?

This useful five-part analytical framework for looking at the phases of innovative projects, is derived from Hopkins (1994), whose questions have been adapted for use here.

## Issues and Implications

### The Right Skills at the Right Time

Each innovation phase requires different qualities of the creative person or innovator and it is rare that these are found in one person. Being both an instigator and consolidator and then being able to live with routinization is unusual. A classic dilemma for organizations is to recognize when changing the guard is necessary, if the organizational task changes. At the outset entrepreneurial drive and risk taking is key; in the consolidation phase administrative and fundraising qualities and the tenacity to follow through and to deal with legislative or policy implementation issues come to the fore.

That is why innovations, as distinct from the creative idea, are often associated with organizations, rather than individuals, so that the diversity of these skills is spread across a team. Yet each phase of an innovation has a different feel organizationally. Similar issues emerge when replicating ideas; the drive and charisma of the first community bank or first cooperative recycling scheme is difficult to duplicate and new rewards and motivations need to be found to sustain enthusiasm, such as 'this is the first type of project here!' What organizational structures are conducive to generating the enthusiasm for continuous innovation? Here we can learn from organizations within the new tech industries such as multi-media or the consultancy world. These often form flexible teams based around specific tasks with a small organizational core to drive the administrative structure. Talent is brought in on an 'as required basis' and, whilst working procedures may have a structured pattern, the make-up of the group undertaking different tasks varies.

The capacity to assess what kind of innovation is right at any given moment is key. Timing is everything. In Helsinki, for example, it may currently be important to open out bureaucratic structures to unleash dormant potential or find ways of harnessing energies in a slightly bizarre way. At a later point in the journey a more consolidating approach might be appropriate, one that takes stock, ponders and considers future moves and only then moves ahead to a new creative plateau.

Closing in when openness is required or opening out when quiet consideration is right can throw plans into disarray, waste resources and effort and jeopardize success. The problem is that those in power often rose on the last wave of need but have now entrenched themselves when in fact different characteristics are required for the next stage. Additionally cycles of renewal and replacement within public authorities are traditionally slower, because they are based on timeless rules.

## *Lack of Trust in and Recognition of Radicals*

The role of radicals, activists, campaigners and grassroots movements is severely underestimated in launching and building momentum for innovations, especially in less technologically advanced areas. Community leaders and social mobilizers have been at the forefront of urban innovations throughout history, they are closest to the issues as they usually live in neighbourhoods with the severest problems (see Hall and Landry, 1997). Most mainstream ideas were started by a radical. The policy implication is for the mainstream to look to, listen to and be sympathetic to the radicals, inside and outside the organization.

The historic role of radicals even stretches to the consultative mechanisms now accepted as part of what makes a modern, caring company or public sector organization. The central role of outsider groups or alternative movements has been documented by Art Kleiner in *The Age of Heretics* (1996). Even the innovative empowerment structures in corporations had their origins in a body of intellectual work in the post-war period whose roots lay in Western and Eastern spiritual traditions, in new types of social science and humanistic psychology and the counter-culture of the 1960s. Their heretical ideas have gradually moved into the mainstream becoming the operating premises of institutions – commercial and public – worldwide.

## Moving from the Outside to the Inside

The weakness of alternative structures is that they usually lack the resources to implement their ideas, and if they do there are problems of continuity and sustainability. Indeed their innovations often address only a symptom of a larger systemic problem, that is too difficult and contentious to tackle, involving entrenched power structures that may be causing the problem in the first place. A way out is to creatively broaden the ambit of concerns. For example, a graffiti problem may only be an expression of a problem somewhere else. Thus the Dortmund–Scharnhorst project to involve graffiti artists cleaning their graffiti as part of a job creation scheme and extending that later to the setting up of a waste disposal business dealt with several problems at once. Brokering some form of acceptance by the official structure is crucial. It is not straightforward. At one moment direct protest action may seem appropriate, at another 'constructive debate' and at yet another setting up an alternative project independently. The final move may be to join the mainstream by becoming part of the political structure in order to pursue certain ideas – often innovations – from within the official structure.

## Scaling Up and Replicating

At each stage of the urban innovation process are distinctive hurdles. In the inception phase lack of belief is a problem; in the implementation phase and as acceptance looms the role of institutional support and funding becomes vital. The step from launching pilot

## THE RADICALS' IMPACT ON SUSTAINABILITY: AN EXAMPLE

The central role of radicals can most clearly be seen in the trajectory of acceptance of sustainability. It came onto the political agenda through intense lobbying over decades by committed authors such as Rachel Carson and her book *Silent Spring* and later more organized outsider environmental groups of which Greenpeace or Friends of the Earth are the best known. This was then legitimized by mainstream bodies such as the Club of Rome with its first report 'Limits to Growth', which brought the wider policy-making world into the discussion. Their latest report *Factor Four – Doubling Wealth and Halving Resource Use* has had a similar effect, whilst most examples are being implemented by commercial firms they were forced to listen to by pressure groups.

Initiatives such as waste recycling; car sharing schemes; social auditing; recycling industrial buildings for alternative uses; or innovative ways of dealing with unemployment have been initially instigated through pressure groups, civil society organizations, activists and even groups treading beyond the law such as squatters who take over buildings. Indeed squatters created innovations that are now seen to contribute to sustainability. Apparently useless spaces were left to degrade and have been regenerated through self-help groups, thus empowering those involved and often housing people who were otherwise homeless. They re-invented new usage combinations in buildings, such as working space combined with living and exhibition space, often providing support services such as cafes and restaurants which later became attractive to the mainstream because of the ambience they created.

These pressure groups in turn, over time, have been able to promote some underlying issues – such as ecological living, social housing, alternative financing mechanisms or concepts of recycling – into the political arena and urban policy. They have then become legitimized, mainstreamed and as a result scaled up. For innovations to achieve maximum impact, they need scaling up and replicating. Sadly the majority of innovations stay small and low key, are not disseminated and thus remain largely unknown. If they do get past these hurdles they do so: 'through a protracted process fraught with obstructions and delays' (Hopkins, 1994).

projects to mainstreaming is fraught with difficulty. A number of choices need addressing. Should the creative idea be incorporated throughout a structure? Should it be separately branded, say by being identified with an agency? Should it be carried out by the originating organization itself? Here dangers emerge since implementing a widespread innovation programme may blunt an organization's capacity to stay innovative. The organization's skill may be to be creative, to conceptualize, innovate or think and not implement. When ideas diffuse and become accepted new organizational dynamics come into play, yet many believe working with established procedures will create the greatest impact, although 'innovations requiring new legislation are unlikely to be implemented, because there are too many decision points at which the idea could be vetoed. It may be more effective to incorporate reform into existing bureaucratic systems and therefore advocate supporting innovation at the level of the street level bureaucrat' (Weatherley and Lipsky, 1977). The danger is assuming the legislative framework is pliable enough to allow for sufficient reconfiguration. Whilst legislation is a cumbersome tool in a period of paradigm shifts every plank of the structure needs rethinking, including legislation. The turning point is incorporating creative ideas into ongoing policy and the agreement to replicate widely. Once they become part of overall policy, innovations usually attain more substantial resources for implementation. An example would be setting up dedicated programmes such as encouraging energy saving in houses. Another approach is to reallocate existing resources to new priorities and re-branding them for a new purpose.

One overall aspect of legislation that needs assessing in the context of the creative city is to provide a legislative context and framework within which creativity can develop. This means creating core legislation such as advanced intellectual property rights or copyright laws that allow innovative activities to flourish within explicit rules. Then applying, adapting or interpreting existing general laws, such as those on finance, so they foster innovation. This highlights the need to create a cascading set of regulatory mechanisms with varying degrees of enforceability and power. At the apex would stand constitutional issues, with a bearing on innovation and creativity, below that a limited number of specific laws, such as setting up a government endowment to encourage innovation; and at the bottom a series of regulations, measures, guidelines, policies and programmes. Within these latter mechanisms a city, region or state can guide policy and create substantial impact.

# URBAN R&D

Everything is in a name. To call an activity 'Urban R&D' gives it credence and legitimacy; it sends out a signal of intentions and has symbolic resonance. The concept of 'Urban R&D' might sound like a glorified name for pilot projects. It is much more and it highlights the importance of pilot projects not as a series of one-offs, but as part of a structured approach to experimentation. It implies mechanisms are present to encourage pilot projects and for a city to have links with any movements that gather and promote urban experiments, best practices and databases thereof. Through this process new practices are encouraged.

In the hierarchy of change, clearly the most profound and transformative learning experiences come from doing something oneself; secondly by visiting a good and relevant urban example with a peer group; and then finally learning about a best practice by reading about it or seeing it on television (Landry, 1995).

## *Urban R&D Budgets and Departments*

When cities have departments called 'Urban R&D' or 'Urban Market Research' it will change their organizational culture. By self-consciously allocating a budget to experiments, perhaps called a 'creativity and innovation fund', imaginative activity would be made legitimate. This might be within an overall budget or within a sub-budget. It may only be 1 per cent of a municipal budget – perhaps not much compared to some companies which may allocate up to 15 per cent – but by labelling an amount the issue is forced onto the agenda and demands political will. It seeks to avoid the situation where overworked managers might say 'I am too busy to think strategically' when it is precisely their lack of strategy which makes them too busy in the first place.

The concept of research and development is embedded in industrial firms, without it they could not survive in competitive markets. Every major multinational has an R&D department, if not they would be deemed irresponsible, storing up problems for the future, not thinking of the sustainability of the company or their next generation of employees, products and services; not protecting their existing assets. The same is true for cities. They are even more complicated than firms and have organizational structures with multiple objectives and targets; provide products and services; have to husband resources; and are answerable in the one case to stakeholders, in the other to citizens. Although they are in competition, which drives the need for self-improvement, they also need to self-improve for other, internal reasons. Enhancing a city's quality of life both makes it attractive to outsiders – say potential investors – but also ultimately reduces costs to maintain the city for itself. If there is less crime, graffiti or vandalism it saves costs. If there are more empowered individuals who are self-motivated costs are saved too. If a city can achieve more with less resources it is competitive, because it can offer its citizens more.

Cities may say 'we already have an "Urban R&D" department, but we don't call it R&D, we call it a strategy division or economic development department'. That is not quite the same. Strategy departments are like a compass or periscope looking at the forward scenery, sensing opportunities and threats and responding as appropriate. It is not a structured response mechanism to self-consciously generate creative inventions; nor do they actively search, develop and implement innovations. Economic development divisions may foster innovations, but only within their circumscribed remit, they do not normally encourage or fund social innovations.

## The Rise of Best Practice and Benchmarking

The concept of best practice has become popular over the last decade as a means of developing a 'culture of excellence within cities' (Badshah, 1996). The interest in best practice has had a different trajectory within business and the public sphere. In business it was linked to benchmarking – a way of measuring a firm's achievements against others. Benchmarking traces its roots to the strategic planning movement which gained momentum in the 1960s. As one of many of the popular strategic planning tools which provided frameworks for managers to think about the issues and challenges facing their organizations, benchmarking enriched strategic planning and is linked to best practice, since it means 'the search for best practices that lead to superior performance'. The Xerox Corporation are believed to have been the first company to have introduced benchmarking in the late 1970s – an innovation that is credited with contributing significantly to the company's turnaround. Benchmarking is a continuous and systematic process of evaluating the services, products and work processes of organizations that are recognized as representing best practices to improve an organization. Benchmarking can take various forms:

- Cooperative: a city might contact another, seen as representing best practice in a particular activity and to seek to share its knowledge.
- Competitive: a city compares what a competitor is doing and how well. The objective is to arrive at a sense of the competitor city's practices and their advantages and without sharing a more developed understanding of its own practices.
- Collaborative: the city makes a self-conscious effort to share knowledge through active joint learning.
- Internal: used by large organizations, such as urban authorities, to identify best in-house practices and to disseminate the knowledge about these practices to others in the organization. (Adapted from Spendolini, 1992).

## *A Beyond Best Practice Observatory*

Urban pilot projects are the lifeblood of a city that seeks forward momentum. As with each analytical technique assessing when to instigate pilot projects depends on an analysis of the situation. When or where to locate pilot projects depends on a truthful assessment of how things are going; if a benchmarking review shows a city is performing well against its competitors or against city specific indicators no action may be required. Nevertheless for a city to advance it either needs its own urban experiments in most areas of concern or be aware of others, even though many experiments will naturally fail. Otherwise it cannot know what does and does not work and will fall back on the tried and tested solutions that may have been invented for a former era. Yet a city cannot do all the urban experiments itself, it needs 'a best and worst practice observatory' in which to gather the best ideas from elsewhere and to assess how they can be appropriately adapted to their city. In this way it can evolve its benchmarking process, maintain its competitive advantage through close contact with best practice models and become a learning city. Yet knowing about best practices is only the start – the creative city constantly attempts to get beyond other people's best practices and to develop its own.

Staying in touch with best practice, whether through direct experience or databases, benchmarking enables authorities to shorten their learning curves, reduce R&D expenditure, save on experimentation costs and the development of pilot projects as well as increase contacts with leading-edge practitioners. To stay ahead of and in touch with interesting and relevant experience a structured and proactive approach to information gathering is a pre-requisite. This allows experiences to be channelled, assessed and monitored and demands continuity and consistency as good information is a competitive resource. Most private sector firms have this understanding and engage in competitor analysis and the like, which is less frequent in local authority worlds. A 'best practice office', whether inside or outside the public structure, offers an institutional mechanism. If given appropriate status, by perhaps working to a 'strategy board' it can underpin, expand and reinforce a culture of creativity and innovation. Crucially, the idea of best practice must be assessed critically to ensure that lessons are applicable, relevant and replicable in divergent urban contexts. A consensus is emerging as to what is 'best', namely 'good projects, that have worked elsewhere, and that may be replicable in my city'. There is increased understanding that best practice is about learning, not ranking. It is this reflexive process that yields continuous learning. In analysing good practices it is most useful to assess how practices came about, what the conditions and critical factors were for success and failure, how they were financed, organized, managed and disseminated.

Cities will claim they do this monitoring, yet rarely is it a publicly accessible, open institutional mechanism whose primary role is to proactively seek best practice issues out and to assess their implications and replicability for the city in question. If it were, there would be public dialogue about where a city is going. Best practices are generally gathered on a project by project basis as needs arise. Christchurch, New Zealand, a winner of the Bertelsmann prize for local authority innovation, is an exception. It scours good ideas from various countries to test their applicability to Christchurch. Their best practice search in the late 1990s was for new performance indicators and internal local authority arrangements.

The office would need to be proactive, making contacts with existing networks, searching for and following up interesting examples garnered from hear-say or databases, according to criteria that are relevant to a city's needs. Drawing attention to good examples, it would have authority to engage public and private partners in discussion about replication. It would be entrepreneurial, spotting opportunities, linkages and synergies. It would publicly bring the leading edge to the city. Over time it might actively research the interests of key stakeholders to tailor information gathering to local needs. There might even be a best practice one-stop information shop in the city to foster debate amongst citizens, as well as having information online. A number of organizations worldwide have been gathering best practice given the shift from emphasizing the discussion of problems to identifying and disseminating solutions. These are listed in the bibliography.

## Experimentation Zones and Programmes

Cities usually introduce experiments within functional areas such as housing or social services, yet problems such as urban deprivation have multiple dimensions that can only be addressed comprehensively. Recent studies show that area-based responses to regeneration are far more effective, linking integrated economic, social, cultural and environmental approaches. This can only be achieved through cross-departmental working and devolving power downwards to the locality and partnership-based structures. It may be an idea to create 'experimentation zones' in a city where interlocking and mutually interdependent and reinforcing policies can be tried out and the classic regulatory and incentive regimes are put on hold. This has happened in a number of instances, although not all called 'experimentation zones', with varying results.

The Emscher Park IBA project was a deliberately planned cluster of over 100 quite substantial projects that simultaneously pursued goals of economic restructuring, physical rehabilitation and environmental improvement. The individual projects are interesting in themselves, but what makes the scheme outstanding is the synergy between them, which makes the whole achievement much greater than the sum of the parts. This experimentation zone was clever, because it helped fund innovations within a spatial area acting as a gateway to resources with strong criteria focused on creative solutions, but it had no planning powers whatsoever. Urban Development Corporations in the UK were a less successful attempt where planning regulations were substantially relaxed and cheap loans made available to get a property-led regeneration process off the ground, but its notion of regeneration was far too limited.

The European Union Urban Pilot Projects scheme, described earlier, is another structured innovations scheme as is the Innovations in American Government Program of the Ford Foundation and Harvard's John F. Kennedy School of Government. Each year 25 awards are given to develop replication materials and put on conferences. Ford funds similar programmes in Brazil, the Philippines, South Africa and Chile (see Tayart de Borms, 1996;

Power and Mumford, 1999 and Urban Pilots Project Annual Report, 1996, 1997).

## Diffusing Urban R&D: The Role of Information Flows and Databases

New computing technology gave an impetus for creating urban best practice databases; a main way of disseminating innovations. Databases exist to share information, act as a lobby and advocacy tool; to encourage cities to document good practices, to foster exchange and transfer useful experience; to motivate and to give confidence to decision-makers. Yet we have reached the end of the first phase of the 'best practice idea' as a number of questions have emerged, including: Who decides what goes into a database and on what basis under what criteria? Who writes descriptions that end up in a database – the project itself, the database provider or evaluator? Either course has strengths and weaknesses. When written by the project you can hear the voices of those involved, and this has a value in its own right. How are the best practices evaluated and monitored? What is the exact definition of a 'best practice'? What impact do they have on the ground? Does the proliferation of databases confuse the user, or alternatively is it valuable to maintain a series of databases whose background philosophy or ideology is different? What about the many examples of best practice that do not find their way into databases. Databases are also a gatekeeping mechanism. The UN database, for example, was built up by a call for best practices, which initially elicited 700 examples. The UN procedure used a two-stage evaluation process involving technical experts with experience of developments and an international jury deciding on selection. Whilst the selection procedure was as objective as possible, certain countries and projects 'had to be included'. Their objective is to develop towards a growing list of 500 global best practices awards with a much bigger back-up list, possibly running into several thousand, which will simply serve as a reference list. (For a full discussion of databases of best practice see Hall and Landry, 1998.)

### Can Databases Drive Urban R&D?

Databases provide a starting point for discovery and a networking tool. All the main database providers recognize that the greatest impact is: 'To actually see and feel a project, to live it in some way.'

This can only occur by face to face contact with key actors involved in any best practice. Yet by spreading information, databases act to speed up the process of innovations transfer. The myriad questions a researcher in a new project needs answering are unpredictable and based on individual circumstances. Beyond basic questions like 'how did a project happen, who was involved, how much did it cost and what was its impact', such questions cannot easily be formatted in a structured and cost-effective way. Most of the organizations that summarize good solutions are faced with a dilemma of how to fulfil the expectations a database generates. Whilst most cities are pleased to be included on a best practice database for promotional and self-affirming reasons, inclusion can have negative effects. Some are overwhelmed by enquiries and visitors which can take time away from actually doing the job. And explaining to visitors what they have done costs time and resources, for which a project is usually not funded.

## *Where Next with Information Flows?*

As the first stage of best practice and innovations databases draws to a close, new issues emerge. In the first rush to produce databases of good urban innovations, many projects included were in their initial stages, whereas innovations with real impact take many years to mature and show their real effects. People forget how an innovation or best practice, that is now ordinary good practice, came about in the first place. Yet real innovations and best practices stand the test of time.

Historic innovations are excluded in best practices described in databases, as they cover predominantly the last five years. For example, the greenbelt initiatives developed in the UK and elsewhere in Europe in the early post-war period remain as relevant today as they did then and their implementation today in many European countries would be regarded as novel. It can still be insructive to include an old innovation in a database, especially as its long-term effects will be much clearer. Many examples highlighted as best practices now will not stand the test of time and may end up as failures.

The combined databases are not truly representative as many are self-selecting. Amsterdam's interesting traffic solutions; Hannover's early light rail system; Munich's advanced pedestrianization; Barcelona's outstanding urban regeneration based on the Olympic Games; or Bologna's youth culture centres are all missing.

As the core audiences are largely municipalities their initiatives are covered well and those of NGOs reasonably well.

Five important categories are weakly represented in databases. The first is very small projects, typically undertaken by voluntary groups. The issue is perhaps not to describe each in detail, since they would run into thousands quite rapidly, but instead to think of describing themes and groupings of initiatives, say on local recycling, self-build or LETS (local exchange trading) schemes that give the reader a flavour of innovation evolution. Secondly, by focusing on one or two examples within an area, like car sharing, one does not get a sense of the movement of innovation that is occurring. For example, the Stattauto scheme in Berlin is described on a number of databases, yet there are now nearly 300 such initiatives in Europe alone. Thirdly, there is no database of culturally inspired innovations. A widely quoted example is how, in 1990, environmental artist Jim Lundy grassed over Melbourne's main thoroughfare, Swanston Street, overnight, with the blessing of Victoria's head of planning, to give it over to public use for a short period. This action raised a heated debate and led to the first pedestrianization programme in central Melbourne. A fourth omission concerns trade union activities, and finally a gap remains with online business best practices. Two other areas are missing: a database of regulatory mechanisms and incentives. National operating context determines much, but it would be useful to know which tax incentives or regulations were used to foster innovative and sustainable urban development. What energy-saving tax regimes exist at a national level that have been applied locally? What levers have cities or governments used to get businesses to act in an environmentally or culturally friendly way? What banking laws exist that foster local development in deprived areas? What tax rebate structures exist to guide urban development towards creative sustainability? What national guidelines exist that can encourage greater use of public transport? Finally, most interesting would be a database of failures. It is unlikely that public authorities would fund such an exercise, whereas a foundation may have fewer qualms. Discussing obstacles to implementation truly reveals important lessons that can be shared.

Lastly there is the problem of evaluation. Objectively assessing a complicated, multi-faceted project can take anything from one day to one week and as there are around 2,000 European examples on the joint databases which might take around 25–30 person years to evaluate and monitor. An approach that focuses on the principles and factors of success is more appropriate when combined with 'themeing' groups of innovations, say in finance, as well as historic innovations that still have something to teach to the present.

# 9

# Assessing and Sustaining the Creative Process

## The Cycle of Urban Creativity

The 'cycle of urban creativity' is a dynamic concept, which attempts to create a form of urban energy that will drive a city like a renewable resource. It is not simply concerned with charging a city with a few volts of electricity to bring a dying corpse back to life. It provides a mechanism to assess the strengths and weaknesses of creative projects in a city at various stages of their development. It is a useful conceptual device and organizing principle that gives an overview of inventive projects and is a primary strategic tool. A city can assess whether there is sufficient encouragement or initiatives to get ideas and projects off the ground, then implemented and circulated so that a new flow of projects and ideas are generated. An urban decision-maker can then ask: 'Are we doing enough to harness the creativity of our citizens and making it work for us?' When self-consciously applied it helps assess whether a creative milieu exists or there is potential to have one. The cycle can be thought of as five stages:

1   Helping people generate ideas and projects.
2   Turning ideas into reality.
3   Networking, circulating and marketing ideas and projects.
4   Delivery mechanisms such as cheap spaces for rent, incubator units or exhibition and showcasing opportunities.
5   Disseminating results to the city, building markets and audiences and discussing these so that new ideas are generated.

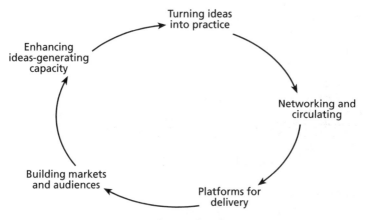

**Figure 9.1** *The Cycle of Creativity*

The fifth stage then stimulates stage one to start over again. If the cohort of roughly 300 people who have gone through the process in Huddersfield do not generate a new set of ideas and projects or do not inspire a new group to think 'if they can do that, so can I' nothing is gained. When the cycle works it provides a collective sense that a city is being changed for the better as cities are often their own worst enemy, putting themselves down and self-deprecating first before an outsider can do so. The cycle then becomes positive, creating a virtuous circle of invention, reflection and reinvention.

The objective is for a city to make judgements about how strong or weak it is within any of the stages, so it can decide how it should or can intervene. For example, how good is our city at generating new product ideas or can our city turn ideas into real products and services? Ideally there should be a balance of projects within each stage. Such judgements are inevitably place specific. Yet it is possible for a city to benchmark itself within each phase against a comparable city to assess how well it is doing. Comparators need to be appropriate. A city like Glasgow in the colder north should not necessarily compare itself across all dimensions with a sunnier Barcelona. It might be more appropriate to compare Glasgow with an equivalent cold northern port city like Gothenburg.

Within technology driven sectors, the technology transfer arena and strategic economic development organizations think through the logic addressed by the cycle of urban creativity. They highlight process cycles like incubation, implementation and dissemination or the balance of projects across the value chain from ideas generation to production, circulation, delivery and dissemination. As yet the concept has not been applied to assessing the overall creativity of a city.

Creative urban projects of various types, from economic to social, cultural and environmental, and different stages in the production process are rarely if ever seen as part of an interconnected creative totality. To apply the cycle of urban creativity in this way will normally be the first time a city has put – side by side as equally interesting, valid and important – a range and combination of projects, large and small. Seen in this way they form part of an integrated milieu. Not everyone would agree that the Helsinki voluntary group, Suburbs Up, which tries to get disaffected youth involved in their estates through cultural initiatives, is as equally creative as Culminatum. This internationally oriented technology transfer project takes ideas through research to saleable product by part-financing and coordinating the collaboration between companies and scientists.

Traditionally the worlds they represent are seen as having little in common; technological and economic creativity has greater status and credibility, even though cultural creativity is gaining legitimacy. Their common factor is their capacity to address or solve problems relevant to Helsinki in new, value adding ways. Yet adding value is seen normally only in a financial context, less often in how a social project might indirectly create monetary value for a community. Simply raising awareness of common creative ground could initiate a learning context, such as how they came up with solutions or overcame obstacles. Creative projects are a city's vanguard. Their common identity is their creative approach, yet there is usually no common language between them. Most projects are not aware of what others are doing; as a rule key people do not know each other, except within like-minded clusters. People still retrench into their disciplines and do not learn across disciplines. Essentially there are a number of divides: between those concerned with the cutting edge of technology and business development and those concerned with cultural activities or social development. In an analysis of 30 innovative Helsinki projects only a few broke the divide, they include: the Arabianranta project with the University of Art and Design leading a long-term integrated area renewal initiative and Valon Voimat – The Festival of Light – which celebrates light in the winter.

The cycle idea encourages interconnections. The continual danger remains that thinking on 'innovation' gets boxed into the technology areas and discussion on 'creativity' into the artistic and cultural sphere. Yet connections between the different creativities – scientific, cultural, social and economic – can create new synergies. The conclusion of an evaluation on Sci–Art, a project which linked artists and scientists and attracted 450 proposals, concludes: 'The forces at work during the process of collaboration between scientist and artist in effect work together to stimulate a new kind of creativity, creating something which is a synthesis out of the scientific and artistic mind' (Cohen, 1998).

## The Cycle of Urban Creativity in Action

Huddersfield, with its Creative Town Initiative, the European Union funded Urban Pilot Project (UPP), is perhaps the first city that has used the 'cycle of urban creativity' for urban strategy development. The cycle can be explained with reference to some of their initiatives. The fact that Huddersfield with 120,000 inhabitants is relatively small shows that the creative city idea does not only apply to larger conurbations at the heart of a country. The aim of Huddersfield's Creative Town strategy is to use the cycle idea to help decision-making. Starting in 1996 the objective is to create, by 2003, a place that tangibly enriches talented individuals and provides opportunities for them to turn concepts into products, thereby helping Huddersfield become a wealth-creating town. Huddersfield's initial focus is to bring about a linkage between arts and cultural creativity and technological creativity. From these connections so many future goods and services will be generated. Over time the focus will broaden to include environmental and social innovations.

The specific objectives are: to raise awareness within the whole community of the strategic importance of creativity and innovation; to aid talented Huddersfield people to turn their ideas into reality; to develop programmes that can help discover and harness hidden creativity and potential; to prepare the key network of organizations within Huddersfield to the organizational changes required to compete in the 21st century; to cluster groupings of talented people in a set of buildings as a means of encouraging critical mass and when appropriate to attract external talent; to circulate best practice experience; to set up a skills and knowledge brokerage service in the locality and beyond; to influence the objectives and focus of other public programmes where they believe they could benefit from a creativity led approach.

## Generating Ideas and Projects: Stage One

The starting point is the existence of creative ideas and ideas generation capacity in a city. This can be measured by the availability of patents, copyrights, brands or trademarks held by individuals, companies or associated with the city as well as the number of new businesses being set up, the amount of people in the city well-known in their field. Even the general buzz and ambience is a measure as this encourages interaction. Most cities have a mass of people who are not reaching their potential either through background, personal history or objective conditions. They may fall into crime, create social disruption or simply feel depressed. This is a cost to a city in terms of remedial services or dealing with the consequences of their actions. It is in a city's interest to spend resources to nurture them and create aspiration.

Huddersfield's response to foster 'ideas generating capacity' has been to initiate projects such as the Creativity Forum; a Creative Skills Development Programme and an extensive computer literacy programme. They in turn have spun off a series of other initiatives. We describe two examples, whose core notion can be appropriately replicated elsewhere.

The Creativity Forum is a programme that stresses the importance of creative solutions to survive and prosper in the new economy. The Forum provides a gateway in an informal setting where 'collisions' can take place between people with creative potential and those with the resources to turn them into reality. In part it acts as a referral agency and meeting point between industry, the university and the community. It matches experienced practitioners with local people who have imaginative ideas or brings together specialists and innovators in diverse fields to meet to assess needs and explore the potential for mutual collaborations. The objective is to establish a climate in the town in which free-ranging dialogue and discourse can take place between people and organizations which, under normal circumstances might not come into contact with each other. In the public events programme creative achievers explain how they got to where they are and seek to inspire others to follow their potential. This they regard as the first step on the ladder of success for the innovators of tomorrow.

The Creative Skills Development Programme – the LAB project – is a personal development and community capacity-building initiative. It has already achieved astonishing results and comprises a series of two-week courses for 20 participants from all age groups who have been unemployed and/or alienated from traditional educational and employment pathways. Through the medium of drama training practical and vocationally transferable skills such as interpersonal communication, teamwork, planning, public presentation are taught as well as a personal development action plan created. Each course ends with participants planning and participating in a challenging practical project. It seeks to address the problem that Huddersfield, like many industrial cities, has of alienated, unfulfilled individuals whose potential talents have not been tapped into and whose energies have turned towards petty crime, vandalism, depression or drug abuse. The objective is to draw these groups more into the mainstream by showing how their latent skills can contribute to the development of Huddersfield as a creative town. The innovative element lies in the application of artistic techniques to the development of transferable vocational skills in unemployed people.

These two examples are linked to Huddersfield's needs and aspirations. As with the other stages of the cycle there are many other ways a city can address ideas-generating capacity including: new ideas competitions; public creativity courses; allowing children to be planners on pilot projects or urban visioning exercises and the many techniques associated with this, such as Open Space Technology, Future Search, Urban Design Action Teams or Community Appraisals.

## Turning Ideas into Reality: Stage Two

Stage two in the cycle asks: 'Is there enough capacity focused on turning ideas into production?' 'Are the people, financial and other resources and productive capacities available to aid the transformation of ideas into marketable products?' 'Is there an adequate training infrastructure to provide the appropriate production skills base for each sector?'

Huddersfield's projects include: The Creative Business Development Training Company, which seeks to provide active learning and business opportunities for young entrepreneurs and innovators in the cultural and knowledge based industries; the associated Micro-Business Innovation Scheme, which provides intensive support to currently unemployed people who have a strong innovative business idea but who lack the support and finance to develop it; The Media Industry Development Scheme, which provides hands-on, customized consultancy services to promising new media businesses rather than generic business advice. One of the brokerage projects, the Advisory Service for Inventors, offers a first-point-of-contact advisory and feasibility assessment service to people with innovatory products and concepts in order to assess likely market potential, to provide initial patent protection and undertake product searches, to assist in developing prototyping and market research. A series of other initiatives seek to connect innovators to investors either within mainstream financial services or through its links to the Business Angels Network, a possibility that was laughed out of court when the initiative started in 1997. The Network now is literally falling over itself to get involved. The conservatism of mainstream financial institutions, and the exclusion of new companies from resources to fund growth, is one of the most serious impediments to the process of turning creativity into enterprise. Through links to the Network it seeks to identify and build up a group of private investors who are interested in supporting innovative entrepreneurs through the injection of equity and expertise.

### Networking, Circulating and Marketing Ideas and Products: Stage Three

To make a creative city sustainable there need to be sufficient marketers, impresarios, managers, agencies, distributors, wholesalers, packagers and assemblers of products. In response Huddersfield has created a series of advocacy, marketing and public visibility projects to help sell the town. The Kirklees media centre office complex, its cybercafe and restaurant/bar have become the public face of the Creative Town Initiative where seminars and exhibitions are held. In the longer term it should develop into a showroom for innovations and a creativity best practice office for projects within Huddersfield and elsewhere. The campaign for creativity and innovation, called Create!, is at the hub of this network to promote and bring together creative thinkers in the town and to promote the town's products. It is linked to the town's marketing arm called 'Huddersfield: Strong Heart, Creative Mind' and in collaboration with them undertakes a variety of inward investment promotional activities as well as opportunities to sell Huddersfield products. The Northern Creative Alliance promotes local and regional design companies and encourages them to stay in the area and reverse its image. It does this through publications and events to promote northern creativity often seen by British people as a contradiction in terms as London is seen as the creative hub.

The challenge of this circulating phase is to get the myriad of potentially chaotic organizations into a creative milieu, to give them a sense of purpose and agency that will lead them to contribute to generating social capital, which in turn will benefit the town as a whole. For this reason Huddersfield has drawn on marketing techniques to develop the Creative Town vision and brand as a means of generating inspiration, involvement and commitment to the concept.

## *Platforms for Delivery: Stage Four*

Creative people and projects need to be based and to sell their products and services somewhere. Creative cities need places, at the right price levels, in which to test ideas, pilot products and exhibit and sell work. A creative city requires land and buildings at affordable prices, which as a rule are in urban fringes or areas whose use patterns are changing, such as former port and industrial zones. Cheap spaces reduce financial risk and therefore encourage experiment. Typically older industrial buildings are re-used as incubator units for new businesses, as artist studios, or as centres for design.

Huddersfield is developing older industrial space with a high-tech focus. The Hothouse Unit project will be equipped with first class IT and communications serviced by an advisor and will be available for start-up businesses; there will also be a series of living/working spaces created to break down the barrier between work and living. The telehome idea consists of residential units with teleworking facilities such as advanced ISDN, a kind of experimental 'home of the future'. The flats will be let to people involved in the Creative Town Initiative or on shorter leases to visiting composers, software engineers, digital artists in residence. The CTI is generating a significant throughput of people working on short- and long-term projects who need accessible and convenient accommodation, and many will need to work at high speed. This project seeks to take creativity into the home.

This strategy of using old industrial sites to inspire creativity is tried and tested and examples abound: the music-focused Custard Factory in Birmingham is in the old Bird's Eye custard making factory; the artist's building Mengerzeile in Berlin is in an old piano factory; the Torpedo Factory in Alexandria near Washington DC is an old munitions factory.

## *Dissemination, Reflection, Evaluation: Stage Five*

How far is the local public aware of creative activity through word of mouth, publications or the media? Is critical debate engendering a response – positive or negative? Is the debate about creativity hitting all levels of the population – the businesses, the young, the old, those with different educational backgrounds, the normally excluded? How good is the city at getting people from diverse economic and social backgrounds to involve themselves in exploring their creative potential? Are projects being evaluated?

Huddersfield has sought to address this in a number of ways primarily through a mass involvement campaign called the Millennium Challenge. Set up by the local newspaper, the *Huddersfield Examiner*, and the Creative Town Initiative and sponsored by Lawrence Batley, a local entrepreneur, to the tune of £400,000, the challenge is to complete 2,000 creative projects before 31 December 2000. As of early 2000 over 1,400 were already promised. These cover five areas: projects concerned with increasing prosperity; improving the visual appeal of the town; making the town a healthier and safer place; providing new learning opportunities; and creating a positive image. The importance of the Millennium Challenge is to embed creativity into a wider network beyond the cohort of 300 intimately connected and benefiting from the CTI and so to create an innovation culture in the town as a whole. The danger was that those directly involved in CTI would be seen merely as a bohemian group focused around a media centre.

Other more externally focused initiatives include an international conference to review, debate and disseminate the outcomes and achievements of the CTI; a website to disseminate creative urban best practices, as well as this creative city book, which is seen as part of the project. This external focus is crucial as Huddersfield's self-belief is much more likely to grow when outsiders claim the town is doing interesting things, rather than the CTI itself.

Using the Creative City Development Scale outlined next, linked to the idea of the five-stage cycle it is possible to form a judgement as distinct from a scientific opinion about where a city stands. Any position on the scale has a set of broad characteristics. A city can define its aspirations about where it wants to be. If it wants to move a point or two up the scale it can assess what is required at the next level, bearing in mind the need to provide an appropriate balance of projects across the stages.

# THE CREATIVE CITY DEVELOPMENT SCALE

This scale, from one to ten, is a simple device to assess relative strengths in terms of creativity. Position one means under-developed and position ten highly creative. It gives a snapshot of an immense amount of complex data and provides a guide for action. Each point on the scale is relative to equivalent comparators and what one would expect of a city of a certain size and location. Lyon can not pretend to be a Paris or Belo Horizonte a Sao Paolo. Crucially the judgement about where a city stands is a trigger for strategic discussion, not the truth. It can be applied to each of the stages noted above. For example a city might be a five in its ideas generating capacity and therefore well-developed, and a number one in disseminating products and ideas and thus extremely bad. Over the last decade Comedia has used this conceptual approach to assess the strength of a number of cities with a particular focus on cultural creativity. Cities assessed include Barcelona, Glasgow, Adelaide, Helsinki, Tower Hamlets in the East End of London and London as a whole. Appendices One to Three give examples of the overall results for Tower Hamlets in 1997, Glasgow in 1991 and its visual arts focusing on the contemporary arts.

The methodology used was a combination of local and external peer groups combined with appropriate supporting research of the dynamics in the city. For example, to assess the strength of Glasgow's visual arts scene – one amongst many reviewed – with some degree of objectivity, two assessments were made: internal peer groups within the city and external visual arts peers groups in the UK, Europe and the US. This included judgements on contemporary Glasgow artists, their impact and status in the UK and beyond; views on educational and training facilities right through the range from schools to advanced scholarship; collections, galleries and exhibitions; the power of local auction houses; opinions on the support structures such as conservation, even artistic supplies; the state of cultural debate in the city and the pulling power of the city. Based on this collection of views, plus objective comparative research, such as the relative power of the local arts market, as well as benchmarking, a conclusion was drawn in terms of Glasgow's status within the UK – perhaps the third most important city; then Europe and then on a worldwide basis. The judgements about where a city falls on a scale can also be made without such extensive background research.

In other cities like Helsinki sectors beyond culture were chosen. For example a patent specialist undertook a review of Helsinki-based patents and found that the city had a relatively large proportion of new patents than would be expected for a city of its size. As long as criteria and indicators of success are established the same logic can be applied to any field from scientific to social innovation. The characteristics for each point in terms of, for example, creative awareness would be:

1        Creativity not even thought of as significant or relevant to urban affairs or a particular stage of the cycle, say ideas generation or marketing; very basic creative activity; minimal self-consciousness about the issues amongst the variety of actors in the city. No public discussion of creativity or innovation issues. Activity, if it exists, is submerged with no public sector encouragement. This city is not looking after its future, it may already be dying on its feet.

2 or 3   The beginnings of a self-consciousness by city decision-makers that innovation questions important. Some encouragement from the public sector, say to celebrate a local achievement; a few sporadic private sector initiatives, but no overall strategy, minimal recognition by the media. A few local entrepreneurs help 'creators' onto the first ladders of opportunity through their usually low-level contacts. Still no concept of the need to embed creativity. Organization and management of city still likely to be traditional. Leakage of talent outside the city still very strong.

4        Much more pressure for recognition of innovation issues by those active in industry and public institutions. A few pilot projects encouraged or research undertaken say by the local university. There may be an alternative culture emerging, that begins to create a 'buzz' about the city or part of the city; this in turn might generate many project ideas, however little means to take risks or implement them. Pressure without and within public institutions to rethink organizational ethos. This is the 'take off' level. Leakage of talent begins to balance out. Some of the creative actors have connections or audiences well beyond the locality.

5 or 6   Places where a certain level of autonomy has been achieved and individual creators can begin to meet their aspirations within the location either through commercial firms, the educational sector or a lively NGO world. Support infra-

structures such as a lively research or alternative scene exist; financial networks well-developed; public/private partnerships and mutual sharing between sectors emerging. Connections to the rest of the country and internationally beginning to be credible. Lively technology transfer or exchange programmes exist across business, education and the public sphere. Evidence of existing success may provide a magnet for others to emulate and lead them to stay in the city. A level of coordinated public intervention is usually introduced, especially in the technology areas. Leakage of talent reversing.

7 or 8　Recognition of the importance of the innovation dynamic in both public and private sectors. City in all its guises capable of nurturing 'creators' so that they can meet their aspirations largely within the location. Integrated thinking at strategic levels apparent, which expresses itself in creative projects that hit multiple targets such as environmental initiatives combining social, cultural and economic goals. Support structure for activity available right across the five spheres from ideas generation, to production, circulation, delivery mechanism and dissemination. City or location within a city capable of having credible links to foreign countries without needing to go through central city or national organizations. Creators live and work in the area and a large proportion of the value added returns to the area, such as through the local production capability or management and administrative services. Research and reflective capacity built up in universities so that engine and cycle of creativity can be sustained and renewed. The location is an attractor of talent, but still lacks a few high-level resources to fulfil its ultimate potential. Political structure at ease with itself, open to new ideas and strategically focused.

9　The location is known as a creative centre nationally and internationally. In its own right it is an attractor of talent and skill. Has practically all facilities, and is nearly self-sufficient. Has the headquarters of important research institutions or innovative companies. Is renowned as a culturally vibrant and vital place and thus attracts imaginative individuals in a variety of sectors from around the world. The city has accrued to itself most value-added services.

10    A virtually self-sufficient place which has established a virtuous cycle of self-renewing, self-critical and reflective creativity; it is an attractor of leaked talent and the location for the self re-inforcing creation of value-added. Has high-level facilities and international flagships, and all types of necessary professional services. Is a centre for strategic decision-making about a range of sectors and looked to as a provider of best practices. Capable of competing equally on an international level with any city.

## Lessons Learnt

The technique is regarded as helpful to cities as it breaks down complex detail and simplifies it sufficiently to remain useful. The comparative element establishes which are the appropriate cities to benchmark against and engenders a lively debate within the internal and external peer groups as to what the 'objective' position of the city is. In itself it becomes an ideas generation process, because gaps, weaknesses and strengths reveal themselves as one proceeds through the five-stage chain; it also becomes a strategy formation procedure because by focusing on where a city stands it automatically suggests where it could be.

Conclusions emerge by assessing strengths across the chain from ideas generation to dissemination. For example, in every city analysed ideas potential was far greater than expected. Inevitably there need to be far more ideas than can be implemented; some turn out to be unsustainable, weak after further examination, do not have a market, are too expensive or even simply no good. This attrition process is normal, which is why one needs such an enormous ideas bank in the first place to ensure wastage can be afforded. Given that so many potential solutions were not even coming to the attention of urban decision-makers, when outsiders often relatively easily bring them to the fore, reveals some structural weakness which lies at the core of why the creative city concept is important. Most firms have a suggestion box, at a minimum, and obviously many more sophisticated methods from R&D departments to the self-conscious search for new products through scanning patent applications and even industrial espionage. Why is there not an urban equivalent of the suggestion box, such as the Institute of Social Inventions 'Book of Visions' or its 'Global Ideas Bank'? Looking at best practice databases from around the world is one way forward, allowing new ideas to emerge from within a city is another.

Most cities were judged quite highly in terms of ideas generation – from four to seven on the scale – though there were practically no sustained mechanisms for encouragement. The next problem emerged at the point of turning ideas into reality, which had slightly lower assessments. There were less problems concerning the technical capacities to implement, say, an environmental recycling scheme or finding a company somewhere to do a prototype. The majority of urban innovations do not require sophisticated high-tech solutions such as self-guiding vehicles or transport control systems. More often attitudinal and mindset shifts were both the issue and the answer, often using the tried and tested in new ways, such as ecological building, or letting a group of women design a housing estate as in Westkamen in the Emscher region.

Most problems lay in the culture of entrepreneurship of the places under examination. Thus for some Glaswegian companies it was easier to get a briefing and agreement for a prototype to be done overnight in Italy or Turkey than in the city itself. Similarly many companies found the trial and error approach necessary for experimenting jarred against the grain. Lack of financial support structures for the first steps of the innovation process – a loan of say £5,000 to £30,000 – was a key problem, rather than the higher figures required later on in a development process. Getting on the first step on the ladder proved to be a real blockage. In addition non-technological innovations, especially those concerned with design, aesthetics or the development of new socially oriented services were difficult to fund.

The major problems revealed themselves in the third segment circulation and marketing where all cities reviewed had major weaknesses and their assessments dipped, even though it is here that a large proportion of the income is made. This is for a number of reasons: in the first tranche of cities much of the survey work looked at cultural potential, such as developing a record label, a film or exhibition, where the excitement of producing the project took higher priority than selling it. The same applies to creative projects beyond the cultural field especially where social commitment was dominant as in developing home services for disabled people or new forms of waste disposal. Secondly, innovations have great difficulty in getting off the ground and much of the initial energy, commitment and financial resourcing was drained by the time marketing questions were in focus. A third reason was that a marketing culture does not come naturally to public authorities or NGOs. A final reason was that resources agglomerate in capital cities, which become central communications nodal points through which strategic decision-making flows and from which income is made, thus taking away talent and resources from the rest of the country. The assessments tended to be between two and five on the scale.

The delivery mechanism phase had far less problems, such as creating structures to house innovative companies, venues for culture or the building of architectural icons to reflect a city's image. This is because urban development agencies or economic development units have worked out procedures and means of evaluating tangible property-based initiatives with expertise to match. A building-based project leaves an unarguable physical legacy, which in the worst case can disguise a programme that might not work. Outcomes are achieved that are more easily measurable. Glamorous buildings in particular can be associated with an individual or an urban leadership. Thus all over the world resources are found for prestige buildings like town halls, opera houses whose costs appear disproportionate to the benefits. Buildings seem to represent a tangible commercial asset should everything go wrong, whereas a failed service experiment leaves nothing behind except perhaps a bad taste. The property development world is usually a willing partner given the fundamental asset positions involved. The assessments tended to be between five and eight on the scale.

Dissemination and creating a culture of debate and critical reflection on achievements was underdeveloped. There was a tendency to be purely celebratory, image-focused and outwardly guarded. Collisions of alternative viewpoints were insufficiently publicly encouraged. The more cities were perceived to be creative the more debate, argument and discussion the city developed. In Glasgow, for example, a celebrated case was called Workers City emerging in its European Cultural Capital year of 1990 in response to a contentious appointment in a local museum. The group felt that the idea of an authentic Glasgow was being hijacked by hype, glamour and promotion not based on a local definition of what Glasgow is to Glaswegians. Yet negative as this intervention seemed to the organizers of the cultural capital celebrations it deepened debate, created a positive conflict and took the city forward by forcing it to confront the issues highlighted. In Adelaide the festival fringe, as it battled in a friendly manner with the mainstream festival, was equally seen as pulling the city out of complacency. A major visioning exercise taking place at the time of the bi-annual festival in 1996 shaped its conclusions around the possibility of Adelaide forming a creative Australian hub around the synergies created in putting the two festivals together.

# New Indicators for Creative Cities

## *Why Indicators?*

Conventional aggregate indicators of economic, social or environmental conditions in national reports, such as GNP (gross national product) do not describe urban dynamics well or translate easily down to the city level. They are of little help in monitoring a city's capacity to be creative or to learn.

Indicators simplify and communicate complex information and their primary purpose is to guide an evaluation process by helping policy-makers act and then assess, measure and monitor the impact of decisions. Indicators are important for several reasons: the debate about what should be an indicator triggers discussion as to what is important to a city; it gives the city a goal and action plan by making explicit which target it wants to reach and so create aspirations; it provides an opportunity to assess strengths and weaknesses and how these might be addressed; and lastly quantification gives legitimacy to activities. In the context of the creative city, which by definition has to be a reflexive, learning city, evaluation is in and of itself perhaps the central process: if a city is to learn from its experiences, it must be committed to effective and ongoing evaluation processes; it must reflect, consider and reconsider; it must think and rethink. You cannot think about being a creative city without integral evaluation mechanisms. The first indicator of a creative learning city is whether it evaluates its performance as a creative learning city (discussions with Francois Matarasso have been helpful to clarify this point).

The process of generating indicators to assess a creative city is simple, flexible and logical. It means clarifying objectives, setting up indicators, choosing methods of recording progress and awareness that the task of indicators is to measure as well as possible and relevantly to the city under review. Indicators are unlikely to be completely objective, although they will strive to be.

Data needs to be looked at in four different ways:

1  Subjective measures of subjective phenomena, for example, how safe do people feel?
2  Objective measures of subjective phenomena, for example, how much do people spend weekly on taxis because they are afraid of walking home at night?

3   Subjective measures of objective phenomena – for example, to what extent are people satisfied with lighting in the neighbourhood or the frequency of public transport?
4   Objective measures of objective phenomena, for example, how frequent is the bus service or how many events has the arts centre put on?

Objective data can be quantified and measured, while subjective data can only be assessed and judged. Some measures will be generic and applicable in any context, others will be locally specific. Some monitoring data will be available at the national level, others at the regional or local level. For some indicators, specific customized research will need to be undertaken.

## Planning Indicators

Before creating indicators some preparatory work is necessary. First a city must make it explicit what it wants to achieve through greater creativity; second to understand the general picture of a creative, learning and innovative city and the way it can be stimulated in the specific urban context. That preliminary work should address the following areas:

- Provide criteria against which the innovative capacity of the city under investigation can be assessed.
- Establish the necessary linkages between educational and training policies and learning and innovation potential in the city under review.
- Enable decision-makers within both the public and private sectors to review how well financing structures are doing in fostering innovation and creativity policies.
- Indicate after reviewing good practice strategies which are most suited to the city at its level of development.
- Help the city assess the extent to which their urban policy framework is encouraging the idea of a creative city.
- Assess the city's organizational capacity to cope with learning, creativity and innovation.
- Give a sense of the time scales necessary for actions to work themselves through to different levels of economic, social and cultural enterprise in the city.

The judgements on these areas will help to define appropriate indicators, which if achieved will create the greatest value-added.

Any process of generating indicators at the city level should bear two principles in mind: create agreement between the urban partners as to what the common objectives and commitments are to be; involve those who will be affected by any changes in determining indicators as well as in measuring whether goals have been met. Effective evaluation of indicators is a partnership process, rather than a quasi-scientific assessment by outsiders: the creative city learns by taking responsibility for its own evaluation. In doing this, it is possible to adapt the five-stage process developed by Francois Matarasso in *Use or Ornament: The Social Impact of Participation in the Arts* (1997).

## 1 Planning
The first stage is to establish a partnership between the stakeholders, defined as those who can affect or are affected by the desire to be a creative city. This might include strategic businesses in the city, the educational sector or social affairs agencies. This partnership is the core not only of the evaluation process but of the creative city itself, and should be seen as quasi-permanent. It is this group which will agree the local definition of the creative city in the context of local needs. Having done this, it can identify the mechanisms and interventions to be included in the evaluation process.

## 2 Indicators
The partners can agree a series of indicators, having identified the areas to be evaluated in relation to their own definition of what their city is trying to achieve through its creative processes. The thinking already done will make it much easier to set indicators linked to creativity goals and plan how to collect the information needed. Allowance must be made to accommodate unforeseen outcomes. Some data (eg school performance) will already be available; other areas (eg democratic vitality) may be assessed through proxy indicators such as voting records. Some indicators may be monitored through sampling.

## 3 Execution
Indicators will be related either to points in time, to periods of time, or sometimes to a combination: thus some will record activity on a particular date, some over a year, and some for a shorter period at

the same time each year. The most effective indicators will be simple enough to be understood by all those involved, and able to be recorded as part of normal professional and management tasks so that they do not impose a heavy additional burden.

### 4 Assessment
The data collected should normally be evaluated on an annual basis, preferably by a person or institution with appropriate skills and experience. It can be prepared in the form of a report to the stakeholder partnership, and will have to make allowance for unforeseen developments since these are to be expected in a really creative city.

### 5 Reporting
This report should then be reviewed by the stakeholder group from the different individual perspectives, contrasted with data from other cities and changes made, as appropriate for subsequent evaluation. Reporting is thus the first stage of the next cycle of the process.

## Measuring the Preconditions for a Creative City

Two instances of indicator sets are elaborated below as examples to show how straightforward the process is. The first is based on the preconditions for a creative city addressed in the chapter 'Embedding Creativity into the Genetic Code' and the second on measuring 'Urban Vitality and Viability' essential for a city to be creative. For example, awareness of crisis or challenge can be measured by the existence of strategic plans, publicly available long-term forecasting data and trend analysis. The need to develop organizational capacity and governance could be tested by the existence of inclusive visioning procedures; the number and diversity of successful partnership networks; how far public officials merely co-opt, cooperate or collaborate with citizens in major decision-making; whether officials decide the agenda and change process or jointly retain responsibility with local stakeholder groups.

Empowerment could be measured by the proportion of major businesses and institutions which use non-hierarchical management processes, the levels of hierarchy in key organizations or levels of responsibility for middle managers, the creation within organizations of new procedures suggested by staff or the number of mentoring schemes supported by business. Open communications and networking could be measured by the density of communication; the number and range of cafes, bars or restaurants. The capacity to break established rules and procedures might be assessed by the number of experimental pilot projects in selected areas or levels of cross-departmental working. How far outsider talent is being harnessed could be tested by the percentage of significant decision-makers who have been brought in from other contexts or disciplines or what percentage of projects in large organizations are on project-based contracts and how important they are in the hierarchy.

The quality of a city's learning can be assessed by the range of lifelong learning initiatives; training and professional development by the proportion of the workforce receiving training or numbers securing additional professional qualifications. A test for attitudes to risk and failure could be how many pilot programmes the city has instigated and how many have been adopted by the mainstream. The level of approval and recognition devices can be measured by how many competitions the city instigates or by how many competitions individuals or institutions have won. The vitality of local democracy by voting patterns, responses to consultation processes, numbers of people involved in local campaigns and voluntary groups dedicated to bringing about change or the effectiveness of local government as an enabler and partner. The quantity and quality of public and private research capacity in universities, government research agencies and private business can be judged by achievements at various levels of education or research track records. The availability of affordable spaces for creative experiment gauged by how the planning regime has sought to guarantee low-value uses. Finally best practice benchmarking can be judged by whether the city has a benchmarking programme or whether keeping up with best practices is integral to the planning of the city's key organizations.

## Measuring the Vitality and Viability of a Creative City

The second set of indicators relevant to the creative city are the 'Urban Vitality and Viability' indicators (Developed by Bianchini and Landry, 1995). Vitality is the raw power and energy of a city which needs focusing to reach viability. Creativity is the catalyst for vitality, which the creative process focuses. It becomes sustainable and viable through innovations which are of long-term benefit to the city. Vitality involves levels of activity – things going on; levels of use – participation; levels of interaction, communication, transaction and exchange; levels of representation – how activity, use and interaction are projected outwards and discussed in the outside world. Viability is concerned with long-term self-sufficiency, sustainability, adaptability and self-regeneration. It is necessary to promote vitality in order to achieve viability. Vitality describes the mass of activities, which in and of themselves are not necessarily good or bad. Activity, use and interaction need to be focused towards a set of purposes, goals and objectives for them to have any substantial, positive impact.

There are various forms of vitality and viability which need to be harnessed through the creative process. For example economic vitality is measured by levels of employment, disposable income and standards of living of people in a catchment area, annual numbers of tourists and visitors, retail performance, property and land values. Social vitality is tested by levels of social interaction and activity as well as the nature of social relations. A socially vital and viable city would be characterized by low levels of deprivation, strong social cohesion, good communications and mobility between different social strata, civic pride and community spirit, tolerance of different lifestyles, harmonious race relations, and a vibrant civil society. Environmental viability and vitality concerns two distinct aspects. Ecological sustainability in relation to variables such as air and noise pollution, waste use and disposal, traffic congestion and green spaces. The second concerns the design aspects including variables such as legibility, sense of place, architectural distinctiveness, the linkages in design terms between different parts of the city, the quality of street lighting and how safe, friendly and psychologically approachable the urban environment is. Cultural viability and vitality concerns the maintenance, respect and celebration of what a city and its population is. It involves identity, memory, tradition, community celebration and the production, distribution and consumption of products, artefacts and symbols, which express a city's distinctive nature.

Nine criteria help assess what a creatively vital and viable city is: critical mass; diversity; accessibility; safety and security; identity and distinctiveness; innovativeness; linkage and synergy; competitiveness; and organizational capacity. These criteria need to be looked at across the four dimensions – economic, social, environmental and cultural. We give some examples of the key issues all of which can be assessed and monitored by indicators: critical mass is concerned with the achievement of appropriate thresholds which allow activity to take off, reinforce itself and cluster. Security is concerned with continuity, stability, comfort, and lack of threat and accessibility with convenience and opportunity.

Economically critical mass involves developing and agglomerating sufficient activities to ensure that economies of scale, inter-firm cooperation and synergies can be obtained. Critical mass thresholds make the organization of complex economic initiatives possible. A diverse economic base strengthens a city's resilience. Economic accessibility provides convenience and ladders of opportunity to contribute to economic life. If economic access or intra-urban linkage is poor then the capacity of the city to creatively renew itself is undermined. Economic distinctiveness means a city can increase its attractiveness and viability by providing products and services that are not available elsewhere. A city's economic competitiveness can be measured by the rank and status of local firms and their products and services locally, nationally and internationally.

Socially critical mass represents the density of social interactions within areas of the city at different times of the day, the week and the year. In a social sense security means the lack of threat to people and property, a sense of trust and bonding with one's fellow citizens. Social accessibility involves the possibility of taking part in city life and a diverse social base implies a variegated and lively civil society and voluntary sector with self-confident organizations likely to be more resilient in times of stress. Social innovativeness includes mechanisms or meeting opportunities that allow positive critical debate to take place. A distinctive identity has positive social impacts as it creates the preconditions for establishing civic pride, community spirit and the necessary caring for the urban environment.

For the environmental dimension accessibility means encouraging participation, because facilities can be easily reached on foot or by public transport. Linkage highlights the importance of the physical relationship between the city centre and its sub-centres to encourage interflow, interaction and exchange. Critical mass focuses on whether there are sufficient historic buildings to form an attractive and marketable heritage quarter. Environmental competitiveness is measured by a city's attractiveness and uniqueness, as well as its location.

Cultural identity and distinctiveness marks out one place from the next through urban symbols, food or manufacturing products. Critical mass, in cultural terms, is the opportunity of experiencing different types of facilities such as enjoying, in the course of the same evening, a French bistro, a Shakespearean play, a late night cabaret in a wine bar and then taking a stroll through a pleasant historic area. Culturally, security involves acceptance, in an open and non-chauvinistic way, of the different identities of a place. Accessibility focuses on whether the cultural identities of the communities that make up the city are legitimized, respected and celebrated. Diversity implies the encouragement of production, consumption and distribution opportunities for different cultural forms and the encouragement of a wide and rich definition of what local culture is about. The cultural dimension of linkage plays a crucial role in showcasing what is best in a city, both in the urban centre and on its peripheries.

Several of the indicators to measure the above exist within national or regional surveys from both public institutions – statistical offices, the police, etc – and the private sector – shoppers surveys, national property data, etc. Some of the more attitudinal indicators need to be measured at the local level, here the work of the New Economics Foundation in London is especially useful.

## Finally

The creative city that wishes to learn will be wise enough to understand that no evaluation process can be true or complete, that at the best it can give an indication of part of what is happening. It will devise the best evaluation systems it can, from a mixture of conventional, tested indicators and ones which push the boundaries of its knowledge and expectation, but it will not fall into the trap of believing that it has a complete picture. It will not be afraid of the unconventional or the hard to measure. It will learn continuously from its own evaluation not only about itself as a learning organism, but about its approach to evaluation, demanding more of itself each time it goes through the cycle. It will see evaluation as a fundamental part of its development and will welcome the involvement of all sectors and outsiders.

## URBANISM AND URBAN LITERACY

### A New Urban Discipline?

Urbanism is the discipline which allows an understanding of the dynamics, resources and potential of the city in a richer way. Urban literacy is the ability and skill to 'read' the city and understand how cities work and is developed by learning about urbanism. Urbanism can become the 'meta urban discipline' and urban literacy a linked generic and overarching skill. A full understanding of urbanism only occurs by looking at the city from different perspectives. By reconfiguring and tying together a number of disciplines penetrative insights, perceptions and ways of interpreting an understanding of urban life emerges. By seeing the city through diverse eyes, potential and hidden possibilities, from business ideas to improving the mundane, are revealed. Traditionally, however, the discourse on urbanism has been dominated by architects and urban designers. Urbanism provides the raw materials for creating urban strategies and decision-making; it requires a set of lateral, critical and integrated thinking qualities as well as core competencies. These draw on the insights of cultural geography; urban economics and social affairs; urban planning; history and anthropology; design, aesthetics and architecture; ecology and cultural studies as well as knowledge of power configurations.

Each discipline contributes its unique quality, traditions and focus necessary to comprehend urban complexities. For example, cultural studies and anthropology bring an understanding and interpretation of inherited ideas, beliefs, values and forms of knowledge, which constitute the shared bases of social action. This is enriched by understanding the signs and symbols in the physical, spoken or visual world, helping to decode what they mean. The sociological focus helps reveal group dynamics and the processes of social and community development; economics the financial and commercial determinants driving urban transition processes. Cultural geography helps clarify the spatial, locational and topographical patterning of cities and design and aesthetics focuses on look and feel. Completely underestimated psychology brings in emotional factors in urban development and how people feel about their environments. Planning finally contributes the set of rules, codes and conventions to carry out the insights gained from these varied forms of knowledge.

## Beyond Planning as Land Use

Planning is a generic concept that applies to any activity with an intention to achieve an objective methodically. Planning establishes courses of action which involve prioritizing as resources are limited. Yet in the urban context it is nearly exclusively associated with land use and development control, important as this function is. For the person in the street this is the urban planner, when in fact a mass of other urban activities involve planning too. This may seem a trivial point, but it causes severe problems. First, it implies that planning falls under the jurisdiction of the land use specialist. More accurately planning departments should be called land use and development control departments. Secondly it usually puts the land use specialist towards the top of the hierarchical tree and so can downgrade the power of people-based departments from business start up to community building specialists. Thirdly, there is a danger that focusing on land use planning oversimplifies issues and looks at problems through one lens leading us away from asking fundamental questions. It remains difficult to get conventional planners to understand that 'my' experience is powerful and felt and may have nothing to do with land use, although it may have land use implications. Importantly it shows there is more than one way of looking at planning a city. Take children's play. The best or most successful play areas are not necessarily those with expensive play equipment that signal 'this is a children's play area'. Children are often contrary on purpose, an area labelled 'play area' may put them off. Instead a strategy involving a craftsperson or artist in collaboration with youngsters, might create a play area in the end, but through the process of creating a play area generate life skills or social responsibility. Alternatively it may be a simple basketball hoop or just space to kick a ball which create vibrant play spaces. This is not the expensive catalogue-based approach to play areas, which attempts to short cut place-making. Thus the answer to an urban problem may not be the obvious discipline of leisure, transport or housing – having grasped the essence of a problem, a circuitous route may touch its deeper heart and may as a secondary consequence deal with the issues at hand.

Fourth, the tight association of planning in general with land use planning is the source of the major criticism that planners do not have a sufficiently broad base of knowledge. If land use planners are to maintain a predominant role it is essential they understand more about culture, history or social dynamics. If their role is to be reduced to an equal status with other disciplines, these forms of knowledge can be present in a team. Ideally whatever the specialism historical, aesthetic and cultural knowledge should become a generic (and required) skill set embedded in all training for those working with cities, as should new skills concerned with understanding networks and communications dynamics. This greater focus on soft infrastructure highlights concern with issues of ambience, feeling and behaviour.

## Gaining Insights through Crossovers

The real power of the notion of urbanism and its linked quality urban literacy comes from emphatically integrating disciplines and the extra dimension added by knowledge gained through synergy. Much of this will be new perceptions such as cultural insights to economics; or psychological ones to geography. Alternatively combinations might be created that could link telecoms and transport and then land use with social networking strategies. This might then justifiably be called communications planning. Valuing the diversity of disciplines might lead to interesting appointments in running cities, such as environmentalists becoming heads of transport as the best environmentalist would surely be better as a transport head than one of the less talented transport planners. An economist might head up social affairs, and an historian physical planning; a social development specialist cultural affairs.

Deep insight comes from a visceral sense of and emotional engagement with the city and so many people already understand and apply urban literacy instinctively, being able to draw threads from different domains of their experience. Urbanism seeks to systematize these spheres of knowledge as these intuitions will be more effective if refined and enhanced through education and training. An interplay is necessary between urban theorists or professionals and those on the front line of urban deprivation who have the potential of helping the professionals deal with problems. This street knowledge is insufficiently used as a rich resource by urban professionals or academics who often live divorced from and as outsiders to the problems they deal with. Community artists have been one of the few groups to tap into this tacit knowledge. A minimum standard of competence from both professionals and the general public is required to participate in creating urban futures. This will have an impact on participation and consultative methods. Consultation is a democratic good and inclusive, but does not by definition lead to creativity. People usually merely reflect what they already know, which may have been influenced by the media or fashion. Thus learning to think out of the box and being more knowledgeable about the city are preconditions for imaginative action. For example, good instincts feed off knowing the history of a city better and by researching a city's possibilities you appreciate more and can generate more ideas to make better decisions as well as facilitate cooperative working.

## A New Language for Urban Affairs

Over time the concepts of urbanism and urban literacy can lead to a new language for urban planning. Some notions of urbanism will initially develop from its component disciplines, later on new concepts will emerge through insights gained by blurring discipline boundaries and crossovers. Language and the concepts underlying it shape our understanding of the world, it effectively circumscribes the limits within which urban strategies can be thought through and so guides our action. By talking about the city in land use planning terms we tend to use the static language of zoning, retail, office, residential or leisure, car parking, active street frontages or public space although more dynamic terms like accessibility are entering the vocabulary. It is like seeing the city from the air and not from the street. To understand the logic of cities more comprehensively, a more active language is necessary, concerned with dynamics, exchanges, flows, resources and networks. For example looking at cities with a cultural approach gives a completely different sense of what an urban resource can be. Rather than simply being a physical manifestation it can be intangible like a city's collection of internal and external images accumulated through history that it might wish to reflect as a brand. That brand in turn is a resource that a city can use to attract investment or generate products identified with the city, as Parma has done with ham.

## Urban Literacy in Action

The purpose of urban literacy is to help create urban strategies and its value becomes apparent when applied in action. Seemingly complex economic and social dynamics are simple to disentangle with its skills. Perhaps literacy is a limiting word as urban literacy is concerned with interpreting and decoding all our experiences and senses: what we see, feel, smell and hear in the city. It seeks to understand the shapes of urban landscapes and why they came about. It tries to sense history in how the city goes about its business. It attempts to feel the city's economy both through obvious signs like a steel plant or whether it is going up or down because of shabbiness or 'for sale' signs. It helps identify social consequences of urban economies in transition as when 'lower value' uses get supplanted by 'higher value' uses. In consequence, in older urban centres traditional shops or communities disappear so erasing memory and history. It helps appreciate aesthetic codes so one understands the meanings of colours, the style of buildings and presentation.

Subconsciously 'trained' in advertising symbolism it intuits and interprets the manifold urban distinctions and identifiers – to whom a shop is targeted, what draws people in and what repels.

Urban literacy helps us recognize the invisible walls of urban ghettos and feel the lack of social capital. With this skill one can read the implied threats by how people look at you. It provides implicit knowledge so you can sniff out cheaper restaurants or the alternative district. Perhaps a whiff of incense or a gothic look, a bike shop, a bookshop specializing in green issues, the vegetarian cafe, an artist studio complex, perhaps in the courtyard of an old light industrial building. If the alternative district is on the turn one or two houses will be done up and there will be a subtle change in stores. A rather upmarket interior designer, a bistro, more gay people – who as risk takers are often adept at spotting urban trends – a bond trader, an acupuncturist. They push prices up, in part destroying in the process that which originally drew them here.

From a distance you see the religious focus – a church, a mosque, an icon – normally the centre of the town. On closer inspection the natural churchgoing community might have drifted to an urban layer further out. That change is read in the shops. No food shops; they have gone out of town and if the town is not powerful enough and can't substitute them it will start to die and become hollow. This is the lifecycle of the city in motion.

The historic names of places always have a purpose and the placement of facilities like markets, often seemingly chaotic at first sight, are thought through at root. The market at the centre will not stand alone, it will often be part of a square. The best of squares explain urban dynamics beautifully. As noted before, the church in one corner denotes religious and spiritual power, the town hall at another signals temporal power; a museum, a cultural space at the third reveals the power of knowledge and learning, and finally the market hall or trading and banking houses reveal commercial and economic power. Today the change in the source of power from the spiritual and heavenly to that of Mammon imposes itself in the built form. Every floor that rises higher into the sky creates more profit, especially if the city is successful and therefore short of space. That is why places like Washington can be relaxing on the eye because regulations from a former civic logic – not to build higher than Capital Hill – have imposed a shape on the city.

Typical corporate buildings make self-centred statements more for themselves rather than their urban context so we feel a loss of urbanity. Good urbanism had its source in how the philosophies and compromises of competing powers and logics play themselves out, as seen in the ideal square. Buildings had conversations with God; with learning; with commerce whose aspirations were tempered by doubt and fearfulness of higher forces. These conversations expressed themselves in different physical forms and resulting codes of civility. The tensions of urban life needed tempering in games or simulations of war such as the annual Palio in Sienna – a ritual horse race around the central square where the Siennese neighbourhoods, the *contrade*, fight it out in controlled combat. For these reasons the public sphere – a means of mediating and finding mutuality between individual desires and collective needs – has always been central to urban life to leaven the pressure of dense urban living.

Today one logic over-rides urban decision-making: the financial calculus. In this process urbanity loses out and with urban literacy we can read these trends. Lack of investment in public infrastructure, which it is claimed does not pay for itself, is one result leading to a lack of caring, few facilities for self-improvement is another. Crucially, public infrastructure does not pay for itself within a narrow financial logic; however, once the costs of various consequences, say social, are calculated then public investment can be cheap.

---

### THE URBAN LITERATE

As Colin Ward notes in *Welcome, Thinner City* (1989): 'a city fancier knew without seeing that there must be a lorry driver's snack bar around the next corner; as accurately as any predecessor centuries earlier would locate a coaching inn. A poor traveller would know where he could find cheap lodgings and the prospect of casual work. An itinerant salesman would know that a shop on that particular site would not pick up enough trade to be safe for credit. A lecher knew where to find their particular kind of bar. Criminologists could take one look at a place and predict the pattern of offences. Wholesalers and hucksters, junkmen and junkies, model aeroplane enthusiasts and people selling leotards to dancing academies all developed a city sense which is a guide to the specialized functions for which cities originally arose.'

## Local Urbanism Centres

Urbanism and urban literacy can be taught formally and informally as university courses, through media reporting or urbanism centres. In the early 1970s there was an attempt to create urban studies centres, sparked off by the post-1968 notion of democratizing planning. Over time most were shut down or became local history centres such as the Living History Unit in Leicester. There is a need for new independent urbanism centres to actively help make urban strategy. The existing architecture centres which showcase designs and plans are far too narrow for what is required and the traditional urban studies centres almost exclusively focus on education. The new centres, funded from a variety of sources, would be formed as a partnership representing a diversity of urban stakeholders and their role would be to provide a research and development function for the city. This includes: advocating and educating, for example by initiating urban literacy projects in schools; showcasing and providing a forum for discussion; initiating exemplary pilot projects especially those which encourage collaboration between different groups within the city. An example is building on the interests and knowledge of the old or the young or of business and community organizations. As an active institution the centres would be self-renewing in their quest to help shape the economic, social and physical life of the city. They would hand over projects that work to appropriate organizations outside rather than seeking to become ever larger themselves.

Part Four

# THE CREATIVE CITY AND BEYOND

# 10

# The Creative City and Beyond

## CONTOURS OF THE NEXT WAVE OF CREATIVITY AND INNOVATION

The Creative City is no more than a beginning, it seeks to flesh out the landscape of an emerging urban world characterized by diversity, disruption, division between the rich and the poor, fluidity and liveliness. Clearly in such a rapidly changing world it raises more questions than it can answer. I hope it has sufficiently invigorated others to take its themes forward and to explore issues not fully addressed. These include: to what extent are micro-innovations of the kind this book has discussed effective in changing the macro environment for innovative development? It begs the question of what should come first: the smaller pilot project that inspires, perhaps leading to broader changes because it is replicated, and thus over time may help change the incentives and regulatory regime; or does the macro regime need adjusting to provide the conducive seedbed to allow pilot projects to take place in the first instance. The jury is out and the answer is perhaps: 'it depends on circumstance and context' and perhaps both need to be worked on at the same time. Secondly, what is the best strategy to mainstream and replicate ingenious projects? Should one start covering a tight geographical area fully or disperse innovations widely, but thinly? Should dissemination occur through state institutions, be left to market forces or through community leaders? Should small-scale projects remain small or be turned into large-scale initiatives with different dynamics and financing requirements? Thirdly, what regulation and incentives structures are most effective in unleashing ingenuity and imaginative action in the city? Fourthly, how long does it take to get creative ideas accepted and turned into reality in a broad-based way and what are the best mechanisms for speeding up the process? For sustainability to come fully onto the agenda took 20 years; for 15 years already there has been a concerted effort to highlight the importance of culture to development, but general acceptance remains a long way off. There is no consensus, yet for the time for deeper seated changes to occur a decade seems to be required. By contrast political change can happen more or less overnight and change priorities and unleash innovative action as happened with the social inclusion agenda under Blair in Britain. Finally many cities are mentioned throughout the book and a few are discussed in more detail. Yet to fully understand why one city rather than its neighbour is innovating requires much more description, research and knowledge of its specific history and context than has been given room here. Peter Hall's *Cities in Civilization* (1998) is the first major attempt to grapple with this issue, covering cities as wide-ranging as Detroit, Athens, Tokyo–Kanagawa and Vienna.

Inevitably *The Creative City* reflects its time and so much emphasis has been placed on sustainability. This powerful concept has represented a paradigm shift whose implications are slowly working themselves through the urban system unleashing innovations, best practices and concepts, such as the ecological footprint idea, along the way. Within a decade many inventions associated with sustainability will seem mundane and other priorities will emerge. However it will be difficult to come up with a concept as strong in its overarching impact as sustainability, especially when seen as something that goes well beyond the environmental aspect. The new economy notion based on knowledge and driven by IT is the obvious shift with foreseeable paradigmatic impacts from which a raft of innovations as to how we do things are likely to emerge.

For what it is worth I sketch below the major arenas within which creativity and innovation are required. There will need to be breakthroughs at the level of paradigm shifts and overarching concepts and then a continuous flow of innovations that over time are taken up as a best practice and then become good practice. Strong concepts can help agenda setting, strategy creation and direct the flow of urban development. They can be revolutionary and unleash creativity as their implications cascade down into the texture of our economic and lifestyle structure. In order to maximize the potential of such conceptual breakthroughs it is usually essential to change the incentives and regulatory regime, as new concepts, such as changing the idea of waste to a resource, often turn a problem on its head and find solutions for things that previously seemed incompatible. They usually require new actors to enter the urban arena, as when third sector organizations took on responsibility for self-help programmes.

The contours of the next wave are already appearing where quantum leaps of new understanding are required, especially areas where problems appear intractable or interconnected. The focus will lie in seven areas which are:

1 *Creating value and values simultaneously:* The emerging economy requires an ethical value base to guide action. It thus ensures the inequalities seen in the increased presence of spatially divided and segmented 'dual cities' are central to any decision-making.

2 *From hardware solutions to software solutions:* In the next phase greater value will be generated by shifting the focus towards 'software' solutions such as improvements in governance, organization and relationships rather than technology.

3 *Doing more with less:* A resource conscious world will focus on resource productivity rather than labour productivity and adapt its incentive structures accordingly, but the concept applies to other domains as well.

4 *Living inter-culturally:* As the world becomes more multicultural it poses a threat and an opportunity and the potential of hybrid forms and inter-cultural projects needs exploring.

5 *Valuing varied visions:* Seeing problems and potential through different eyes requires a self-conscious effort to ask, re-value and adapt what the specific creative contributions are that might come from the young or the old; from women or men; ethnic majorities and minorities; the well-connected or the excluded and to harness these for the overall goals of the city.

6 *Recombining the old and the new imaginatively:* Re-connecting the past with the present and re-presenting it in the future reveals untold assets. History is a huge undervalued resource and recombining the old and new can trigger untold solutions by imaginatively linking ideas, perspectives, traditions, materials used, institutions and structures created.

7 *The Learning City:* The key to sustainable creativity. The city of the future needs to be a learning city reflecting on and responding to achievements and obstacles. Only by embedding reflexiveness and learning into every crevice of a city's inner workings can it sustain its creative momentum.

The above can only happen under the following conditions, which also set an agenda for new waves of innovation:

- A massive effort is required to imaginatively rethink incentives, so that reward and penalty mechanisms provide the preconditions for establishing creatively sustainable cities.
- Many brilliant projects are hidden from view. Cities are generally unimaginative in telling their stories both to their citizens and outsiders. Ingenious and effective visibility strategies need to be invented to disseminate urban innovations to drive creativity using all forms of media from the written word, to theatre or electronic media in formats that go beyond best practice databases, which themselves were a significant innovation.
- And finally everything impacts on how we plan cities and who should plan them. My view is that what is required are urban strategists with a deep knowledge of urbanism who use the knowledge of conventional planning as part of their toolkit rather than being dominated by it.

## Creating Value and Values Simultaneously

The emerging economy requires an ethical value base to guide action given the inequitable distributive effects of globalization and destructive impacts of unfettered development on cities. The situation today has similarities to the philosophical dilemmas the Industrial Revolution brought into focus where unfettered individualism needed to be tethered to a broader public interest. The value base should be revisited to balance individual and collective needs relevant to the 21st century. This requires reassessing and broadening what we mean by value; creating value and adding value and finding forms of action and evaluation that combine the creation of value and values simultaneously.

Capitalism is good at creating and assessing value defined by a narrow financial calculus. Yet the system as a whole has no intrinsic or self-conscious value base from within itself that guides it inexorably towards the solution of public interest needs. Unless simultaneously constrained and goaded the system largely ignores the consequent costs of its actions on the environment or its distributional effects. Improving future urban problems requires preventative action rather than dealing with after-effects.

Firms need to quantify and audit the value they return to society more broadly, assessing for example: how did our actions contribute to enhancing skills? How did they effect levels of crime or graffiti if any? How did they impact on the environment or cultural needs? Social, cultural and environmental impact auditing linked to financial auditing needs to become commonplace. This process attempts to link value to values. Within this broader definition of accounting, initiatives that currently seem 'unprofitable' and 'unachievable' become 'profitable'. For example, a recycling project that gives unemployed people work within a self-help voluntary structure achieves multiple objectives that can be calculated. The management structure may be empowering and has social impacts; it creates work and products and has an economic impact and its focus is environmental. It can change a lifestyle pattern so waste is separated, revolutionizing behaviour and contributing more than a technological fix. It may have had, as an incentive, a grant to get it going, yet is still commercial given the costs of dealing with the alternatives of unemployment. Any value calculations need to include the costs of not dealing with a problem or costing the value of wasted potential. Fostering social and human capital should thus be at the centre of urban regeneration, because a more knowledgeable and intelligent, trained workforce helps develop economic prosperity. Building social capital means addressing social exclusion, which is not the same as dealing with poverty as not all poor people are socially excluded.

The aim of connecting value and values requires the following: first, moving away from rigidly ideological and fundamentalist positions and the black and white logic that, for example, simplistically stated capitalism is either all good or all bad. Secondly, recognizing the value and virtues in each position. For example, free marketeers seeing the limits of the market, or grassroots activists appreciating how a market can be useful. Thirdly, finding creative urban strategies that make money out of the socially useful. The Ruhr area has done this by exploiting environmental technology and using their degraded environment as the test bed rather than promoting defence equipment. Finally, devising inventive incentive structures to guide value creation in the context of fostering collective values.

## From Hardware Innovations to Software Solutions

What the city requires in one period may be less of a problem in the next. Urban innovations and their underlying creativity in recent centuries were focused largely on physical infrastructures –

the sewage systems, the great transport advances, train and road networks and later IT infrastructures or improvements in building techniques and project management allowing ever larger structures to be built. They were the most visible signs of the changing city. There were more invisible advances in sanitation and public health and utilities or the identification of the causes of diseases, which increased urban quality of life.

The needs of the 21st century are different. Every period of history needs its own form of creativity. Today's is more 'synthetic', able to bring the seemingly disparate together; to understand the underlying ecologies and logics that make self-regulating systems work; the capacity to shape relationships where networks are so widely dispersed; new organizational forms and a revitalized democracy that harnesses people's commitment, motivations and potential. The key applications of creativity will lie in the realm of democracy, organization, governance and management – social and political innovations – as much as in new technology. They are likely to generate more value added than technologically driven productivity advances. Building civic capacity and leadership is a software infrastructure as essential as roads and airports.

The challenge is immense, for example, the concept of democracy is under pressure from a number of sources. On the one hand we have seen a growth of democracy, a concept conceived in Europe, yet in the East a more autocratic version is emerging. Democracy needs to be renewed under pressure from alternative concepts as to how it should operate and where its focus should be as the supranational, national and urban fight it out. They question the relationship between the individual and the state. There is also a loss of faith in democracy as currently conceived and interesting responses are emerging like citizen's juries, electronic voting or participatory decision-making. All are attempts at renewing the mandate and building trust as part of a bigger issue of re-conceiving relationships between individuals, within organizations and between organizations. It raises questions such as: 'What forms of hierarchy are conceivable within a world of more empowered individuals or should hierarchy disappear?' or 'What is representation when democratic voting cycles are inadequate to meet needs for participation?' or 'How can power and responsibility be devolved to the third sector?'

Governing, organizing and managing better can make the difference between success and failure. They are the new sources of competitiveness – good, strategic and effective governance and management arrangements are just as much a competitive tool as is a piece of technology.

## Doing More with Less

The 'doing more with less' principle can be applied to many fields, but is easiest to grasp in terms of environmental issues. Yet the movement towards new indicators and forms of evaluation and auditing opens up other vast areas to assess the principle. They include the governance and management arena allowing one to assess how loose organizational structures built on trust can achieve more value by applying fewer inputs. It depends on how leaders use power to bind a community together and release the power in others. As a result a meeting of three that can achieve objectives comprehensively is better than if it requires a mass of report-backs. Similar benefits are to be expected with other social innovations, as when empowered individuals achieve more than those in a straight jacket.

The 'Factor Four – Doubling Wealth and Halving Resource Use' idea has already been described. It shifts the focus away from rewarding labour productivity to resource productivity bolstered by incentive and regulatory structures that would lead to a surge of innovatory activity. The examples come from the environmental sphere like revolutionizing energy productivity in products in general use to show possibilities: air-conditioning, lighting or super-windows. The same logic can apply to rewarding materials productivity from electronic books, residential water efficiency to recycling; or transport productivity from car-sharing to video-conferencing.

For the system to work a shift in incentives structure is necessary so utility prices like electricity can be structured to reward regulators and consumers for finding ways of reducing bills, not for selling customers more of a commodity. Another example is rethinking how fees for professionals are paid. Architects, engineers or consultants do not get rewarded for saving resources or costs; the practice adopted worldwide is to charge according to the amount of materials used thus increasing resource use as does charging a percentage of overall cost. Richard Garwin invented the concept of 'feebates' – a fee charged for inefficiency and a rebate rewarding efficiency (see von Weizsäcker et al, 1998, pp 191–7). Thus in a building that wastes water or energy the owner pays a fee for the inefficiency and a rebate when they are more efficient. As Paul Hawken noted (1993) 'Competition in the marketplace should not be between a company wasting the environment versus one that is trying to save it. Competition should be between companies which can do the best job in restoring and preserving the environment.'

## Living Inter-culturally

Increased personal mobility has made countries and cities more mixed, but also fractured the homogenous sense of community and identification with place. Living with strangers is the quintessential urban experience and these strangers will increasingly come from far-flung places. In a village, by contrast, everyone knows each other and community is clearly bounded. This can be seen as a threat or an opportunity. On the one hand it can destabilize communities as immigrants bring in habits, attitudes and skills alien to the original community, on the other it can enrich and stimulate possibilities by creating hybrids, crossovers and boundary blurring. It is most apparent in the cultural and food industries and can be seen in the new hybridized Australian food culture, the world music phenomenon or bangra music of Asian Britons or in fashion – Rifat Ozbek, Hussein Chalayan working out of London or Yohji Yamamoto out of Paris. The challenge for urban policy-makers is to find further ways to be inventive with mutual understanding between cultures and ideas of tolerance. This should go well beyond ethnic festivals and imaginative ways of mixing forms of science like Chinese and Western medicine or mixing architectural traditions. The West has a lot to learn from Muslim traditions in urban design and architecture. Yet this requires a major shift. Planners have to recognize that the tradition has something to offer in the first place and then find ways of communicating seriously with Muslim theorists and practitioners.

So far multi-culturalism has been the predominant policy goal, which means strengthening the separate cultural identities of ethnic groups. This is important, it is crucial to feel confident about who one is, but it is not enough if there is little communication between cultures, perhaps reinforcing stereotypes and prejudices. We need to move one step further towards inter-culturalism which builds bridges, helps foster cohesion and conciliation and produces something new out of the multi-cultural patchwork of our cities. In this way local culture and ingenuity is re-shaped. Creativity may be encouraged by fragmentation, but certainly not by marginalization. Inward-looking ethnic ghettos are unlikely to contribute to solving the wider problems of cities. The creative challenge is to alleviate the fear of change in cities.

## Valuing Varied Visions

By tapping into different forms of creativity imaginative solutions can emerge, because the pool of ideas and perspectives is enlarged. The majority of decisions are made by a narrow slice of the population, in our more paternalistic society usually men, which leads to a waste of resources. This is more than a question of consulting diverse groups or letting them participate, but it has to do with giving people the means to develop new approaches, solutions and even paradigms themselves. For example, the feminist critique of functionalist urban planning that emerged from the 1970s proved a fertile ground. By linking into the direct experience of ordinary women, women architects and planners highlighted the fact that the city, for many women, was an obstacle course. They noticed before anyone else by responding to the real anger that change had to occur. For those with prams road curbs, underpasses, multi-storey car parks and stairs were difficult to negotiate and so the idea of putting ring-roads underground or ramps became more common. Reclaiming the city, its safety regime, its squares, its night time and even the idea of the 24-hour city emerged from these debates, as people began to think about the urban calendar, opening hours, work schedules, time issues and service provision. The resulting solutions, often creative, were of benefit to all. Celebrating the distinct voices of sub-groups is important but ultimately reductive, the more interesting challenge is to see how their creativity can benefit the public at large. The time has come to take into account views of the city of the socially excluded and to bring their ideas to bear on decision-making. The same logic applies to any other perspective – the young, the old or a minority group. The task is to validate the insights of ordinary people by linking them with supportive and credible professionals who might hold similar views and who can thereby develop an alternative framework. This sympathetic intelligentsia can give people the belief that it is possible for them to implement their ideas. Indeed in terms of the broader objectives of the Creative City it may be women who are more in tune with the softer sensibilities that the concept implies with its focus on sociability, integrated thinking, networking and human capacities. Indeed, the future may be female (see Leonard Shlain, 1998, *The Alphabet versus the Goddess*).

## *Recombining the Old and New Imaginatively*

History can be mined for the future in myriad ways. The presence of the past in the present gives a sense of weight and significance to any urban endeavour and the constructive clash and recombination of past and future reaps unusual rewards. It is as easy to go overboard with an infatuation of the new as it is with pining for the past. In certain places there is too much obsession with the past in others too little appreciation. Erasing memory is like throwing an asset away. Yet the past is too often left exclusively to antiquarians, nostalgics and historians. The exciting challenge is to bring into a coalition for urban strategy making those with a historical perspective and those dealing with the here and now. The result is enriched decision-making. The art of blending the old and the new requires refocusing to see history as a resource. An equally rich potential can emerge from the historical ideas bank and asking old questions afresh, such as about democracy or the good life, or what enlightenment or being a rational person would mean today. Easiest and most visibly impressive are the interventions in the built fabric, such as inserting the Pei pyramid into the Louvre, placing an intricate wire structure on top of the Tapies museum in Barcelona or the conversion of a munitions factory in Karlsruhe into a massive Centre for Media Technology.

## TOWARDS THE LEARNING CITY

In the future the 'learning city' notion will be a more powerful metaphor than that of the 'creative city'. Yet I believe the focus on creativity is more crucial now to ensure an ideas bank is generated from which innovations emerge and a city can learn in the first place. Responding creatively to urban needs is not a once and for all activity. The city of the future needs to take things further by becoming a learning city. It needs to reflect on and respond to achievements and obstacles, continuously assessing as part of a structured programme. An analogy is how aircraft maintenance is based on schedules of the life expectancy of each component part. Only by embedding reflexivity into every crevice of a city's inner workings can it sustain its creative momentum. Creativity and leadership need to be treated as a renewable, developable resource that can be depleted when unwisely used.

A true learning city is one which develops by learning from its experiences and those of others. It is a place that understands itself and reflects upon that understanding – it is a 'reflexive city' and self-evaluation is a defining feature. The key characteristic of the learning city is the ability to develop successfully in a rapidly changing socio-economic environment. Where the unconcerned city flounders by trying to repeat past success for far too long, the learning city is creative in its understanding of its own situation and wider relationships, developing new solutions to new problems. The essential point is that any city can be a learning city. It is not a factor of size, geography, resources, economic infrastructure or even educational investment (though this will play an increasingly important role if a city is to sustain itself as a learning organism in the emerging knowledge economy). To some extent, it might be argued that the fewer natural or historical advantages a city enjoys, the more important it is that it should re-think itself as a learning city. The learning city is thus strategic, creative, imaginative and intelligent – it looks at its potential resources in a far more comprehensive way. It sees a competitive edge in the seemingly insignificant; it turns weaknesses into strengths, it makes something out of nothing. It is a rich and complex place (see Landry and Matarasso, 1998).

Only if learning is placed at the centre of a city's daily experience can individuals continue to develop their skills and capacities; organizations and institutions harness the potential of their workforce and respond flexibly and imaginatively to opportunities and difficulties; cities act responsively and adapt flexibly to emerging needs; societies understand that the diversity and differences between communities can become a source of enrichment, understanding and potential. The challenge is to promote the conditions in which a 'learning city' can unfold. A learning city is much more than a place whose members are simply well-educated; it goes well beyond learning in classrooms. It is a place where individuals and organizations are encouraged to learn about the dynamics of where they live and how it is changing; a place which on that basis changes the way it learns to grasp the opportunities at work and leisure, formally and informally; a place in which all its members are encouraged to learn; finally and perhaps most importantly, a place that can learn to change the conditions of its learning democratically.

As our cities face unprecedented and continuing change it erodes the possibility of ever recovering the traditions of stability.

In the current period of transformation stable views of occupations, economies, religions, organizations and value systems have been lost. We must learn to live 'beyond the stable state' (Schon, 1971) in continuing processes of transformation and cannot expect new stable states that will endure even for our own lifetimes. We must learn to understand, guide, influence and manage these transformations and make the capacity for undertaking change integral to ourselves and to our institutions. In other words, become adept at creating and learning. We must be able not only to transform our institutions, in response to changing situations and requirements; we must invent and develop institutions, networks or partnership forms which are 'learning systems', capable of bringing about their own continuing transformation – and we must learn about learning (Cara et al, 1998).

## From Planning to Urban Strategy Making

Everything said affects planning and I am aware of the complexity of the debate on the future of planning and will not cover it in detail. Some say planning should be more consultative and participatory as the discipline is too technocratic and incomprehensible to citizens because it expresses itself in a form that has little meaning in terms of day to day experience. For example, Patsy Healey (1997) believes in collaborative planning, which views planning as a system of communication with planners skilled in creating debate and communication. Planning is then an active process which looks for and values different types of knowledge and understanding of a given city. Others believe that planning's role of control embodies a mindset disposed to saying 'no'. This lies uncomfortably with the needs of changing cities where a flexible, anticipatory mindset disposed to saying 'yes' within a framework of principles is called for. These may include the need for distinctiveness, mixing the old and the new, sustainability or development that does not erase memory yet innovates. This lack of balance, critics say, leads to exaggerated responses either thoughtlessly dismembering places or over protecting cities so they are locked into a time warp. Critics also claim planners underestimate social dynamics, which are as significant as land use or property prices. Some argue planning should be more culturally sensitive. Increasingly multi-cultural cities should reflect diversity as Italian, American, Spanish, Asian or Islamic planning has different priorities. Finally I argue that those in planning from land use to urban marketing are not creative enough, because they limit what they see as resources and underestimate the diverse ways of improving or solving problems. In part their mindscape is at fault and in part the uncreative bureaucratic process they are bound into. Yet if they get it right they can and do create physical spaces and opportunities that act as a stimulus for imaginative action so that the city works well as a creative system. This might require new leaders and certainly new training.

The central question remains: what is the philosophy, purpose and future role of urban strategists (formerly planners) and what should their education be? The 'team' that plans cities, both administrative insiders and the strategic private sector or community groups outside, should in their entirety represent a diversity of roles: facilitators, visionaries, leaders, public servants, investors, advocates and technical specialists, with a wide range of intellectual resources to match.

My conclusion is that planning needs to adapt to a changing world and its inner focus be superseded by the notion of urban strategy. This is easier said than done and will require much ingenuity. Planning should be a vision-driven and deliberative, rather than narrowly technical, process. Through planning, a city decides what public goods it wants. Planning involves turning a vision into practice by being simplified so it is rooted in principles, strategically focused and tactically flexible on implementation. In this way the vision does not get lost in a plethora of detail. The overall vision guides judgement from land use to aesthetics and provides a level of certainty and standards necessary for the community at large, developers and investors. People accept difficult decisions provided there is transparency, consistency and a level playing field in enacting a policy framework. The vision thus needs to balance complex and contradictory needs and be generated by people with different backgrounds, perspectives and interests. It requires an active process of participation to develop consensus by minimizing or resolving conflict over implementation. Such a vision may be driven by notions such as sustainable and equitable development or better design, aesthetics and local distinctiveness or even a desire to make a community happy – a language long lost in the political arena. Planning should enable and rarely need to deliver itself; it should guide and rarely need to control.

Planning can be effective in a market economy if it is underpinned by a principled ethos with regulation at a minimum and a forceful and ingenious incentives structure focused on taxation and other fiscal control measures. Planning needs more power and less power. More to create imaginative incentives to get the private sector and other actors to contribute and less of powers that stifle creative action. By these means planning controls should attempt to integrate and coordinate investment and action, both public and private, reflecting the interests of the various stakeholders whilst striking the proper balance between certainty and flexibility, efficiency and justice. Value accruing from planning decisions should be brought back to a fund of benefit to the community as a whole. As a democratically driven process planning should energize representative local democracy by being linked to a strategic community vision. It requires a new set of indicators and statistical basis, allowing for more sophisticated evaluations of the economic impact of planning decisions by taking into account environmental and social diseconomies. These will help planning facilitate change creatively. It implies that planners should exercise judgement, which has drawbacks if the wrong person applies it. But it has always been so and there will always be political discussion; the issue is to make decisions more explicit, transparent and accountable drawing on new mechanisms including citizens' juries. Urban strategy making is thus both much broader in scope than the classic town planning idea, involving a wider range of expertise, indicators and criteria for what it is trying to achieve and should also be more strategic in that it is more conscious of eco-system implications, regional impacts and creative needs. The path to reconciling planning as a creative process with tight regulatory systems is difficult. It does not mean the regulatory process has to be abandoned, rather that the regulatory process needs to be more flexible and matched with innovative incentives and recognition devices. It is vital to reward achievements to bolster the new ways of doing things. A small example might be buildings which use less energy should have a plaque saying how much money they are saving daily in comparison to the building next door or they might get an additional local tax rebate bonus. (The UK Town and Country Planning Association's Inquiry into the Future of Planning was helpful in thinking through this section and especially Roger Levett's contribution.)

## Coda

Now it's over to you. The fun bit can begin: to create and re-create your city how you want it. The slogan I believe captures the essence of future planning is: 'strategically principled and tactically flecxible'. The solutions will be infinitely diverse and the solutions are out there to be grasped. Some merely require imagination, others require confronting deep power structures and entrenched attitudes of mind. I hope *The Creative City* has provided a spark to drive your imagination even further. It is the real world applications that count and these will modify the toolkit outlined and embellish it.

# Appendix 1

# Cultural Industries in
# Tower Hamlets

**Table A.1** *Development scale assessment of cultural industries in Tower Hamlets (1997)*

| (Average) | Beginnings (4–5) | Production (3–4) | Circulation (3) | Delivery Mechanism (3) | Promotion (3) | Overall score and comments |
|---|---|---|---|---|---|---|
| **Visual arts** | 7–8 | 7–8 | 4 | 3 | 4 | **6** |
| painting | 9 | 8 | 3 | 3 | 5 | |
| sculpture | 7 | 6 | 3 | 3 | 5 | |
| graphic arts | 4–5 | 3–4 | 3 | 3 | 2 | |
| **Crafts** | 5 | 4 | 4 | 3 | 3 | **3–4** |
| **Performing arts** | 2–3 | 2–3 | 2 | 1–2 | 2 | **2** |
| traditional | 2 | 1–2 | 1 | 1–2 | 2 | weak |
| dance | 2–3 | 3 | 5 | 1–2 | 1 | |
| new forms | 4 | 2–3 | 2 | 1–2 | 2 | |
| **Mime** | 2 | 1 | 1 | 1 | 1 | **1** |
| **Cabaret** | 3 | 2 | 1–2 | 3 | 2 | **2** |
| **Music** | 4–5 | 4 | 3 | 2 | 3 | **3** |
| opera, classical | 5 | 5 | 4 | 4 | 5 | |
| jazz | 3–4 | 2 | 2 | 2 | 2 | |
| popular | 5 | 3 | 2 | 2 | 2 | |

|  | Begin-nings | Prod-uction | Circul-ation | Delivery Mech-anism | Prom-otion | Overall score and comments |
|---|---|---|---|---|---|---|
| *(Average)* | *(4–5)* | *(3–4)* | *(3)* | *(3)* | *(3)* | |
| **Audio-visual** | | | | | | |
| | 2 | 2–3 | 2–3 | 1–2 | 1–2 | **1–2** |
| film | 2 | 2 | 3 | 1 | 1 | generally weak |
| TV | 3 | 3 | 2 | n/a | 2 | in all sub-sectors |
| video/ corporate | 2 | 2 | 2 | 2 | 1 | |
| photography | 3 | 3–4 | 3 | 2 | 2 | |
| **Multimedia** | 3 | 3 | 2 | 2 | 2 | **2–3** |
| **Publishing** | 6 | 6 | 6 | 6 | 6 | **6** |
| books | 2 | 1 | 2 | 2 | 2 | imbalanced |
| newspapers/ magazines | 8 | 8 | 8 | 8 | 8 | (newspapers so strong) |
| **Fashion** | 5–6 | 5–6 | 6 | 6 | 4 | **6** |
| designer | 4–5 | 4 | 2–3 | 2 | 2 | great potential |
| mass | 6 | 8–9 | 8 | 8 | 6 | |
| **Design** | | | | | | |
| **general** | 2 | 2 | 2 | 2 | 2 | **2** |
| **Industrial** | | | | | | |
| **design** | 4 | 2 | 1–2 | 1–2 | 1 | **2** |

*Note:* The grid is assessed on a scale between 1 and 10, where 1 is very weak, 3–4 is quite weak and 10 extremely strong. The original report had commentaries for each of the grades given.

# Appendix 2

# Glasgow's Cultural Strengths

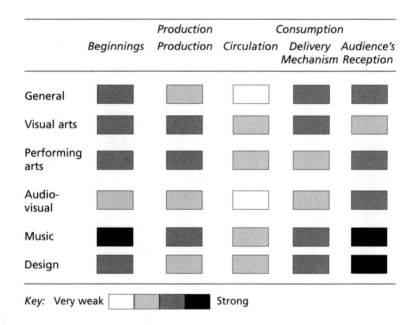

|  | Beginnings | Production Production | Circulation | Consumption Delivery Mechanism | Audience's Reception |
|---|---|---|---|---|---|
| General |  |  |  |  |  |
| Visual arts |  |  |  |  |  |
| Performing arts |  |  |  |  |  |
| Audio-visual |  |  |  |  |  |
| Music |  |  |  |  |  |
| Design |  |  |  |  |  |

Key: Very weak ▢ ▨ ▦ ■ Strong

# Appendix 3

# Visual Arts in Glasgow

**Table A.3** *Glasgow's position in the visual arts relative to other cities, with an emphasis on contemporary arts (1991)*

| Glasgow compared to British cities | | Glasgow in the European context | | Glasgow in the World context | |
|---|---|---|---|---|---|
| London | 10 | London | 8 | New York | 9/10 |
| *Glasgow* | *5* | Cologne | 6 | London | 6/7 |
| Leeds | 4/5 | Madrid | 6 | Cologne | 6 |
| Liverpool | 4 | Berlin | 5 | Los Angeles | 5/6 |
| Edinburgh | 3/4 | Paris | 5 | Madrid | 4/5 |
| Manchester | 3 | Amsterdam | 4 | Paris | 4 |
| Newcastle | 3 | Barcelona | 4 | Berlin | 3/4 |
| Bristol | 2/3 | Frankfurt | 4 | Chicago | 3/4 |
| Cardiff | 2 | Helsinki | 3 | Frankfurt | 3/4 |
| Oxford | 2 | Rome | 3 | Amsterdam | 3 |
| Southampton | 2 | Basel | 2/3 | Sydney | 3 |
| | | Zurich | 2/3 | Rome | 2 |
| | | *Glasgow* | *2* | Tokyo | 2 |
| | | Milan | 2 | *Glasgow* | *1* |

*Note:* The table shows Glasgow's position in 1991. Positions are subject to change, eg by 2000 London and Berlin's positions had improved. 1 is very weak, 3–4 is quite weak and 10 extremely strong.

# Bibliography

The references in this bibliography have been divided into two groups. The first list includes general references and those focusing on the themes of cities and urban cultural policy. The second list includes those with a focus on creativity and thinking.

## CITIES AND URBAN CULTURAL POLICY

Amin, A and Thrift, N (1994) *Globalization, Institutions and Regional Development in Europe*, Oxford: Oxford University Press

Andersson, A E (1987) *Culture, Creativity and Economic Development in a Regional Context*, Strasbourg: Council for Cultural Co-operation, Project no 10, Seminar no 5

Argyle, Michael (1987) *The Psychology of Happiness*, London: Routledge

Badshah Akthar (1996) *Our Urban Future: New Paradigms for Equity and Sustainability*, London: Zed Press

Bauman, Zygmunt (1997) *Postmodernity and its Discontents*, New York: New York University Press

Bianchini, F and Ghilardi Santacatterina, L (1997) *Culture and Neighbourhoods: A Comparative Report*, Strasbourg: Council of Europe

Bianchini, F and Landry, C (1995) *Assessing Urban Vitality and Viability*, Bournes Green: Comedia

Bianchini, F and Parkinson, M (1993) *Cultural Policy and Urban Regeneration: The West European Experience*, Manchester: Manchester University Press

Borja, J and Castells, M (1997) *Local and Global: Management of Cities in the Information Age*, London: Earthscan

Brotchie, J and Batty, J (1995) *Cities in Competition: Productive and Sustainable Cities for the 21st Century*, Melbourne: Longman

Camagni, R (1995) 'The Concept of Innovative Milieux and its Relevance to Public Policy in Europe's Lagging Regions', *Papers in Regional Science*, 74(4), p317

Cantell, T (1999) *Helsinki and a Vision of Place*, Helsinki: City of Helsinki Urban Facts

Cara, S, Landry, C and Ransom, S (1999) 'The Learning City in the Learning Age', Richness of Cities Working Paper 10, Bournes Green: Comedia

Carson, R (1962) *Silent Spring*, Boston: Houghton Mifflin

Castells, M (1989) *The Informational City: Information Technology, Economic Restructuring and the Urban-Regional Process*, Oxford: Blackwell

Castells, M (1996) *The Rise of the Network Society*, Oxford: Blackwell

Castells, M and Hall, P (1994) *Technopoles of the World: The Making of 21st Century Industrial Complexes*, London: Routledge

Christie, I and Nash, L (eds) (1998) *The Good Life*, London: Demos Collection

Clarke, D (ed) (1997) *The Cinematic City*, London: Routledge

Clifford, S and King, A (eds) (1993) *Local Distinctiveness: Place, Particularity and Identity*, London: Common Ground

Cohen, Sarah (1998) *Evaluation of the Sci–Art Programme*, Wellcome Trust

Cooke, P (ed) (1995) *The Rise of the Rustbelt*, London: University College London

Cooke, P and Morgan, K (1994) 'The Creative Milieu: a Regional Perspective on Innovation', in Dodgson, M and Rothwell, R, *The Handbook of Industrial Innovation*, Aldershot: Elgar

Cornwall, A (1995) 'Towards Participatory Practice, PRA and the Participatory Process', Draft Paper, Department of Anthropology, School of Oriental and African Studies, London

Coyle, D (1997) *The Weightless World*, London: Capstone

*Demos Quarterly* (1994) 'Liberation Technology', *Demos Quarterly*, 4

*Demos Quarterly* (1995) 'The Time Squeeze', *Demos Quarterly*, 5

Ekins, Paul (1992) *Wealth beyond Measure: An Atlas of the New Economics*, London: Gaia Books

European Business Network for Social Cohesion (1996) Corporate Initiatives: 100 Case Studies, Brussels

Fleming, Tom (ed) (1999) *The Role of the Cultural Industries in Local and Regional Development*, Manchester: Manchester Institute for Popular Culture

Gaffikin, F and Morrissey, M (1999) *City Visions: Imagining Place, Enfranchising People*, London: Pluto Press

Gilbert, R, Stevenson, D, Girardet, H and Stren, R (1996) *Making Cities Work: The Role of Local Authorities in the Urban Environment*, London: Earthscan

Girardet, H (1992a) *The Gaia Atlas of Cities*, London: Gaia Books

Girardet, H (1992b) *Cities: New Directions for Sustainable Living*, London: Gaia Books

Girouard, Mark (1985) *Cities and People*, New Haven: Yale University Press

Global Ideas Bank, www.globalideasbank.org/

Graham, S and Marvin, S (1996) *Telecommunications and the City: Electronic Spaces, Urban Places*, London: Routledge

Graham, S and Marvin, S (1998) 'Urban Planning and the Technological Future of Cities', Richness of Cities Working Paper 3, Bournes Green: Comedia

Greenhalgh, E, Landry, C and Worpole, K (1998) 'New Departures', Richness of Cities Working Paper 1, Bournes Green: Comedia

Greenhalgh, E and Worpole, K (1999) *The Richness of Cities*, Bournes Green: Comedia

Habitat, 'Best Pratices Database for Human Settlements', www.bestpractices.org/

Hall, P (1995) 'The roots of urban innovation: culture, technology and the urban order', *Urban Futures*, 19, pp41–52

Hall, P (1998) *Cities in Civilisation*, London: Weidenfeld

Hall, P and Landry, C (1997) *Innovative and Sustainable Cities*, Dublin: European Foundation for the Improvement of Living and Working Conditions

Hall, P and Markusen, A (1985) *Silicon Landscapes*, Boston: Allen Unwin

Hall, P and Preston, P (1988) *The Carrier Wave: New Information Technology and the Geography of Innovation, 1846–2003*, London: Unwin-Hyman

Hall, P and Castells, M (1994) *Technopoles of the World: The Making of 21st Century Industrial Complexes*, London: Routledge

Hawken, P (1993) *The Ecology of Commerce*, New York: Harper Business

Healey, P (1997) *Collaborative Planning: Shaping Places in Fragmented Societies*, London: Macmillan

Healey, P, Cameron, S, Davoudi, Simin, Graham, S and Madani-Pour, A (1995) *Managing Cities: The New Urban Context*, Chichester: Wiley

Healey, P, Khaker, A, Motte, A and Needham, B (1997) *Making Strategic Spatial Plans: Innovation in Europe*, Basingstoke: Taylor and Francis

Hopkins, Ellwood (1994) *The Life Cycle of Urban Innovations*, Working Paper 2, UNDP/UNCHS/World Bank

Hudson, R, Dunford, M, Hamilton, D and Kotter, R (1997) 'Developing Regional Strategies For Economic Success: Lessons From Europe's Economically Successful Regions?' *European Urban and Regional Studies*, 4(4), pp365–73

Jacobs, J (1984) *Cities and the Wealth of Nations*

Jenkins, Deborah (1998) 'Partnerships and Power: Leadership and Accountability in Urban Governance', Richness of Cities Working Paper 4, Bournes Green: Comedia

Jenks, Chris (1993) *Culture: Key Ideas*, London: Routledge

Joseph Rowntree Foundation (1991 onwards) *Search*, quarterly publication, review of research of the foundation on social and economic exclusion issues, York

Kelly, K (1997) 'New Rules for the New Economy: Twelve Dependable Principles for Thriving in a Turbulent World', *Wired*, September

Kelly, Kevin (1999) *New Rules for the Economy*, London: Fourth Estate

Kilper, H and Wood, G (1995) 'Restructuring Policies: the Emscher Park International Building Exhibition', in Cooke, P (ed) *The Rise of the Rustbelt*, London: University College London

Kleiner, Art (1996) *The Age of Heretics: Heroes, Outlaws and the Forerunner of Corporate Change*, London: Nicholas Brealey

Kuhn, Thomas (1962) *The Structure of Scientific Revolutions*, Chicago: University of Chicago Press

Kunzmann, K (1995) 'Developing the Regional Potential for Creative Response to Structural Change', in Brotchie, J and Batty, J *Cities in Competition: Productive and Sustainable Cities for the 21st Century*, Melbourne: Longman

Kunzmann, K (1997) 'The Future of the City Region in Europe', in Bosma, K and Hellinga, H (eds), *Mastering the City: North European City Planning 1900–2000*, Rotterdam, NAI

Landry, C with Kelly, O (1994) *Helsinki: A Living Work of Art: Towards a Cultural Strategy for Helsinki*, City of Helsinki Information Management Centre

Landry, C with Greenhalgh, E and Worpole, K (1995a) *The Innovative Capacity of the Swedish Public Library System*, Swedish Council for Cultural Affairs

Landry, C with Mulgan, G (1995b) *The Other Invisible Hand: Remaking Charity for the 21st Century*, London: Demos

Landry, C with Greene, L, Matarasso, F and Bianchini, F (1996) *The Art of Regeneration: Cultural Development and Urban Regeneration*, London and Nottingham: Comedia in Association with Civic Trust Regeneration Unit, Nottingham City Council

Landry, C (1997) *From the Art of the State to the State of the Art: Bulgaria's Cultural Policy in Transition*, The Council of Europe

Landry, C (1998a) *From Barriers to Bridges: Re-imagining Croatian Cultural Policy*, The Council of Europe

Landry, Charles (1998b) 'Helsinki: Towards a Creative City', Report for the City of Helsinki

Landry, C and Bianchini, F (1995) *The Creative City*, London: Demos

Landry, Charles and Matarasso, Francois (1998) *The Learning City-Region: Approaching problems of the concept, its measurement and evaluation*, Paris: OECD

Landry, C, Bianchini, F, Ebert, R, Gnad, F and Kunzmann, K (1996) *The Creative City in Britain and Germany*, London: Anglo-German Foundation for the Study of Industrial Society

Landry, C, Ransom, S and Cara, S (1998) *The Learning City in the Learning Age*, Bournes Green: Comedia

Lash, S and Urry, J (1994) *Economies of Signs and Space*, London: Sage

Leadbeater, Charles (1997) *The Rise of the Social Entrepreneur*, London: Demos

Leadbeater, C and Goss, S (1998) *Civic Entrepreneurship*, London: Demos

Lehan, Richard (1998) *The City in Literature: An Intellectual and Cultural History*, Berkeley: University of California

Levine, Robert (1997) *A Geography of Time*, New York: Basic Books

Lundvall, B A (1992) *National Systems of Innovation: Towards a Theory of Innovation and Interactive Learning*, London: Frances Pinter

Lundvall, B A (1994) 'The Learning Economy: challenges to economic theory and policy', paper presented at the EAEPE Conference, Copenhagen, October

Lynch, Kevion (1981) *Good City Form*, Cambridge MA: MIT Press

MacGillivray A, Weston, C and Unsworth, C (1998) *Communities Count: A step by step guide to community sustainability indicators*, London: New Economics Foundation

Matarasso, Francois (1993) *Regular Marvels*, Leicester: Community Dance and Mime Foundation

Matarasso, Francois (1997) *Use or Ornament: The Social Impact of Participation in the Arts*, Bournes Green: Comedia

McNulty Bob, (1994) *The State of the American Community: Empowerment for Local Action*, Washington: Partners for Livable Communities

Meadows, D H, Meadows, D L, Randers, J and Behrens, C W (1972) *The Limits to Growth*, New York: Universe Books

Melucci, Alberto (1989) *Nomads of the Present*, Philadelphia: Temple University Press

Melucci, Alberto (1996) *Challenging Codes: Collective Action in the Information Age*, Cambridge: Cambridge University Press

Melucci, Alberto (1996) *The Playing Self: Person and Meaning in the Planetary Society*, Cambridge: Cambridge University Press

Mercer, C (1995) *Urban Cultures and Value Production*, Proceedings of the Conference Cities and the New Global Economy, Melbourne: OECD

Mitchell, W (1995) *City of Bits: Space, Place and the Infobahn*, Cambridge: MIT

Montgomery, J (1996) 'Developing the Media Industries: An overview of strategies and possibilities for the local economic development of the media and cultural industries', *Local Economy*, 11(2), pp158–68

Morgan, K (1997) 'The Learning Region: institutions, innovation and regional renewal', *Regional Studies*, 31(5), pp491–503

Mulgan, Geoff (1995) 'Missionary Government', *Demos Quarterly*, 7

Murray, Robin (1999) *Creating Wealth from Waste*, London: Demos

Nelson, Jane (1996) *Business as Partners in Development: Creating Wealth for Countries, Companies and Communities*, London: Prince of Wales Business Leaders Forum

Nyström, Luise (1999) *City and Culture: Cultural Processes and Urban Sustainability*, Karlskrona: Swedish Urban Environment Council

O'Connor, J and Wynne, D (1996) *From the Margins to the Centre: Cultural Production and Consumption in the Post-Industrial City*, Aldershot: Arena

Ohmae, K (1993) 'The Rise of the Region State', *Foreign Affairs*, Spring, pp10–19

Osborne, D and Gaebler, T (1992) *Reinventing Government: How the Entrepreneurial Spirit is Transforming the Public Sector*, Reading, Mass: William Patrick

Osborne, D and Plastic, P (1997) *Banishing Bureaucracy: The Five Strategies for Reinventing Government*, Reading, Mass: Addison-Wesley

Parnes, S J (1992) *Source Book for Creative Problem Solving*, Buffalo, NY: Creative Education Foundation Press

Perri 6 (1997) 'The Wealth and Poverty of Networks', Demos Collection 12: London

Piore, M and Sabel, C (1984) *The Second Industrial Divide*, New York: Basic Books

Porter, Michael (1990) *The Competitive Advantage of Nations*, New York: Free Press

Power, Anne and Mumford (1999) *The Slow Death of Great Cities? Urban Abandonment or Urban Renewal?* Joseph Rowntree Foundation: Brussels

Pratt, Andy (1998) *A Third Way for the Cultural Industries*, London: LSE

Putnam, R (1993) *Making Democracy Work: Civic Traditions in Modern Italy*, Princeton: Princeton University Press

Rickards, Tudor (1996) 'The Management of Innovation: Recasting the Role of Creativity', *European Journal of Work and Organizational Psychology*, 5

Robinson, G and Rundell, J (1994) *Rethinking Imagination: Culture and Creativity*, London: Routledge

Rötzer, Florian (1995) *Die Telepolis: Urbanität im digitalen Zeitalter*, Berlin: Bollmann

Rushkoff, D (1994) *Cyberia: Life in the Trenches of Hyperspace*, San Francisco: Harper

Sassen, S (1994) *Cities in a World Economy*, Thousand Oaks: Pine Force Press

Saxenian, A (1994) *Regional Advantage: Culture and Competition in Silicon Valley and Route 128*, Cambridge, Mass: Harvard University Press

Schon, D (1971) *Beyond the Stable State: Public and Private Learning in a Changing Society*, New York: WW Norton

Scott, A J (1988) *New Industrial Spaces*, London: Pion

Scott, A J (1998) *Regions and the World Economy: The Coming Shape of Global Production, Competition and Political Order*, Oxford: Oxford University Press

Seabrook, Jeremy (1996) *In the Cities of the South: Scenes from a Developing World*, London: Verso

Shlain, L (1998) *The Alphabet versus the Goddess: The Conflict Between Word and Image*, London: Penguin

Sieverts, Thomas (1991) *IBA Emscher Park: Zukunftswerkstatt für Industrieregionen*, Cologne: Rudolf Müller

Spendolini, Michael (1992) *The Benchmarking Book*, New York: Amacom

Storper, M (1997) *The Regional World: Territorial Development in a Global Economy*, New York: Guilford Press

Storper, M and Scott, A (1993) 'The Wealth of Regions: Market Forces and Policy Imperatives in Local and Global Context', Working Paper 7, Lewis Centre for Regional Policy Studies: UCLA

Tayart de Borms Luc (1996) *Corporate Initiatives: Putting into Practice the European Declaration of Business against Social Exclusion*, Brussels: European Business Network for Social Cohesion

Urban Pilots Project Annual Report (1996, 1997) Brussels: Joseph Rowntree Foundation

von Weizsäcker, E, Lovins, A B and Lovins, L H (1998) *Factor Four: Doubling Wealth, Halving Resource Use*, London: Earthscan

Ward, Colin (1989) *Welcome, Thinner City*, London: Bedford Square Press

Weatherley, R and Lipsky, M (1977) Street Level, Bureaucrats and Institutional Innovation, Working Paper 44, Joint Center for Urban Studies of MIT and Harvard University

Worpole, Ken (1997) 'Nothing to Fear? Trust and Respect in Urban Communities', Richness of Cities Working Paper 2, Bournes Green: Comedia

Worpole, Ken (ed) (1997–98) Richness of Cities Working Papers 1–12, Bournes Green: Comedia

# CREATIVITY AND THINKING

Albery, N, Irvine, L and Evans, S (1997) *Creative Speculations: A Compendium of Social Innovations*, London: Institute for Social Inventions

Albery, N and Mezey, M (eds) (1994) *Reinventing Society*, London: Institute for Social Inventions

Albery, N and Wienrich, S (1999) *Social Dreams and Technological Nightmares*, London: Institute for Social Inventions

Albery, N with Yule, V (1992) *A Book of Visions: An Encyclopedia of Social Innovations*, London: Institute for Social Inventions

Assagoli, A (1973) *The Act of Will*, New York: Viking Press

Birch, P and Clegg, B (1996) *Imagination Engineering: The Toolkit for Business Creativity*, London: Pitman

Buzan, Tony (1974) *Use Your Head*, London: BBC Books

Buzan, Tony with Barry (1993) *The Mindmap Book: Radiant Thinking, The Major Evolution in Human Thought*, London: BBC Books

Capra, Fritjof (1997) *The Web of Life: A new Synthesis of Mind and Matter*, London: HarperCollins

Cook, Peter (1998) *Best Practice Creativity*, Aldershot: Gower

Covey, Stephen R (1992) *The Seven Habits of Highly Effective People*, London: Simon & Schuster

Csikszentmihalyi, Mihaly (1992) *Flow: The Psychology of Happiness*, London: Rider

Csikszentmihalyi, Mihaly (1996) *Creativity: Flow and the Psychology and Discovery of Invention,* New York: Harper Perennial

De Bono, E (1971) *The Use of Lateral Thinking*, London: Pelican

De Bono, E (1982) *Lateral Thinking for Management*, London: Pelican

De Bono, E (1990a) *Master Thinkers Handbook*, London: Penguin

De Bono, E (1990b) *Six Thinking Hats*, London: Penguin

De Bono, E (1993) *Water Logic*, London: Penguin

De Bono, E (1995a) *Parallel Thinking: From Socratic to de Bono Thinking*, London: Penguin

De Bono, E (1995b) *Teach Yourself To Think*, London: Penguin

De Bono, E (1996) *Serious Creativity*, London: HarperCollins Business

Dennison, Paul and Gail (1986) *Brain Gym. Simple Activities for Whole Brain Learning*, CA: Edu-Kinesthetics

Dilts, Robert and Epstein, Todd A (1995) *Dynamic Learning*, California: Meta Publications

Dryden, Gordon and Vos, Jeannette (1994) *The Learning Revolution: A Lifelong Programme for the World's Most Finest Computer: Your Amazing Brain,* Aylesbury: Accelerated Learning Systems

Edwards, Betty (1986) *Drawing on the Artist Within*, New York: Simon & Schuster

Egan, Kieran (1992) *Imagination in Teaching and Learning*, London: Routledge

Fritz, Robert (1984) *The Path of Least Resistance: Becoming the Creative Force in Your Own Life*, London: Butterworth

Fritz, Robert (1991) *Creating*, London: Butterworth

Fritz, Robert (1994) *Corporate Tides: Redesigning the Organisation,* London: Butterworth

Fryer, Marilyn (1996) *Creative Teaching and Learning*, London: Paul Chapman

Gardner, Howard (1984) *Frames of Mind: The Theory of Multiple Intelligences*, London: Heinemann

Gardner, Howard (1991) *The Unschooled Mind*, New York: Basic Books

Gardner, Howard (1993) *Creating Minds: An Anatomy of Creativity seen through the Lives of Freud, Einstein, Picasso, Stravinsky, Eliot, Graham and Gandhi*, New York: Basic Books

Gardner, Howard (1996) *Leading Minds: An Anatomy of Leadership*, New York: Basic Books

Gardner, Howard (1997) *Extraordinary Minds: Portraits of Extraordinary Individuals and an Examination of our Extraordinariness*, New York: Basic Books

Green, Andy (1999) *Creativity in Public Relations*, London: Kogan Page

Hopson, Barry and Scally, Mike (1989) *Wake Up Your Brain: Creative Problem Solving*, London: Lifeskills

Jensen, Eric (1996) *Brain-Based Learning*, California: Turning Point Publishing

Kearney, Richard (1988) *The Wake of the Imagination*, London: Routledge

Knight, Sue (1995) *NLP at Work: The Difference that makes a Difference in Business*, London: Nicholas Brealey

Lynch, Dudley and Kordis, Paul L (1990) *Strategy of the Dolphin. Winning Elegantly by Coping Powerfully in a Turbulent World of Change*, London: Arrow Books

Morgan, Gareth (1986) *Images of Organization*, Newbury Park: Sage

Morgan, Gareth (1989) *Creative Organization Theory: A Resource Book*, Newbury Park: Sage

Morgan, Gareth (1993) *Imaginization: The Art of Creative Management*, Newbury Park: Sage

New Economics Foundation (1997) *Participation Works: 21 Techniques of Community Participation for the 21st Century*, London: NEC

Petty, Geoffrey (1997) *How to be Better at Creativity*, London: Kogan Page

Rosen, Robert with Brown, Paul (1996) *Leading People: The 8 Proven Principles for Business Success*, London: Penguin,

Senge, P (1992) *The Fifth Discipline: The Art and Practice of the Learning Organization*, Sydney: Random Books

Senge, P, Kleiner, A, Roberts, C, Ross, R and Smith, B (1994) *The Fifth Discipline Fieldbook: Strategies and Tools for Building a Learning Organization*, London: Nicholas Brealey

# Interesting Websites

## URBAN CREATIVITY AND INNOVATION WEBSITES

Comedia
   www.comedia.org.uk

EGPIS (European Good Practice Information Service)
   cities21.com/egpis/

European Academy of the Urban Environment
   www.eaue.de/

EuropeanCommissionUrban Pilot Projects
   www.inforegio.org/urban/upp/frames.htm

European Sustainable Cities
   ourworld.compuserve.com/homepages/European_Sustainable_Cities/
   homepage.htm

European Urban Forum
   www.inforegio.cec.eu.int/urban/forum/

Forum on Creative Industries
   www.mmu.ac.uk/h-ss/sis/foci/welcome1.html

Global Ideas Bank (Institute for Social Inventions)
   www.globalideasbank.org/

Habitat – Best Practices Database for Human Settlements
   www.bestpractices.org/

Huddersfield Creative Town Initiative
   www.creativetown.com

*The Innovation Journal*
   www.innovation.cc/index.html

International Council for Local Environmental Initiatives
   www.iclei.org/iclei/casestud.htm

International Institute for Sustainable Development
   iisd1.iisd.ca/default.htm

International Urban Development Association
   www.inta-aivn.org/

Megacities
   www.megacities.nl/

Randers Urban Pilot Project
   www.undervaerket.dk/

RSS (European Regional Development Fund and Cohesion Fund Projects)
   www.inforegio.org/wbover/overstor/stories/D/RETD/st100_en.htm

SCN (Sustainable Communities Network)
   www.sustainable.org/casestudies/studiesindex.html

United Nations Management of Social Transformations
   www.unesco.org/most/bphome.htm#1

# CREATIVITY WEBSITES

Charles Cave
   www.ozemail.com/~caveman/creative/content.xtm

Creativity Net
   www.links.management.org.uk/Categories/Creativity.htm

De Bono, Edward, related sites
   www.aptt.com
   www.edwdebono.com

The Fritz Group
   www.fritzgroup.com

Healthcare Forum
   www.well.com/user/bbear/rosen.htm

Kao, John (author of *Jamming*)
   www.jamming.com/

Morgan, Gareth (of Imaginization)
   www.mgeneral.com
   www.imaginiz.com

Mulder, Bert – New Media and the Power of Culture
   kvc.minbuza.nl/homepage.html

Russell, Peter (author of *The Brain Book*)
   www.peterussell.com

# About Comedia

Founded by Charles Landry in 1978, Comedia is a small strategically oriented organization that acts as facilitator, mentor and consultancy, with a focus on the future of cities and maximizing cultural resources. It has carried out work in over 30 countries including Australia, Bosnia, The Netherlands, Bulgaria, Germany, Spain, Italy, Finland, Russia, Poland, South Africa, Scandinavia, the US, Ukraine, Croatia, New Zealand and Yemen. Comedia has undertaken several hundred projects concerned with revitalizing public, social and economic life through cultural activity; quality of life studies; cultural industry development projects and city and regional strategies.

Most recently Comedia has been involved in five major programmes: an international initiative on creative cities, their vitality and viability; the social and economic impact of culture; the notion of the informed citizen; the role of public parks and public space; the future of the non-profit sector. Landry has lectured widely in Europe, North America and Australia and spent 1998/1999 at the World Bank advising them on their strategy for culture and cities. He is regarded as an international authority on the use of culture in city revitalization; creativity in cities; the cultural industries and city futures.

Further details can be found on the Comedia website **www.comedia.org.uk**, or by contacting Comedia at:

*Comedia*
*The Round*
*Bournes Green*
*Near Stroud*
*Gloucestershire GL6 7NL*
*UK*

*email: creativecity@hotmail.com*

# Index